TAKING SIDES

Clashing Views on Controversial

Issues in Early Childhood Education

TAKING SIDES

Clashing Views on Controversial

Issues in Early Childhood Education

Selected, Edited, and with Introductions by

Karen Menke Paciorek
Eastern Michigan University

McGraw-Hill/Dushkin
A Division of The McGraw-Hill Companies

For Maxine G. Roberts, Ph.D.,
Professor Emeritus at the University of Pittsburgh
For providing me with a strong foundation to enter the
profession and continuing to show interest and support
throughout my career. I am grateful for all you have done
for me and the field of early childhood education.

Photo Acknowledgment
Cover image: © 2002 by PhotoDisc, Inc.

Cover Art Acknowledgment
Charles Vitelli

Manufactured in the United States of America

First Edition

123456789BAHBAH5432

Library of Congress Cataloging-in-Publication Data
Main entry under title:
Taking sides: clashing views on controversial issues in early childhood education/selected, edited, and with introductions by Karen Menke Paciorek.—1st ed.
Includes bibliographical references and index.
1. Early childhood education. 2. Education, preschool. 3. Education, primary.
I. Paciorek, Karen Menke, *ed.* II. Series.
372.21

0-07-248054-8
ISSN: 1537-0712

Printed on Recycled Paper

Preface

T he study of young children, their families, and those who care for and educate them is an ever-changing field. What complicates the study of issues that
affect young children is the fact that for many topics, research cannot be carried
out as true experimental studies. Subjects cannot be randomly assigned to an
employed versus nonemployed mother cohort, parents who spank versus parents who do not spank, or a high-quality versus poor-quality early childhood
setting. Many independent variables come into play when examining the effects of life on young children and their families. Parental education, parental
occupation and income, marital status and lifestyles, public education available, and geographical location can affect the ways in which children are raised
and educated. Caring for and educating young children is often viewed as something that comes naturally to most people. Little, if any, preparation or prior
knowledge is required. But when examining the many issues involving the raising and educating of children, one can see how knowledge of the issues that
affect young children's development can be valuable when making important
decisions.

Plan of the book The 18 issues in this book have been selected to appeal to
students in early childhood education courses or seminar discussion classes,
parents, or school administrators and boards who choose to examine the issues.
The issues are divided into two parts: Children in Families and Society, and
Children in Educational Settings. There is not a suggested order for discussing
the selections. The group can decide as a whole which order they would like to
investigate the separate issues. As the editor, I carefully chose the 18 issues to
represent current controversial topics in the field of early childhood education.
Each issue is posed in the form of a question. I then conducted a thorough
search of the literature and read many hundreds of articles. From those readings I chose the two best selections that represented a yes- and no-side to the
issue for a total of 36 different selections. The selections were chosen from a
variety of sources, including magazines, professional early childhood journals,
as well as other professional education journals and Web sites. Each issue is
prefaced by an *issue introduction* that explains why the issue is controversial,
how it may have been viewed historically, or how it varies from state to state.
The *postscript* provides thought-provoking questions as well as additional information about the controversy and suggested readings for follow-up study. Of
course, the reader may view the issue from other angles than are presented in
this book. Controversial issues generally do not have a right or wrong side, just
different ways of viewing an issue. People usually form an opinion after becoming educated about an issue by having read and discussed the many points
surrounding the topic. The aim of the Taking Sides series is to provide the reader

with a vehicle for becoming more knowledgeable about controversial issues so that they may be able to carry on a thoughtful, informed discussion with others.

A word to the instructor   An *Instructor's Manual With Test Questions* (multiple-choice and essay) is available through the publisher for the instructor using *Taking Sides* in the classroom. A general guidebook, *Using Taking Sides in the Classroom,* which discusses methods and techniques for integrating the pro-con approach into any classroom setting, is also available. An online version of *Using Taking Sides in the Classrom* and a correspondence service for *Taking Sides* adopters can be found at http://www.dushkin.com/usingts.

    Taking Sides: Clashing Views on Controversial Issues in Early Childhood Education is only one title in the Taking Sides series. If you are interested in seeing the table of contents for any of the other titles, visit the Taking Sides Web site at http://www.dushkin.com/takingsides/.

    For exploration of other issues in early childhood education I suggest the instructor review the current edition of *Annual Editions: Early Childhood Education* and *Sources: Notable Selections in Early Childhood Education,* 2d ed., both published by McGraw-Hill/Dushkin.

Acknowledgements   My husband Michael and sons Clark and Clay deserve my heartfelt appreciation and love for their support during the writing of this book. Their suggestions and ideas were always welcome. I am fortunate to have two wonderful parents, Audrey and Kenneth Menke, who raised my sister and me to be accepting of all, and to broaden our horizons through travel, reading, and thoughtful discussions. For that I am thankful. In addition, I want to thank the administration at Eastern Michigan University for supporting me with a sabbatical leave award so I was able to complete this project, and my colleagues Sue Grossman and Judy Williston for their extra effort while I was gone. Ted Knight at McGraw-Hill/Dushkin has been extremely supportive and accessible throughout this project. His attention to detail as well as his experience was valuable to me as I chose the issues to be presented. To my friends Linda Edwards, Cindy Ferriman, Joni Gallagher, Joyce Huth Munro, and Judy Wollack, thank you for the encouragement and diversions. As always, I welcome your feedback on any book I edit for McGraw-Hill/Dushkin, especially this first edition of *Taking Sides: Clashing Views on Controversial Issues in Early Childhood Education.* Feel free to contact me at karen.paciorek@emich.edu. I look forward to hearing from you.

Karen Menke Paciorek
Eastern Michigan University

Contents In Brief

Contents

Susan W. Haugland, a professor emeritus in child development, raises many of the key issues related to the use of computers by young children. She asserts that young children should use computers as long as attention and careful consideration is given to the age of introduction, support provided, and teacher training. The Alliance for Childhood released a report that critically examines the use of computers by young children and concludes that there are many more appropriate activities for children to be involved in that will also enable them to succeed in the future.

Psychologist Lawrence Kutner supports time-out when effectively managed by parents or teachers. Mary Ellis Schreiber, a consultant for the Early Childhood Conflict Resolution Program, argues that time-out is an ineffective tool for guiding the behavior of young children due to the fact that the children do not learn from it.

Professors of education Betty Jo Simmons, Kelly Stalsworth, and Heather Wentzel assert that there are many correlations between children viewing violent acts on television and displaying aggressive behavior. Professor of psychology Jonathan L. Freedman states that many of the studies done on children's television viewing were flawed and provided inaccurate findings. He does not find a strong correlation between television viewing and aggressive behavior.

Lynn Rosellini, a writer for *U.S. News & World Report*, explores the dilemma many parents face related to widespread disapproval of spanking. Rosellini maintains that spanking is the most viable option for disciplining children. Nadine Block, director of the Center for Effective Discipline, argues that parents and teachers should not legally be allowed to use the same force on children that would not be allowed against an animal. She states that adults should find more acceptable methods of discipline.

Lawrence J. Schweinhart, research division chair of the High/Scope Educational Research Foundation, and David P. Weikart, founder and former president of the High/Scope Educational Research Foundation, examine three curriculum models for at-risk preschoolers and conclude that a child-initiated active learning curriculum is best. Siegfried Engelmann, director of the National Institute for Direct Instruction, states that a preschool curriculum approach that is highly structured and teacher directed can best help at-risk children catch up to affluent children in learning.

Nancie L. Katz, a writer for the *Christian Science Monitor*, examines families who chose to keep their children out of kindergarten for a year after they were eligible to go age-wise. Katz cites research that finds that children with October to December birthdays are retained at a higher rate and that the parents who retained their children are pleased with their decision to do so. Samuel J. Meisels, professor of early childhood education at the University of Michigan in Ann Arbor, discusses three school-readiness policy myths that are strongly held by parents and teachers. He presents arguments to dispel these myths and suggests that children should attend kindergarten when they are age eligible.

Assistant professors Patricia Clark and Elizabeth Kirk present a review of the literature on full-day kindergarten and report that the majority of studies on the subject found increased academic performance along with additional benefits for children participating in full-day programs. Professors Deborah Olsen and Edward Zigler assert that there is a need for half-day programs for all children as well as a full-day program. Parents should be able to choose what is best for their children.

Anthony D. Pellegrini, a professor at the University of Minnesota, and David F. Bjorklund, a professor at Florida Atlantic University, conducted numerous studies examining student behavior before and after recess as well as academic performance. They state that there is a strong correlation between recess and higher academic performance. Kelly King Alexander, a contributing editor for *Parents* magazine, asserts that many school administrators have no choice but to eliminate nonacademic time from the daily school schedule due to the need for as much educational activity as possible.

Associate professor Wendy C. Kasten argues that multi-age classrooms are stable and effective learning environments for children. Kasten asserts that students benefit from the consistency and close relationship with their fellow students and their teacher. Assistant professor DeWayne A. Mason and professor Roland W. Doepner III contend that multi-age classes contain inferior curriculum to accommodate the lower-level students in the class.

Steve Zemelman, Harvey Daniels, and Marilyn Bizar, all faculty at the Center for City Schools, National-Louis University, assert that a whole-language approach to reading is supported by 60 years of research that confirms its positive results. Members of the National Reading Panel conclude that students need a strong foundation in systematic phonics instruction in kindergarten through sixth grade in order to be successful readers.

John A. Zahorik, a professor emeritus at the University of Wisconsin–Milwaukee, asserts that the research on class size reduction indicates that smaller class size translates into higher academic achievement in the primary grades. Eric A. Hanushek, the Paul and Jean Hanna Senior Fellow at the Hoover Institution of Stamford University, states that the small academic gains, found mainly among poor kindergarten children, do not warrant the cost of nationwide class size reduction programs.

Joellen Perry, a writer for *U.S. News & World Report,* states that for many families, grade retention is successful. She asserts that to many parents and children, the only solution for getting back on the right track in school is to start again. For these children, repeating a grade offers them a chance at having a positive learning experience. William A. Owings, superintendent of Accomack County Public Schools in Virginia, and Susan Magliaro, an associate professor at Virginia Tech, maintain that grade retention is not a positive experience for children when it happens or later in their school careers. Grade retention does more harm than good in the long run and other options should be considered before retaining a child.

Karen Rasmussen, associate editor for *Educational Leadership,* states that classroom teachers spend a great deal of time at the beginning of the school year developing positive working relationships with students and their families. Multi-year assignments allow these relationships to flourish over a minimum of a two-year period of time, making possible more learning progression in the second year. Allan S. Vann, principal at the James H. Boyd Intermediate School, counters that there may be significant disadvantages in having a child stay with the same teacher and peers for more than one school year. The disadvantages often outweigh the potential benefits of multi-year assignments.

Introduction

Early Childhood Education

Karen Menke Paciorek

Issues affecting the care and education of young children have always been controversial. Parents and teachers make educational decisions based on their own childhood, their involvement with children on a daily basis, their educational level, and their perception of what is best for their children or the children in their educational setting. For those of us who make early childhood education our profession, we strive to provide optimal care and educational experiences for all children in the classroom. We diligently work to educate families, advocate for resources and support, and develop appropriate learning experiences that will meet the needs of all young children. We are rewarded daily with smiles, stories of achievements, and opportunities to participate in the education and development of young children who will grow to be contributing members of society. Our job as citizens that are concerned for the care and education of young children is not new, neither are many of the issues we face. Some of the issues chosen for this book have been discussed by educators and families for over 100 years. For issues involving modern technology, the debate is in its infant stages.

The one-room school houses that once dotted the rural territories of the United States and Canada were the initial discussion settings for many education issues. As the population grew, the importance of making the best decisions grew, as well. When making decisions affecting children, passion runs deep. Many adults view educational experiences for today's children based on memories and experiences of when they were younger. Some assert that if a certain practice was good enough for them, and seemed to work, then it will also be good for the current generation of children.

Historical Perspective of Care and Education of Young Children

For many thousands of years little was known about the development of children. Parents were uninformed about rudimentary skill development, such as crawling, walking, and talking. Much of family life depended on basic survival, and healthy children were prized for their ability to help in the fields or in the home. The period of time we know today as childhood did not exist for most children years ago. For wealthy families, care was provided by nursemaids and education was conducted by private tutors. Children would rarely see their parents and males were often trained to take over the family business. Learning outside of the family business operation was not a high priority for most. For the majority of children who lived in poverty, life was extremely difficult and often involved hard physical labor that began at an early age. Care was provided by the parents as they went about their daily work, and education was minimal, if at all. The skills necessary for survival were more important than educational skills.

As countries throughout the world explored and traded, more knowledge was gained and more resources became available. Religious influence into the care and education of young children brought a more humane focus and efforts were made to provide quality educational experiences for young children. The philosophies concerning the care and education of young children was dominated by European men in the fifteenth and sixteenth centuries. Men such as Martin Luther, John Amos Comenius, John Locke, Jean-Jacques Rousseau, Johann Pestalozzi, and Friedrich Froebel laid the foundation for a child-centered, exploratory-based learning environment. Books, materials, and music were developed specifically for children and school settings were established for their education. As exploration moved west, influences from Europe, Asia, and Africa were spread to North America. In the late 1870s the American kindergarten movement gained momentum. The 1876 Centennial Exposition in Philadelphia had an exhibit of a kindergarten classroom complete with a teacher and young children who went about their day of playing and learning while millions of visitors watched. Women became more influential in the care and education of young children as many struggled to balance family duties and work during the Industrial Revolution in the late 1800s and early 1900s. Elizabeth Peabody, Susan Blow, Patty Smith Hill, Margaret and Rachel McMillan, and Maria Montessori worked diligently to educate others about current educational trends and practices.

The genenral public wasn't yet ready to accept public education for children under the age of six at this time, but many private kindergartens flourished. Unfortunately, there were many children who were left to fend for themselves or who were cared for by siblings or relatives as parents worked hard to provide for the family. Child care outside of the home was almost nonexistent. Educational settings grew as the population in cities and rural areas grew. At this point, the first generation of children who had more education than their parents was being raised. Education began to be viewed as a viable option for a better life. Parents wanted their children to learn to speak English, no matter what their native language may have been. They also wanted them to learn to read and to attend school. Kindergartens, modeled after the work of German educator Friedrich Froebel, were spread throughout the United States. Formal schools were built and a school attendance calendar was developed based on the seasons. The summer months were designated as time off from school. In the cities, this allowed children to avoid the classroom during the hottest months of the year. In rural areas, children had the summer months of off due to the fact that this was the time that they were needed most to help with chores on the family farm. That academic calendar still operates today for most schoolchildren even though air conditioning is available in classrooms and even though the majority of American families no longer live on farms.

Programs for Young Children in the Past 100 Years

The late 1890s brought prosperity for many families. The United States had re-built cities after the Civil War and industry grew as products were exported all over the world. The education of young children became a concern. Many people were especially concerned about the lives of young children who were living in unstable families or in poverty. Day nurseries were opened to care for children as young as two years of age. Children were given daily health assessments and were provided with warm, nutritious meals. Information on childrearing was shared with the mothers. Nursery schools were started for middle-class children, providing them with social experiences as well as opportunities for large-muscle development through free play. Colleges and universities began to offer classes in child development and opened child-care centers on the campus for students to observe young children in groups. Professional organizations were formed and information and research about appropriate practices for teaching young children began to be disseminated through conferences and seminars. In 1909 President Theodore Roosevelt convened the first White House Conference on Children. These conferences, held every ten years, highlight children's health and well-being. Most of the recommendations that came forth from the White House Conferences over the years were not legislated, but some progress was made. A Children's Bureau in the Department of Labor was organized as a result of the 1909 conference.

The Great Depression of the 1930s brought a new dimension to programs for young children—government funding. Up until that time, day nurseries and nursery schools were supported by private charities, colleges and universities, or tuition. The depression put many people out of work, including elementary teachers. In rural areas schools closed due to lack of funds, and in the cities children left school to get jobs. The United States government developed a massive federal relief program in 1933 called the Works Projects Administration (WPA) that had the aim of providing jobs for unemployed Americans. Many of our public parks, zoos, and town halls were built by WPA workers. Nursery schools were started so the unemployed teachers could obtain paying jobs. These schools and parent education programs were coordinated through a national advisory agency. Although the 1,700 WPA nursery schools were created to augment temporary relief programs and existed for only 10 years, their effects are still evident today. These programs did not just provide basic services such as food, they were also comprehensive programs of preschool education. Children received physical, social, and intellectual development in a safe and nurturing environment. This massive federal program employed 3,775 teachers over the course of its existence, of which only 158 had previous nursery school experience.

The new focus of psychologist John Watson in the 1920s and 1930s on helping children to become detached from their mothers had a profound impact on preschool education and pedagogy. Watson strongly urged parents to never hug and kiss their children or let them sit in their laps. This advice caused many to wonder exactly what the role of parents and teachers in the early care and education of young children should be. As a result of this confusion by many on the abilities and needs of young children, child development professors and teachers at laboratory nursery schools began to regularly observe, record, and write on the behavior of children. Advice was given to parents, and knowledge about child development was disseminated to families and the community. Parent education was seen as a way to make an impact on the lives of young children. The study of young children received attention from noted psychologists and educators, such as G. Stanley Hall, Jean Piaget, Lev S. Vygotsky, John Dewey, Arnold Gesell, and Erik Erikson.

As conflicts throughout the world escalated in the 1930s and early 1940s, the need for the federal government to once again become involved in the care and education of young children was the result. The Lanham Act was passed by Congress and was in effect from 1940–1946. The early childhood centers that were developed as a result of this act were designed to provide child care for children whose mothers were employed in industries supporting government efforts during World War II. Since many men at that time were needed in the military, women, many of whom were mothers, were needed to work in the factories. Maternal employment was not a controversial issue then. The war effort required mothers to work, so they answered the call of duty without repercussions from those in society who did not approve of mothers working. The out-of-family care options available for the children of working mothers ranged from nonexistent for mothers working at the B-24 bomber plant in Willow Run, Michigan, to new child-care centers built for the children whose mothers were employed at the Kaiser Ship Yards in Portland, Oregon.

In 1943 Edgar Kaiser was concerned that the Lanham child-care centers located in Portland neighborhoods were not convenient for his workers. He sought to build his own child-care centers and staff them with employees from the shipyard. Kaiser found out that one should not staff programs for young children with untrained staff. The general community at large, and the early childhood community specifically, quickly educated Kaiser as to the importance of quality early childhood programs. He responded by supporting what many called the best child care there ever was. In addition, he recognized the importance of high-quality staff and recruited some of the best in the field to establish the centers and started teachers at what was considered a very high salary. The two Kaiser Centers served 1,125 children each from eighteen months of age to six years of age and were open 24 hours a day, 7 days a week, 364 days a year. These were services that were unheard of at the time. Mothers could pick up cooked meals at the end of the day, have their children's hair cut, drop off clothes to be mended, or have school-age children cared for during school breaks. So what happened to these marvelous programs after the war? If the best child care that America ever had was available 60 years ago, then we have not made much progress since then, and it can be argued that child care has never achieved the level of quality and comprehensiveness as it did at that time. As James L. Hymes, who served as manager of the Child Service Centers, stated in 1970 at a conference on industry and day care, "We did it all at a tremendous expense." He went on to say, "I have to end by saying this was wartime. This was a cost-plus contract. I am taken with how costly good services to children and families have to be. I am taken with how costly bad services always are."

The war ended and fathers returned home to seek employment or to attend college, and mothers stayed home to care for the children. The federal government's involvement in the care of young children ended for the second time. The 1950s were a decade of expansion and prosperity for many Americans. The economy rebounded, and suburbs blossomed overnight outside of major cities. Full-day child care was extremely limited, but half-day preschool programs began to open in order to serve middle-class children. These children were living in families with many options available. However, children living in poverty were less fortunate. They had limited options for formal education before entering the first grade.

When the Murfresboro, Tennessee, public schools recognized the difficulty that children living in poverty were having when they entered the first grade, they looked to George Peabody College in Nashville, Tenessee. Kindergarten was not universally available then, so first grade was often the initial school experience for many poor rural children. In 1962 Susan Gray and Rupert Klaus from the psychology department enlisted the help of doctoral students to develop a six-week summer program called the Early Training Project. Up until that time it was believed that an early intervention program for children living in poverty could not help. The curriculum was aimed at teaching disadvantaged children language skills and other skills necessary for success in elementary school. Gray and Klaus gathered data and found that their program caused children to be better prepared for the first grade. In fact, the earlier the intervention, the greater the gain, according to research findings. The final report, prepared to justify the funding they had received from the federal government for the program, was sent to the Department of Health, Education, and Welfare. The results meshed with the goals of the Economic Opportunity Act of 1964, and the outcome was the establishment of the Head Start Program on February 12, 1965. This became the third time the federal government provided services for young children in order to fulfill economic goals. The Head Start Program serves at-risk children who are three and four years old. Head Start includes many types of programs in a variety of settings. All Head Start child development centers were initially based on five major components: health, nutrition, education, parental involvement, and social and psychological services. Many question why Head Start has had to constantly struggle financially for its basic existence. With the vast amount of evidence that supports early intervention programs, why are more funds not available to meet the needs of all children?

As one can see, there are recurring themes in the past century related to programs for young children:

1. Federal involvement in early childhood education has primarily been in response to economic or social crises in the country, not as a result of the needs of young children.
2. Much of the focus and money has been spent on children from disadvantaged or at-risk families as opposed to all children.
3. Early childhood education was viewed as a panacea, the solution to all social ills in society. This was, and is, huge pressure to put on an overworked and underpaid profession, especially when longstanding federal commitment to programs for young children has not been forthcoming.

Current Trends and Issues

The last quarter of the 20th century was marked by an increase in single-parent families and the participation of mothers with young children in the workforce. There was also an increased mobility of families that resulted in a lack of extended family upon which to rely for child care and other child-rearing assistance. The decreasing availability of extended family child care, coupled with the problem of ensuring that outside child care is high-quality and that the staff is compensated at an appropriate level, has become a major dilemma. In what was once a private family matter, child care has entered corporate boardrooms and community discussion groups as parents struggle to provide for their families and care for their young children simultaneously. Much attention has been paid to the lack of quality early childhood programs being available for all children and the high turnover of teaching staff. Teachers who can make more money at other jobs leave the teaching profession at a national rate of approximately 40 percent each year. The long-term effects for young children who spend the majority of their formative years in poor-quality child care are still being investigated. Teachers in elementary schools are encountering children who show effects of having participated in a wide range of child care situations during their early years. Educational requirements for teaching staff in child-care centers range from no requirements in 29 states and the District of Columbia to 90 hours of college credits in Maryland. The effects of poverty on children are being met with success through quality early childhood programs, but there are not enough programs available. There are also not enough teachers prepared to work with young children from a variety of backgrounds. The United States has yet to address the problem with sufficient resources and attention to sufficiently meet the challenge of early care and education.

Children from diverse types of families attend the same schools. Parents may not speak English, children may have disabilities, and the beliefs of many parents regarding educational practices may differ greatly from what is actually practiced in the school. It is the job of educators to meet each child at his or her level and move him or her forward. The need to accommodate programs instead of making young children change to fit into programs has never been more true than it is today. The focus in many schools has changed to one of preparing the schools for the many different students who will attend. Teachers of young children need to be constantly aware of the needs and abilities of each child in the classroom. Teachers are under great pressure to improve academic standards, elevate failing schools to acceptable levels, and produce children who score passing marks on state-mandated tests. It is incumbent on early childhood education teachers to use their knowledge of child development and to use current research on the best practices in order to advocate for what is most appropriate for young children. State and federal policies will be proposed as legislators and business leaders work to improve academic performance. Early childhood education plays a key role in any reform due to the fact that it is the initial learning setting for all children. The importance of the strong foundation that can be forged during the years from birth through eight must be shared with others. We must also address the need for the appropriate resources required to prepare every child for a lifetime of learning. One must also keep in mind that technology is changing the way we live our lives. Educators need to be wise consumers of all available resources.

Public policy efforts are more crucial today than ever. Teachers have more responsibilities than just teaching children. They must inform parents of the kind of learning experiences children are receiving in their classrooms and must stay professionally involved to keep up with current trends.

The research released in the late 1990s that provided information about the development of the human brain has shed some light on the importance of learning during the early years. But once again, it is critical to note that early childhood education should not be viewed as the magic solution to what ails America. Quality early childhood programs, staffed by well-prepared teachers who are knowledgeable about child development, are only one part of the puzzle. We need a society that values young children and is willing to make both financial and emotional commitments to the education of future generations.

The good news for the early childhood education profession is that there has been tremendous growth in professional organizations, journals, and conferences. There are many articles in weekly news magazines on children's issues, and the availability of products for young children has flooded the market. However, with this new information one must exercise caution when judging the developmental abilities and needs of young children. Many parents want information on parenting, and the proliferation of information about the abilities of young children has only served to confuse many on what are the best ways to raise children in today's world. A number of the issues contained in this book are controversial because they may directly conflict with what has been standing practice for many generations. Some are new issues that Americans have not had time to consider at length.

A Call to Action

In many professions a body of research guides its practice. I am continually amazed that in education, unlike other fields, the research is often not heeded. Our grandmothers and great-grandmothers would tell us years ago that for a simple kitchen burn, the best remedy was to slather the burn area with butter. Numerous studies conducted have found that running a burn under cold water is the best treatment. Medical personnel today use that research when educating others about burns. They do not continue to recommend the use of butter, especially since it has been proven to make the burn worse. For many of the issues in this first edition of *Taking Sides: Clashing Views on Controversial Issues in Early Childhood Education,* it was difficult to find a yes- or no-side to an issue. But that does not mean that a certain practice is not occurring. Far from it. In many cases we continue to carry out unsound educational practices even though there is no research to back up the practice. It is my hope that the reader will use sound research to guide decisions that are made regarding the care and education of young children.

When editing the two editions of *Sources: Notable Selections in Early Childhood Education,* I realized just how little the field of early childhood education has changed over the years. Many of the educational principles upon which quality early childhood programs are based are deeply rooted in practices from centuries ago. Educational philosophies have a cyclical pattern where they are all the rage for a period of time, then fall out of favor with the general public for years before being revived again. Change is evident. What must be kept in mind is that we must learn from change and make improvements to practices based on what is learned.

Whether you are a student preparing to enter the field of education, a parent of young children, or a seasoned teacher or administrator, the issues in this book will be of interest. Throughout the United States, local school board members are wrestling with many of these issues. Decisions affect budgets, educational performance, and the views parents in the community have of the school system. Informed decisions can be made based on a thorough study of the issues. Understanding the issues can also lead to additional research. For many of the topics presented in this book, there has been limited research on the issue and how it affects young children. This can serve as a reminder to public policy specialists and researchers who investigate issues affecting children and their families. More data is needed on many topics in order to make informed decisions. I invite you to read and reread the articles in this book. Engage in discussions with colleagues, neighbors, and friends. Develop an informed opinion that is not carved in stone, but one that could be altered based on new information or new experiences with the issue.

Development Tracker

This Development Tracker Web site provides a year-by-year guide of child development from the toddler years through twelfth grade. A range of skills is provided for each age and grade level. Topics include intellectual skills, social skills, and physical changes.

`http://www.women.com/family/tracker/`

Early Childhood Education Clearinghouse: Facts in Action

The Early Childhood Education Clearinghouse: Facts in Action site is designed to put research-based knowledge and tools into the hands of those who serve in the early childhood education field, as well as those who influence or make policies that affect that field. On this site one can find summaries of recent research, important facts and statistics, and legislative and administrative policy updates.

`http://www.factsinaction.org`

A Parent's Guide to Early Brain Development

A Parent's Guide to Early Brain Development provides answers to frequently asked questions about brain development. This page is part of the Web site for the I Am Your Child Campaign and Foundation, which seeks to raise public awareness about early childhood development.

`http://www.iamyourchild.org/brainfacts/index.html`

Technology and Young Children

At the Technology and Young Children Web site one will find resources and links for parents and educators on the appropriate use of computers, criteria for evaluating Web sites, and the use of technology with learning centers. This site also offers a forum for discussion and research relating to technology and young children.

`http://www.techandyoungchildren.org`

The Media Scope

Media Scope is a national nonprofit research and policy organization that works to encourage responsible and creative, yet nonviolent, portrayals in television, the Internet, video games, music, and advertising.

`http://www.mediascope.org`

PART 1

Children in Families and Society

*E*very family is different and operates with its own traditions, practices, and beliefs. Parents make decisions based on their own experiences and the values they hold for their children. How parents support, guide, and educate their children changes as they gain experience as parents and as their children grow up. In addition, the society in which the family lives, which can mean the extended family, the community, and state and country, all make decisions that affect the family. The issues in this part relate to young children as they grow up in their families and in society at large.

- Is Early Maternal Employment Harmful to Young Children?

- Should Brain Science Guide Educational Practice?

- Should Young Children Use Computers?

- Is Time-Out an Effective Discipline Technique?

- Does Television Viewing Cause Violent Behavior in Young Children?

- Is Spanking an Effective Method of Discipline?

- Should Superhero Play Be Discouraged?

- Should Parent Participation in Schools Be Required?

- Does Homework in the Primary Grades Improve Academic Performance?

ISSUE 1

Is Early Maternal Employment Harmful to Young Children?

YES: Andrew Peyton Thomas, from "A Dangerous Experiment in Child-Rearing," *The Wall Street Journal* (January 8, 1998)

NO: Elizabeth Harvey, from "Short-Term and Long-Term Effects of Early Parental Employment on Children of the National Longitudinal Survey of Youth," *Developmental Psychology* (March 1999)

ISSUE SUMMARY

YES: Attorney Andrew Peyton Thomas asserts that early maternal employment affects young children in a negative way. He describes the caring for young children by someone other than their mother as the warehousing of infants for the increased accumulation of material goods.

NO: Professor Elizabeth Harvey counters that a child is not necessarily harmed when his or her mother returns to work, even if the child is under three years of age. Harvey maintains that some positive effects can be gained by the mother returning to work.

Few issues cause as much disagreement, whether in professional research journals, or neighborhood PTA meetings, than the effects of maternal employment on the development of children. Many mothers who stay home with their young children fully agree with research that suggests that children cared for by someone other than a parent will display negative behaviors on many fronts. These findings provide validation that their staying at home and forgoing a career will have a positive effect on their child's development. On the other hand, mothers who work outside of the home are also provided with evidence that shows that their employment will not negatively affect their young child's development. Some mothers work part-time to reap the benefits of being at home with their children and being employed. Many new mothers-to-be dread the question they are often asked after they are asked when the baby is due. When people ask, "What are you going to do about work?" some new moms freeze and feel a sense of panic.

For hundreds of years, there was no reason to question the effects of maternal employment. Mothers worked for the economic survival of the family. Whether the mother was a new immigrant or working to support children due to the illness or death of her spouse, many mothers throughout history have worked during their childbearing years. But those times were also vastly different from today. Mothers had their children near them, whether they were in the shops their family ran or on the family farms. It was not until the Industrial Revolution that mothers began to work in factories and were faced with child-care issues. Often the care was provided by an older sibling. Families were larger and the older children were readily available. Many families also had support systems that are not always available today. Extended family often lived nearby, or neighbors and friends cared for children. Child care in the United States on a large scale did not start until the 1940s. During World War II, mothers were needed to work in the factories to help in the war effort while fathers were serving in the military. There had been child-care programs on a much smaller scale throughout the country before World War II, but it took the war effort to bring to the forefront the issue of working mothers and the need for outside care. After the war, the fathers returned home and many mothers quit their jobs to continue caring for their children.

The 1960s and 1970s brought new educational and employment opportunities for women that were never available before. Women were pursuing careers instead of just temporary jobs, but many also wanted to include having children as a part of their life. The issue of maternal employment began to appear in magazines and journals as women worked not just for the economic survival of the family, but to make contributions to the economy, for personal gain, and for future financial security. There were few child-care options available and working mothers sometimes faced criticism from family, society, and, even employers. Researchers, parents, and others wanted to know how maternal employment would affect children. Would they grow up not knowing their mothers? Would these children be more aggressive or develop other undesirable character traits not found in children whose mothers did not work outside of the home? The literature in the 1970s and 1980s contained many studies of maternal employment.

In the following selections, Andrew Peyton Thomas argues that young children should not be cared for outside of the home. He calls on religious leaders to speak against the selfishness and accumulation of wealth by parents who are more concerned with money than their children. Elizabeth Harvey examines data concerning the long-term effects of early maternal employment. Harvey concludes that there are few, if any, ill effects and that there can be significant financial benefits.

Andrew Peyton Thomas

 **YES**

A Dangerous Experiment in Child-Rearing

A harmful social phenomenon is fast gaining popular acceptance—a vice so common that the problem is rarely even discussed, and almost never forthrightly. A new Census Bureau study makes clear the magnitude of the problem. Examining nearly 57,000 households across the U.S., the bureau found that 55% of new mothers return to the work force *within one year* of giving birth. In 1976, by contrast, the figure was only 31%. Ours is now a day-care culture. And the Clinton administration appears determined to keep it that way. [Clinton] proposed a $21.7 billion program of new spending and tax breaks to subsidize day care.

It is one thing for both parents to work outside the home when their kids are older. But for both parents in a majority of families to be employed before their children can even walk is startling. We are witnessing a momentous experiment in the raising of children. Yet there are few stirrings in the culture suggesting anything but a complacent acceptance of this revolution in child rearing. Few political, cultural or religious leaders have spoken out against the growing practice of abandoning infants to paid strangers. Yet recent research, not to mention common sense, tells us that this quiet overhaul of American families is a profound tragedy whose bitter fruit will be reaped for decades to come.

"Psychological Thalidomide"

Social science confirms that babies raised in day-care centers and similar institutions are often emotionally maladjusted. Child development expert Edward Zigler of Yale has gone so far as to call day care "psychological thalidomide." Research beginning in the early 1970s has found that such children are more likely to be violent, antisocial and resistant to basic discipline. A 1974 study in the journal *Developmental Psychology* reported that children who entered day care before their first birthday were "significantly more aggressive" and more physically and verbally abusive of adults than other children.

A 1985 study by Ron Haskins in Child Development, another scholarly journal, compared two groups of day-care children and found that those who had spent more time in day care suffered from proportionately greater ill effects, regardless of the quality of care. Teachers were more likely to rate these early-care children as "having aggressiveness as a serious deficit of social behavior." Similarly, Jay Belsky of Pennsylvania State University warns, based on his research, that full-time day-care babies are at risk of "heightened aggressiveness, non-compliance and withdrawal in the preschool and early school years."

Other studies have concluded that lengthy stays in day-care centers impair children's mental ability. In 1995, the National Institute of Mental Health published a joint U.S.-Israeli study that found children raised in Israeli communes known as *kibbutzim,* who received 24-hour day care, were at significantly greater risk of developing schizophrenia and other serious mental disorders. Last April the National Institute of Child Health and Human Development released a long-term study of 1,364 children from 10 states. The study, which examined children from diverse ethnic and socioeconomic backgrounds, reported that a child's placement in day care provided a "significant prediction" of poorer mother-child interaction and reduced cognitive and linguistic development.

These are remarkable findings, especially given that social scientists, in the main, hold no brief for traditional family values. But if you are a parent skeptical of this social science, ask yourself this straightforward question: Do you truly believe that a stranger can care for your child as well as you can?

Defenders of day care often say it is essential for women's equality in the work force. This simplistic notion, however, ignores the experiences of real men and women. Often it is fathers who are the biggest fans of day care: They like the extra income their wives can bring in by depositing children in institutions during the day. It is mothers who usually feel the sting of guilt, that despised but just gadfly of conscience.

Americans today are sophisticated at rationalizing vice, but the justifications offered for day care are surprisingly thin. The most common excuse is that young couples need the extra money. But *U.S. News & World Report* found that the median income for two-earner families is $56,000, compared with $32,000 for male-breadwinner homes. At neither salary is a four-member family lacking for necessities. Per capita disposable income, adjusting for inflation, is more than twice as high today as it was in 1950, and three times as high as in 1930. Families are spending much of this money on luxuries like bigger homes (new homes are 38% larger now than in 1970)—not on their kids.

The notorious au pair trial presented this reality in stark relief: Two physicians imported a teenage indentured servant, paid her slave wages, entrusted her with raising their two children and then were outraged when many Americans did not entirely sympathize with them after one of the children died in the young woman's care.

Childhood was never perfect. Small children were once forced to sweep chimneys and pick grapes, and often children lost parents entirely to disease and war. But that is precisely why the destruction of the 1950s nuclear family is so tragic. The 1950s set a standard for family life that probably has never been equaled anywhere. Children were raised by two parents in a safe, comfortable home, and Mom was almost always there to look after them when they were young. The self-centered popular culture unleashed in the 1960s mocked and ultimately shattered this paradigm. Now we are institutionalizing the worst aspects of this cultural revolution by warehousing infants merely so that we might accumulate ever-nicer possessions.

If these dire trends are to be reversed, our leaders must assert themselves. To begin with, religious leaders should decry the selfishness and materialism that lead parents to put their careers ahead of their children.

Politicians always do well to leave moral condemnations to the pulpit, and such a sermon would not win them many votes today. Yet they would likely become heroes to many working mothers if, instead of simply ignoring this issue, they handled it with sincerity and skill. A Roper poll . . . reported that 75% of Americans think that mothers who work outside the home and have children under age three threaten family values. A survey of American women . . . by the Pew Center found that 81% thought the job of mothering is more difficult today than it was 20 or 30 years ago, and 56% thought they did a less capable job than their own mothers. Even among women who work full time, only 41% were confident that their situation was good for their children.

Can't Have It All

There are several policy changes that elected officials should consider. The federal child care tax credit, which subsidizes day care at the expense of stay-at-home parents, should be reassessed. In a growing number of jurisdictions, judges are pressuring divorced mothers, even those with small children, to go to work, by reducing child-support payments based on their potential income. This practice should be ended legislatively. Lawmakers should also consider offering tax credits for businesses that accommodate mothers or fathers who leave the work force during their child's critical first five years. And, of course, Congress should reject Mr. Clinton's ill-considered plan to subsidize day care.

Above all, we must see through the canard that tells us that when it comes to the ancient clash between career and family, we are now clever enough to be able to "have it all." For when we knowingly sacrifice our children's well-being for the sake of money or careers, are we even truly worthy of our children's love?

NO

Elizabeth Harvey

Short-Term and Long-Term Effects of Early Parental Employment on Children of the National Longitudinal Survey of Youth

The past several decades have seen an increase in the number of employed mothers, with a particularly large increase in the frequency with which mothers of young children are employed (Bureau of the Census, 1994). Researchers who have reviewed the literature on the effects of maternal employment on children's development have agreed that there is little evidence of negative effects when children are older (Belsky, 1988, 1990; Hoffman, 1961, 1974, 1989). However, there remains debate about the effects of *early* maternal employment on children. After reviewing the literature, Belsky (1988) concluded that maternal employment during infancy had ill effects on children's well-being. Specifically, he concluded that infants who were in nonmaternal care for more than 20 hr per week week at elevated risk for being insecurely attached at age 1 and were more disobedient and aggressive between ages 3 and 8. However, his conclusions have been criticized on several counts. For example, it has been argued that the studies Belsky reviewed failed to take into account background variables that may have been confounded with maternal employment and children's well-being (e.g., Clarke-Stewart, 1988, 1989). In addition, Clarke-Stewart noted that many of these studies were based on nonrepresentative samples. Finally, she argued that the measures of attachment used in these studies may not have predictive validity for children of working mothers and that more longitudinal studies are needed to determine effects on children's later functioning.

In recent years, several studies have addressed some of these criticisms using the National Longitudinal Survey of Youth (NLSY). The NLSY is a survey of women who have been interviewed annually since 1979 when they were 14 to 22 years old. Beginning in 1986, children of these women were also assessed. Six published studies have used this sample to examine the longitudinal effects of early maternal employment on children's development, controlling for various family background variables. The results of these studies have been surprisingly mixed considering they used the same data set. The sample size and longitudinal

Adapted from Elizabeth Harvey, "Short-Term and Long-Term Effects of Early Parental Employment on Children of the National Longitudinal Survey of Youth," *Developmental Psychology*, vol. 35, no. 2 (March 1999). Copyright © 1999 by The American Psychological Association, Inc. Adapted by permission. Notes and references omitted.

design of the NLSY make it potentially valuable for illuminating the effects of early maternal employment. However, rather than shedding light on this issue, conflicting results of studies based on these data have added further confusion.

Although these six studies all used the same data set, they each used quite different methodological approaches with respect to sample selection, construction of independent and dependent variables, and selection of control variables. The present study sought to resolve some of these differences through a reanalysis using an updated version of the NLSY that contained a much larger and more representative sample. In this article, I examined the six studies, explored how their methodological differences might have yielded discrepant results, evaluated their methodological strengths and limitations, and reanalyzed the effects of early parental employment by drawing on the strengths and addressing the limitations of these six previous studies.

A Comparison of Methodological Approaches and Findings

Of the six previous studies, none used the exact same sample. Slightly different age ranges were selected, and three studies did not include all races. Four studies included the Peabody Picture Vocabulary Test—Revised (PPVT-R) as a dependent variable, and four studies used the Behavior Problems Index (BPI). Vandell and Ramanan (1992) conducted the only study that examined school achievement. There was surprisingly little overlap across studies in the construction of maternal employment variables. There was also considerable variation in the background variables used as controls. The number of control variables varied from 4 to over 25. Mother's IQ, race, and family income or poverty status were the only variables that were controlled across all six studies. Child gender was the only moderating variable examined in all six studies. Only one study directly evaluated potential mediators of early maternal employment.

It is therefore less surprising that these studies yielded very different findings. In general, the Vandell and Ramanan (1992), Parcel and Menaghan (1994), and Greenstein (1995) studies found no adverse effects of early maternal employment on PPVT-R or behavior problems, and Vandell and Ramanan (1992) found some positive effects on children's Peabody Individual Achievement Test (PIAT) scores. Desai, Chase-Lansdale, and Michael (1989) found negative effects on PPVT-R scores only for boys from high-income families, and Bayder and Brooks-Gunn (1991) found negative effects on PPVT-R and behavior problems for White families only. Belsky and Eggebeen (1991) found adverse effects on their variable called ADJUST, a composite of BPI scores and temperament variables, but when they examined BPI scores alone, they did not find significant effects.

Because the studies were based on the same data set, the conflicting results must be due to one or more of the methodological variations, although it is not clear which. . . .

The Present Study

The more recent NLSY provides the opportunity to reexamine the effects of early parental employment on children's development, addressing a number of important limitations of these six previous studies as follows: (a) A larger, more representative sample was used that should significantly increase the generalizability of results; (b) selection factors were distinguished from mediating variables; (c) control variables were selected using both theory and empirical decision rules; (d) the sample contained a wider age range of children allowing for an evaluation of short-term and long-term effects of early employment; (e) children from all races were included; and (f) whenever possible, continuous variables of early parental employment were used rather than artificially creating categorical variables. Thus, by drawing on the methodological strengths and addressing the methodological weaknesses of previous studies of early parental employment, it is hoped that this study will more fully realize the potential of the NLSY to address this topic.

Past research and theory have been conflicting regrading the effects of early parental employment, making it difficult to make specific predictions regarding the presence or direction of effects. Although previous inconsistent results are likely caused by methodological differences, the studies differ in too many ways to determine which findings are correct. Thus, the goal of this study is to examine whether and when early parental employment affects children's emotional, cognitive, and academic development.

Method

The NLSY Sample

The NLSY is a survey of approximately 12,600 individuals who have been interviewed annually since 1979 when they were 14 to 22 years old. This survey oversampled African American, Hispanic, and economically disadvantaged White individuals. The economically disadvantaged White oversample was dropped in 1990 for financial reasons. In 1986, 1988, 1990, 1992, and 1994, the survey conducted child assessments on offspring of the female participants.

Children of all races who were between 3 and 12 years of age at any of the five child assessment dates and who were born in 1980 or later (several background variables were unavailable for children born before 1980) were included. To assess possible developmental differences in the effects of early employment, I examined four different age groups separately: 3- to 4-year-olds, 5- to 6-year-olds, 7- to 9-year-olds, and 10- to 12-year-olds....

It should be noted that there is partial overlap of participants across these four age groups; each age group contains some participants who were also included in another age group. Of the 4,924 children who were 3- to 4-year-olds, 3,371 were also in the 5- to 6-year-old group. There were 4,486 children in the 5- to 6-year-old group, 3,203 of whom were also in the 7- to 9-year-old group. There were 3,711 children in the 7- to 9-year-old group, 1,951 of whom were also in the 10- to 12-year-old group. There were 2,095 children in the 10- to

12-year-old group. Thus, some of the data in this study are longitudinal and some are cross-sectional. (These figures are based on the number of children in each age group who had scores on at least one of the child outcome measures. The actual number of participants for each analysis varies because not all children were administered all measures.) In addition, although this sample is more representative than samples used in previous studies of early maternal employment (Bayder & Brooks-Gunn, 1991; Belsky & Eggebeen, 1991), it still does not represent women who bear children after age 34 and is still somewhat socioeconomically disadvantaged.

Measurement of Variables

Early maternal employment variables   Five indexes of early maternal employment were used. They were constructed on the basis of mother's reports of how many weeks after their children's birth they returned to work and their estimates of the average number of hours they worked per week during each quarter-year of the first 3 years of their children's lives.

For an evaluation of whether early employment status affects children, the first variable indicated whether or not the mother was employed at some time during the child's first 3 years (*employment during the first 3 years*); mothers who reported returning to work by the 156th week after their child's birth were coded 1 and mothers who did not return to work in the first 3 years were coded 0. The second, third, and fourth variables were applicable only for women who were employed at some point during the first 3 years. The second variable was the number of weeks after the child's birth before the mother returned to work (*timing of early employment*), the third variable was the average number of hours per week that she worked when she returned to work (*early employment hours*), and the fourth variable was the number of quarters the mother did not work after she had returned to work (*discontinuous employment*). Early employment hours was constructed by identifying the quarter-year during which the mother returned to work and calculating the average number of hours per week she worked from this quarter-year until the child's third birthday (not including quarters during which she reported working 0 hr). Many of the previous studies on the NLSY have included a variable representing whether or not mothers worked during the first year of the child's life. Although the timing of early maternal employment should capture the effects of employment during the first year, a variable *employment during the first year* was also included to facilitate comparison of the results of this study with the findings of previous studies.

Note that employment during the first 3 years and early employment hours could have been combined into one variable by assigning mothers who were never employed during the first 3 years a score of 0 hr. However, doing so assumes that the difference between not being employed and being employed 5 hr per week is the same as the difference between working 35 hr per week and working 40 hr per week. That is, it could not be assumed that not being employed is simply one end of the employment intensity dimension. Early employment status (comparing being employed with not being employed) might have a different effect on children than the intensity of employment and was therefore examined separately.

Early parental employment variable   Mothers reported the average number of hours per week that their spouses spent at their jobs every year from 1979 to 1994. The variable for *early paternal employment hours* consisted of an average of the spouse's job hours over the first 3 yearly assessments following the birth of the child.

Child outcome measures   Five child outcome variables were examined: compliance, behavior problems, cognitive development, self-esteem, and academic achievement. For children who were in one of the four specified age ranges at more than one assessment date, their multiple scores were averaged to obtain the best possible estimate of their functioning.

Compliance was assessed using a six-item subscale from the Temperament scale, which was developed for the NLSY. This scale correlates modestly but significantly with later behavior problems (Center for Human Resource Research, 1995). Higher scores indicate greater compliance.

Children's behavior problems were assessed using the BPI, which was developed to measure behavior problems in children age 4 and older. Many items were derived from the Child Behavior Checklist (Achenbach & Edelbrock, 1981) and other child behavior scales (Graham & Rutter, 1968; Kellam, Branch, Agrawal, & Ensminger, 1975; Peterson & Zill, 1986; Rutter, 1970). The parent reports the frequency with which the child exhibited each of 28 specific problems (1 = *often true,* 2 = *sometimes true,* 3 = *not true*). Standard scores (based on all children, not same sex) were used, with higher scores indicating more behavior problems. This scale has demonstrated good construct validity (Center for Human Resource Research, 1993).

Children's self-esteem was measured using the global self-worth subscale of the Self-Perception Profile for Children. This is a self-report measure that assesses children's sense of self-competence in the domain of academic skills and general self-worth (Harter, 1985). It correlates highly with teacher ratings and has good reliability (Harter, 1985). This measure was administered to children age 8 years and older.

Children's cognitive development was assessed using the PPVT-R (Dunn & Dunn, 1981), a widely used test of receptive language. This measure was administered to all children age 3 years and older. It was administered to all children in 1986 and 1992, and only to children without a previous valid score in 1988, 1990, and 1994. Children's academic achievement was measured using the PIAT. Three subtests from the PIAT were administered to children age 5 years and older: mathematics, reading recognition, and reading comprehension. Standard scores were used for both the PPVT-R and PIAT. Both cognitive measures have good reliability and validity (Dunn & Dunn, 1981; Dunn & Markwardt, 1970).

Selection factors   Theory and previous research suggested a number of family background variables that might act as selection factors for early employment. The following background variables were created for examining the effects of early maternal employment: family income, mother's education, mother's age at the child's birth, child gender, mother's IQ, child's race, birth order of the child, and marital status. For the effects of parental employment, the following background characteristics were used: gender, child's race, and birth order of the child. Father's IQs were not assessed in the NLSY. Mother's reports of these variables at the first assessment following the birth of the child were used, except for income, which was based on reports regarding the year before the child's birth. Mother's intelligence was assessed using the Armed Forces Qualification Test (AFQT), which was administered to all NLSY participants in 1980. The AFQT consists of the sum of scores on four subtests of the Armed Services Vocational Aptitude Battery: word knowledge, numeric operations, paragraph comprehension, and arithmetic reasoning.

Moderating variables   On the basis of theory and research, the following variables were examined as possible moderators of the effects of early parental employment: marital status, race, gender, family income, and job satisfaction. The six NLSY studies yielded conflicting findings regarding the moderating effects of these variables, but each variable was supported by at least one study. Job satisfaction was assessed by asking individuals to indicate how they felt about their current jobs on a 4-point scale from 1 = *like it very much* to 4 = *dislike it very much*. Previous studies have suggested that job satisfaction predicts child functioning (Brody, Stoneman, & MacKinnon, 1986; Gold & Andres, 1978), and it was thought that this would more directly assess the moderating effects of occupational complexity reported by Parcel and Menaghan (1994).

Results

... These simple correlations suggest that before controlling for selection factors, mothers' working early in the child's life is generally associated with more positive child outcome; however, more intense maternal employment (working more hours) is associated with less positive child outcome. Early parental employment tended to be associated with more positive child outcomes....

Discussion

This study examined the effects of early parental employment on children's later cognitive, academic, behavioral, and emotional functioning using the 1994 NLSY. It sought to clarify conflicting results from previous NLSY studies by addressing several previous methodological limitations. Consistent with previous studies, family characteristics including family income, parents' education, mothers' IQ and age, and child race and birth order were related to both early parental employment variables and child outcome variables. Therefore, the effects of early parental employment were examined controlling for these background characteristics.

The results of this study revealed few simple effects of early parental employment. There were no significant main effects of early maternal employment status. Among mothers who were employed during the first 3 years, the only significant effects of the timing of the return to employment and discontinuity of early employment were on compliance in 3- to 4-year-olds and these effects were small; returning to work later and greater discontinuity were associated with somewhat higher compliance....

The results partially supported the hypothesis that early parental employment has a positive effect on children's development by increasing family income. This positive pathway seemed to affect children's behavior problems and academic achievement but not children's compliance, self-esteem, or language–cognitive development. All of these indirect effects existed largely in the absence of any total effects of early parental employment on behavior problems and academic achievement. This suggests that early parental employment may have both positive and negative effects on children's development that counteract each other. This study has identified one potential positive effect. Future studies are needed to explore other positive and negative pathways. This mediating effect of family income also highlights the importance of distinguishing between selection factors and mediating variables. Controlling for income after birth may yield misleading results; one should not control for a benefit of early employment in examining its effects....

These results should be interpreted within the context of the limitations of the study. Although the sample in the present study was more representative of the general population of mothers than previous studies, the sample is still younger and of lower SES [socioeconomic status] than average; these results may not be generalized to older, higher SES parents. In addition, this study addressed ethnicity in only a limited way. Finer distinctions within each of the racial groups should be made in future studies. Of course, this study was also limited by its correlational design. Although attempts were made to statistically control for third variables, other important background variables may have been omitted; the few significant results that were found may have been due to unmeasured third variables. Finally, data regarding the quality of child care were not available in this data set. Previous research indicates that this is an important contextual variable (Belsky, 1990; NICHD Early Child Care Research Network, 1997b). Although maternal employment appeared to have little effect on these children's development, quality of early child care may have a much larger impact. Further study is needed in this area.

Nonetheless, this study adds to the existing literature in several ways. This study had an unusually large sample size, providing more power to detect effects, particularly interaction effects that are notoriously difficult to detect (McClelland & Judd, 1993). This greater power allows more confidence that nonsignificant effects represent no or negligible effects. In addition, the sample was more representative than previous studies. Also, continuous parental employment variables were examined whenever possible rather than artificially created groups formed by categorizing continuous variables. This study used a longitudinal design to examine the long-term effects of early parental employment; previous longitudinal studies have only examined the relatively short-term effects on children. Finally, this is one of the few studies to examine both early maternal and paternal employment variables, recognizing the importance of examining the role of fathers in children's development.

In sum, findings reported by previous NLSY studies may have been some-what sample and method specific. When methodological limitations were addressed in the present study, few of the previous findings were replicated, and no consistent evidence of substantial effects of early parental employment on children's later development was found.

POSTSCRIPT

Is Early Maternal Employment Harmful to Young Children?

Currently, 66 percent of women who are mothers of children under the age of three are in the workforce. Therefore, the concern over the well-being of their children is a key issue. Harvey's conclusion that there are no significant main effects of early maternal employment, along with her assertion that early maternal employment can have positive effects on children's development by increasing family income, was controversial.

Those who defend stay-at-home mothers are usually those who see the mother in the home environment as the best way for children to be raised. But what are the options for children who have mothers who are not caring and attentive, or for children living in environments where they are not safe, fed, or kept warm during the day? Is the mothers' care and the home environment always the best for children?

Instead of using energy to either defend or condemn working mothers, would efforts to provide appropriate child care for all children be a better way to use our resources? There are cases where a single parent is raising children or where both parents must work to support the family. What quality options exist for these parents and children? What can be done to improve these options?

Suggested Readings

Belsky, J. and Eggebeen, D., "Early and Extensive Maternal Employment and Young Children's Socioemotional Development: Children of the National Longitudinal Survey of Youth," *Journal of Marriage and the Family* (vol. 53, 1991).

Conaway, R. A., "Misleading APA Press Release Results in Media Brouhaha," *Mothers at Home,* http://www.mah.org/apa2.htm (May 1999).

Greenstein, T. N., "Are the Most Advantaged Children Truly Disadvantaged by Early Maternal Employment?" *Journal of Family Issues* (vol. 16, no. 2, 1995).

Holcomb, B., *Not Guilty! The Good News About Working Mothers* (Simon & Schuster, 1998).

Parcel, T., Nickoll, R., and Dufur, M., "The Effects of Parental Work and Maternal Employment on Children's Reading and Math Achievement," *Work and Occupations* (vol. 23, no. 4, 1996).

ISSUE 2

Should Brain Science Guide Educational Practice?

YES: Sharon Begley, from "How to Build a Baby's Brain," *Newsweek* (Spring/Summer 1997)

NO: John T. Bruer, from "Brain Science, Brain Fiction," *Educational Leadership* (November 1998)

ISSUE SUMMARY

YES: Sharon Begley, senior editor for *Newsweek,* presents research on how early experiences can affect the development of the brain.

NO: John T. Bruer, president of the James S. McDonnell Foundation, cautions against putting too much emphasis on brain science and maintains that more research should be done before changing current educational practices.

Researchers now know that 50 percent of brain development occurs during the first year of life. There are implications from this research that are related to windows of opportunity, parent education, and the provision of quality child care. The National Education Goals Panel found that over 50 percent of infants and toddlers in the United States are not living in environments that will provide them the stimulation and assistance thought by some to be vitally important for future success in school. There are many children under the age of three who face one or more of the following risk factors: poor prenatal care, inferior postnatal care, poverty, lack of sufficient parental attention, and parents who isolate themselves from their children. Children being raised in these environments are facing great odds as they begin a life of learning.

In their 1994 report, "Starting Points: Meeting the Needs of Our Youngest Children," the Carnegie Corporation found that there are five pivotal points that Americans should take into consideration as they work to prepare all children for successful lives. The points are:

- Brain development occurs prenatally, and in the first few years, at a rapid pace.

- Brain development is affected by environmental influences.
- Environmental influences are long-lasting.
- Early environments affect the number of brain cells and the connections between the cells.
- Early stress negatively affects brain function.

Connections, or synapses, are formed during the early years and help children think and learn as they grow. Children who lack early brain stimulation have brains that are not as active, and they are not able to engage in complex thought processes nor can they form lasting, secure relationships. Early experiences strengthen the synapses so that the brain will be better able to absorb and acquire new information as children grow and learn.

Does early brain research have implications for the many parents who adopt children from orphanages in developing countries? Many of these babies are left in cribs during the day and only receive human contact when they are changed or given a bottle. Should these adoptive parents be worried about their children's future learning potential and capacity to form secure adult relationships as a result of their early experiences? If early brain development is so critical, what help is available for those children who, because of medical or other reasons, did not receive sufficient early stimulation for the approximately 100 billion neurons with which a healthy child is born?

In the following selections, Sharon Begley reports on the research examining early brain development and asserts that the first three years are critical to future learning. She stresses the need for quality early experiences for the stimulation of neuron development in order to form synapses in the brain. John T. Bruer cautions against jumping to conclusions about the brain-science findings. He points out that for centuries children have been raised in homes by parents who may not have paid 100 percent of their attention to the growth and development of their babies. Yet many prominent citizens have made significant contributions to humanity without having had special toys, attention, or materials available to them. Bruer finds the attention to early brain development to be a passing fad.

How to Build a Baby's Brain

You cannot see what is going on inside your newborn's brain. You cannot see the electrical activity as her eyes lock onto yours and, almost instantaneously, a neuron in her retina makes a connection to one in her brain's visual cortex that will last all her life. The image of your face has become an enduring memory in her mind. And you cannot see the explosive release of a neurotransmitter —brain chemical—as a neuron from your baby's ear, carrying the electrically encoded sound of "ma," connects to a neuron in her auditory cortex. "Ma" has now commandeered a cluster of cells in the infant's brain that will, as long as the child lives, respond to no other sound.

You cannot see any of this. But Dr. Harry Chugani can come close. With positron-emission tomography (PET), Chugani, a pediatric neurobiologist at Wayne State University in Detroit, watches the regions of a baby's brain turn on, one after another, like city neighborhoods having their electricity restored after a blackout. He can measure activity in the primitive brain stem and sensory cortex from the moment the baby is born. He can observe the visual cortex burn with activity in the second and third months of life. He can see the frontal cortex light up at 6 to 8 months. He can see, in other words, that the brain of a baby is still forming long after the child has left the womb—not merely growing bigger, as toes and livers and arms do, but forming the microscopic connections responsible for feeling, learning and remembering. For doing, in short, everything that a brain is born to do but that it is born without knowing how to do.

Scientists are just now realizing how experiences after birth, rather than something innate, determine the actual wiring of the human brain. "Only 15 years ago," reports the Families and Work Institute in the just-release study "Rethinking the Brain," "neuroscientists assumed that by the time babies are born, the structure of their brains [had been] genetically determined." But by [1996] researchers knew that was wrong. Instead, early-childhood experiences exert a dramatic and precise impact, physically determining how the intricate neural circuits of the brain are wired. Since then they have been learning how those experiences shape the brain's circuits.

At birth, the brain's 100 billion or so neurons form more than 50 trillion connections (synapses). The genes the baby carries—from the egg and sperm that made him—have already determined his brain's basic wiring. They have formed the connections in the brain stem that will make the heart beat and lungs respire. But that's all. Of a human's 80,000 different genes, fully half are believed to be involved in forming and running the central nervous system. Yet even that doesn't come close to what the brain needs. In the first months of life, the number of synapses will increase 20-fold—to more than 1,000 trillion. There simply are not enough genes in the human species to specify so many connections.

That leaves experiences—all the signals that a baby receives from the world. Experience seems to exert its effects by strengthening synapses. Just as a memory will fade if it is not accessed from time to time, so synapses that are not used will also wither away in a process called pruning. The way to reinforce these wispy connections has come to be known as stimulation. Contrary to the claims of entrepreneurs preying on the anxieties of new parents, stimulation does not mean subjecting a toddler to flashcards. Rather, it is something much simpler—sorting socks by color or listening to the soothing cadences of a fairy tale. In the most extensive study yet of what makes a difference, Craig Ramey of the University of Alabama found that it was blocks, beads, peekaboo and other old-fashioned measures that enhance cognitive, motor and language development—and, absent traumas, enhance them permanently.

The formation of synapses (synaptogenesis) and their pruning occurs at different times in different parts of the brain. The sequence seems to coincide with the emergence of various skills. Synaptogenesis begins in the motor cortex at about 2 months. Around then, infants lose their "startle" and "rooting" reflexes and begin to master purposeful movements. At 3 months, synapse formation in the visual cortex peaks; the brain is fine-tuning connections allowing the eyes to focus on an object. At 8 or 9 months the hippocampus, which indexes and files memories, becomes fully functional; only now can babies form explicit memories of, say, how to move a mobile. In the second half of the first year, finds Chugani, the prefrontal cortex, the seat of forethought and logic, forms synapses at such a rate that it consumes twice as much energy as an adult brain. That furious pace continues for the child's first decade of life.

Research on language has shown how "neuroplastic" an infant's brain is, and how that plasticity lessens with age. Patricia Kuhl of the University of Washington studies the "auditory maps" that infants' brains construct out of phonemes (the smallest units of sound in a language, such as "ee" or "l"). At first, neurons in the auditory cortex are like laborers to whom jobs have not yet been assigned. But as a newborn hears, say, the patter of English, a different cluster of neurons in the auditory cortex is recruited to respond to each phoneme. Each cluster then fires only when a nerve from the ear carries that particular sound, such as "pa" or "ma." If one sound is clearly distinct from another, as "ra" and "la" are in English, then the neurons whose job it is to hear one will lie far from those whose job it is to hear the other. (Kuhl makes noninvasive electrical measurements, through the babies' scalps, to identify which neurons fire in response to a particular sound.) But if the sounds are nearly identical, as "ra" and "la" are in Japanese, then the two sets of neurons are so close that the baby will have trouble distinguishing the two phonemes. By 12 months, an infants' auditory map is formed. He will be unable to pick out phonemes he has not heard thousands of times for the simple reason that no cluster of neurons has been assigned the job of responding to that sound. And the older he gets, the more he will struggle to learn a new language: fewer unassigned neurons are available for the job of hearing new phonemes.

Experience counts in building vocabulary, too, and at a very young age. The size of a toddler's vocabulary is strongly correlated with how much a mother talks to the child, reports Janellen Huttenlocher of the University of Chicago. At 20 months, children of chatty mothers averaged 131 more words than children of less talkative mothers; at 2 years, the gap had more than doubled, to 295 words. "The critical factor is number of times the child hears different words," says Huttenlocker. The effect holds for the complexity of sentence structure, too, she finds. Mothers who used complex sentences (those with dependent clauses, such as "when . . ." or "because . . .") 40 percent of the time had toddlers who did so 35 percent of the time; mothers who used such sentences in only 10 percent of their utterances had children who did so only 5 percent of the time.

Only "live" language, not television, produced these vocabulary- and syntax-boosting effects. Why doesn't all the gabbing on TV stimulate language development? Huttenlocker suspects that "language has to be used in relation to ongoing events, or it's just noise." That may hold for other sorts of cognition, too. Information embedded in an emotional context seems to stimulate neural circuitry more powerfully than information alone. A child will more readily learn the concept of "more" if it refers to the happy prospect of more cookies, and "later" if it is attached to a frustrating wait for a trip to the playground, than if the word is presented in isolation from things the baby cares about. There is nothing mysterious about this: adults form a memory much more readily if it has emotional context (how did you hear that the space shuttle had exploded?) than if it doesn't (what's the difference between a sine and a cosine?). Causality, a key component of logic, is also best learned through emotion: if I smile, Mommy smiles back. A sense that one thing causes another forms synapses that will eventually support more abstruse concepts of causality. Feelings, concepts and language begin to be linked in this way in the months from 7 through 12.

Another route to brain wiring seems to be tapping into its natural harmonies. In the last year, new studies have nailed down how music affects spatial-temporal reasoning—the ability to see a disassembled picture of, say, a rabbit and mentally piece it back together. Such reasoning underlies math, engineering and chess. In a study published . . . in the journal *Neurological Research,* scientists report how spatial-temporal reasoning in 3- and 4-year-olds was affected by weekly piano lessons. After six months, the budding Horowitzes—all of whom scored at the national average on tests of spatial recognition—scored 34 percent *above* average on this reasoning skill. None of the other children (who had received computer keyboard and mouse lessons, singing lessons or nothing at all) had improved. What explains the effect? Physicist Gordon Shaw of the University of California, Irvine, suspects that in playing the piano, "you are seeing how patterns work in space and time." When sequential finger and key patterns make melodies, neural circuits that connect positions (keys) to sounds in space and time (the melody) are strengthened. "Music training produces long-term modifications in neural circuitry," says Shaw. What scientists do not know is whether the effects of early music training endure—whether the preschoolers will be math wizards in high school.

The downside of the brain's great plasticity is that it is acutely vulnerable to trauma. "Experience may alter the behavior of an adult," says Dr. Bruce Perry of Baylor College of Medicine, but it "literally provides the organizing framework" for the brain of a child. If the brain's organization reflects its experience, and the experience of the traumatized child is fear and stress, then the neurochemical responses to fear and stress become the most powerful architects of the brain. "If you have experiences that are overwhelming, and have them again and again, it changes the structure of the brain," says Dr. Linda Mayes of the Yale Child Study Center. Here's how:

- Trauma elevates stress hormones, such as cortisol, that wash over the tender brain like acid. As a result, regions in the cortex and in the limbic system (responsible for emotions, including attachment) are 20 to 30 percent smaller in abused children than in normal kids, finds Perry; these regions also have fewer synapses.
- In adults who were abused as children, the memory-making hippocampus is smaller than in nonabused adults. This effect, too, is believed to be the result of the toxic effects of cortisol.
- High cortisol levels during the vulnerable years of zero to 3 increase activity in the brain structure involved in vigilance and arousal. ("It's called the locus ceruleus.) As a result the brain is wired to be on hairtrigger alert, explains Perry: regions that were activated by the original trauma are immediately reactivated whenever the child dreams of, thinks about or is reminded of the trauma (as by the mere presence of the abusive person). The slightest stress, the most inchoate fear, unleashes a new surge of stress hormones. This causes hyperactivity, anxiety and impulsive behavior. "The kids with the higher cortisol levels score lowest on inhibitory control," says neuroscientist Megan Gunnar of the University of Minnesota. "Kids from high-stress environments [have] problems in attention regulation and self-control."

Trauma also scrambles neurotransmitter signals, ratcheting up some and depressing others. Since neurotransmitters play key roles in telling growing neurons where to go and what to connect to, children exposed to chronic and unpredictable stress—a mother's boyfriend who lashes out in fury, an alcoholic uncle who is kind one day and abusive the next—will suffer deficits in their ability to learn. "Some percentage of capacity is lost," says Perry. "A piece of the child is lost forever."

That is tragedy enough, of course, but it is made even greater by the loss of what could have been. Babies are born into this world with their brain primed to learn. But they cannot do it alone.

NO

John T. Bruer

Brain Science, Brain Fiction

[Recently], a flood of articles in popular and professional publications have discussed the implications of brain science for education and child development. Although we should consider ideas and research from other fields for our professional practice, we must assess such ideas critically. This is particularly true when we look at how a vast, complex field like brain science might improve classroom instruction.

Three big ideas from brain science figure most centrally in the education literature, and educators should know four things about these ideas to make their own critical appraisals of brain-based education. My own assessment of recent articles about brain research is that well-founded educational applications of brain science may come eventually, but right now, brain science has little to offer education practice or policy (Bruer, 1997, 1998).

Three big ideas arise from brain science: (1) Early in life, neural connections (synapses) form rapidly in the brain: (2) Critical periods occur in development; and (3) Enriched environments have a pronounced effect on brain development during the early years. Neuroscientists have known about all three big ideas for 20 to 30 years. What we need to be critical of is not the ideas themselves, but how they are interpreted for educators and parents.

Early Synapse Formation

Synapses are the connections through which nerve impulses travel from one neuron to another. Since the late 1970s, neuroscientists have known that the number of synapses per unit volume of tissue (the *synaptic density*) in the brain's outer cortical layer changes over the life span of monkeys and humans (Goldman-Rakic, Bourgeois, & Rakic, 1997; Huttenlocher & Dobholkar, 1997; Rakic, Bourgeois, & Goldman-Rakic, 1994). Not surprisingly, human newborns have lower synaptic densities than adults. However, in the months following birth, the infant brain begins to form synapses far in excess of the adult levels. In humans, by age 4, synaptic densities have peaked in all brain areas at levels 50 percent above adult levels. Throughout childhood, synaptic densities remain above adult levels. Around the age of puberty, a pruning process begins to eliminate synapses, reducing synaptic densities to adult, mature levels.

The timing of this process appears to vary among brain areas in humans. In the visual area of the human brain, synaptic densities increase rapidly starting at 2 months of age, peak at 8 to 10 months, and then decline to adult levels at around 10 years. However, in the human frontal cortex—the brain area involved in attention, short-term memory, and planning—this process begins later and lasts longer. In the frontal cortex, synaptic densities do not stabilize at mature levels until around age 16. Thus, we can think of synaptic densities changing over the first two decades of life in an inverted-U pattern; low at birth, highest in childhood, and lower in adulthood.

This much is neuroscientific fact. The question is, What does this inverted-U pattern mean for learning and education? Here, despite what educators might think, the neuroscientists know relatively little. In discussing what the changes in synaptic density mean for behavior and learning, neuroscientists cite a small set of examples based on animal research and then extrapolate these findings to human infants. On the basis of observations of changes in motor, visual, and memory skills, neuroscientists agree that basic movement, vision, and memory skills first appear in their most primitive form when synaptic densities begin their rapid increase. For example, at age 8 months, when synapses begin to increase rapidly in the frontal brain areas, infants first show short-term memory skills for places and objects. Infants' performance on these tasks improves steadily over the next four months. However, performance on these memory tasks does not reach adult levels until puberty, when synaptic densities have *decreased* to adult levels.

Thing to Know No. 1: Neuroscience suggests that there is no simple, direct relationship between synaptic densities and intelligence.

Increases in synaptic densities are associated with the initial emergence of skills and capacities, but these skills and capacities continue to develop after synaptic densities decrease to adult levels. Although early in infancy we might have the most synapses we will ever have, most learning occurs later, after synaptic densities *decrease* in the brain. Given the existence of the U-shaped pattern and what we observe about our own learning and intelligence over our life spans, we have no reason to believe, as we often read, that the more synapses we have, the smarter we are. Nor do existing neuroscientific studies support the idea that the more learning experiences we have during childhood, the more synapses will be "saved" from pruning and the more intelligent our children will be.

Neuroscientists know very little about how learning, particularly school learning, affects the brain at the synaptic level. We should be skeptical of any claims that suggest they do. For example, we sometimes read that complex learning situations cause increased "neural branching" that offsets neural pruning. As far as we know, such claims are based more on brain fiction than on brain science.

Critical Periods in Development

Research on critical periods has been prominent in developmental neurobiology for more than 30 years. This research has shown that if some motor, sensory, and (in humans) language skills are to develop normally, then the animal must have certain kinds of experience at specific times during its development.

The best-researched example is the existence of critical periods in the development of the visual system. Starting in the 1960s, David Hubel, Torsten Wiesel, and their colleagues showed that if during the early months of life, cats or monkeys had one eyelid surgically closed, the animal would never regain functional use of that eye when it was subsequently reopened (Hubel, Wiesel, & LeVay, 1977). They also showed that closing one eye during this time had demonstrable effects on the structure of the visual area in the animal's brain. However, the same or longer periods of complete visual deprivation in adult cats had no effect on either the animal's ability to use the eye when it was reopened or on its brain structure. Only young animals, during a critical period in their development, were sensitive to this kind of deprivation. They also found that closing *both* eyes during the critical period had no permanent, long-term effects on the animals' vision or brain structure.

Finally, they found that in monkeys, "reverse closure" during the critical period—opening the closed eye and closing the open eye—allowed a young deprived animal to recover the use of the originally deprived eye. If the reverse suturing was done early enough in the critical period, recovery could be almost complete. These last two findings are seldom mentioned in popular and educational interpretations of critical-period research.

Over the past three decades, hundreds of neuroscientists have advanced our understanding of critical periods. We should be aware of three conclusions about critical periods that these scientists generally endorse. First, the different outcomes of closing one eye, both eyes, and reverse suturing suggest that it is *not* the amount of stimulation that matters during a critical period. If only the amount mattered, closing both eyes should have the same effect on each eye as it had when only one eye was closed. Neuroscientists believe that what matters during critical periods in the development of the visual system is the *balance* and *relative timing* of stimulation to the eyes. What does this mean? For one thing, it means that more stimulation during the critical period does not necessarily result in a better-developed visual system.

Second, neuroscientists have learned that critical periods are quite complex and that different critical periods exist for different specific functions (Daw, 1995). For example, within the visual system are different critical periods for visual acuity, binocular function, and depth perception. For humans, even in an early developing system like vision, these periods can last until early childhood. For language, the critical period for learning phonology—learning to speak without an accent—ends in early childhood, but the critical period for learning a language's grammar does not end until around age 16.

Neuroscientists now also think that for each specific function of a sensory system, like vision, there are three distinct phases within the critical period.

First, there is a time of rapid change during which a function, like depth perception, quickly matures. During the second phase, sensory deprivation can result in deterioration or loss of that function. After the period of sensitivity to deprivation, there seems to be yet a third phase of the critical period. During this phase, the system retains sufficient plasticity to compensate for deprivation and regains near-normal function if appropriate sensory experience occurs.

Given these complexities, neuroscientists know that it makes little sense to speak of *a* critical period for vision or for any other sensory system, let alone of *a* critical period for brain development. Critical periods are simply windows of learning opportunity that open and then slam shut.

Finally, neuroscientists are beginning to understand why critical periods exist and why critical periods have adaptive value for an organism. They believe that as the result of evolutionary processes, highly sensitive neural systems, like vision, have come to depend on the presence of environmental stimuli to fine-tune their neural circuitry.

Relying on the environment to fine-tune the system results in neural circuits that are more sensitively tuned than they ever could be if they were hard-wired by genetic programs at birth. Relying on the presence of certain kinds of stimuli just at the right times would seem to be a highly risky developmental strategy, especially for a system like vision that is fundamental to survival. The reason it is not risky is that the kinds of stimuli needed during critical periods—patterned visual input, the ability to move and manipulate objects, noises, the presence of speech sounds—are ubiquitously and abundantly present in any normal human environment. Nature has made a bet that the stimuli will be present, but nature has placed its money on an almost sure thing. The brain expects certain kinds of stimuli to be present for normal development, and they almost always are, unless a child is abused to the point of being raised in a deprivation chamber. William Greenough and his colleagues (1992) have characterized the kind of brain modification that occurs as a result of critical periods "experience-expectant brain plasticity."

Thing to Know No. 2: If critical periods are a result of our evolutionary history and nature's bet on almost sure things occurring in a child's environment, then neuroscientific research on critical periods is likely to have little relevance to formal education.

From what we know to date about critical periods, they contribute to the development of basic specieswide abilities, like vision, hearing, or language. For this reason, despite what we read, the specifics of home or preschool environments matter little, if at all, to how children's sensory and motor systems develop.

For similar reasons, critical periods say little about formal education. Formal schooling instructs children about the social and cultural particulars, not about evolution-based, specieswide skills and behaviors. Currently, we have no reason to think that there are critical periods for the acquisition of culturally and socially transmitted skills, like reading, mathematics, or music, just to name a few of the favorite examples. As far as we know, people can acquire these skills at any age; can benefit from instruction at any age; and can increase their intelligence and expertise, given the right opportunities, at any age (Greenough, 1997).

The Effects of Enriched Environments

Neuroscientists have been studying the effects of enriched environments on rats' behavior and brain development for nearly 50 years. Some of the best and most current of this work is that of Greenough and his colleagues at the University of Illinois (1992). In this research, neuroscientists study how raising rats in different environments affects their brain structure. Typically, scientists study the effects of two contrasting environments. Some rats are raised alone in small cages with only food and water available. This "isolated environment" is the typical laboratory environment for a rat.

Other rats are raised in large, group cages that also contain novel objects and obstacles. Greenough calls these environments *complex,* rather than enriched. He points out that complex environments are enriched only in comparison with a rat's typical lab cage. Neuroscientists use complex environments to mimic the rats' wild or natural environment. They are not special, accelerated rodent learning environments. One should not think of them as high-quality infant care or Head Start for rats. One should think of them more as attempts to create New York City subway tunnel conditions in the laboratory.

In electron microscopic studies, Greenough and his colleagues found that young rats raised in complex environments have 25 percent more synapses per neuron in the visual areas of their brains than do rats raised in isolation. However, increases in synapses per neuron ratios do not occur to this extent in all brain areas, and some brain areas show no effects of complex rearing at all. On the basis of this research, we can see that it is definitely not the case, as we often read, that complex environments result in a 25 percent increase in brain connectivity.

More important, however, 15 years ago, Greenough and his colleagues established that the brains of *adult* rats also form new synapses in response to complex environments. Other studies in monkeys and humans have definitively established that the adult brain remains highly plastic and capable of extensive neural reorganization throughout life. The brain's ability to reorganize itself in response to new experiences is what makes it possible for us to learn throughout our lives. The ability of the mature brain to change and reorganize, a finding seldom mentioned in the education literature, is a new, exciting finding of brain science (Nelson & Bloom, 1997).

Thing to Know No. 3: Research on complex environments and related findings tells us that the brain can reorganize itself for learning throughout our lifetimes.

This new insight runs counter to our current fixation on early development and critical periods. However, in thinking about how this research relates to educational practice and policy, we must be careful not to confuse *complex* with *enriched*. Neuroscientists use *complex* as a descriptive term for a laboratory simulation of a wild or natural environment. Education writers tend to use *enriched* as a value-laden term. In the popular and education literature, enriched environments tend to be culturally preferred, middle-class environments. These environments tend to include things that the writers value —Mozart, piano lessons, playing chess—and to exclude things that they scorn —video games, MTV, shooting pool. These writers tend to identify enriched environments with Cambridge, Massachusetts, and Palo Alto, California, and deprived environments with Roxbury and East Palo Alto.

As far as neuroscience goes, all these activities and environments are equally complex—and neuroscience says nothing about which are more or less enriched than others. In assessing claims about environments and the brain, we should be aware of how easy it is to slide from describing complexity to prescribing enrichment. We should be careful not to use neuroscience to provide biological pseudo-argument in favor of our culture and our political values and prejudices.

Educators should know one final thing.

Thing to Know No. 4: Research on early synapse formation, critical periods, and complex environments has a long history. Yet, we have little understanding of what this research might mean for education.

Our appeals to this research are often naive and superficial. Other brain-related themes popular in the education literature—emotional intelligence, the social brain, the brain in the entire body, the intelligent immune system, downshifting—have a much less reliable grounding in neuroscience. Educators seeking to base practice on the best science might want to assess recommendations stemming from these ideas even more carefully and critically.

References

Bruer, J. T. (1997). Education and the brain: A bridge too far. *Educational Researcher,* *26*(8), 4–16.

Bruer, J. T. (1998). Let's put brain science on the back burner. *NASSP Bulletin, 82*(598), 21–28.

Daw, N. W. (1995). *Visual development.* New York: Plenum.

Goldman-Rakic, P. S., Bourgeios, J.-P., & Rakic, P. (1997). Synaptic substrate of cognitive development: Synaptogenesis in the prefrontal cortex of the nonhuman primate. In N. A. Krasnegor, G. R. Lyon, & P. S. Goldman-Rakic (Eds.), *Development of the prefrontal cortex: Evolution, neurobiology, and behavior* (pp. 27–47). Baltimore: Paul H. Brookes.

Greenough, W. T. (1997). We can't focus just on ages zero to three. *APA Monitor, 28,* 19.

Greenough, W. T., Withers, G. S., & Anderson, B. J. (1992). Experience-dependent synaptogenesis as a plausible memory mechanism. In I. Gormezano & E. A. Wasserman (Eds.), *Learning and memory: The behavioral and biological substrates* (pp. 209–299). Hillsdale, NJ: Erlbaum.

Hubel, D. H., Wiesel, T. N., & LeVay, S. (1977). Plasticity of ocular dominance columns in monkey striate cortex. *Philosophical Transactions of the Royal Society of London B., 278,* 307–409.

Huttenlocher, P. R., & Dabholkar, A. S. (1997). Regional differences in synaptogenesis in human cerebral cortex. *Journal of Comparative Neurology, 367,* 167–178.

Nelson, C. A., & Bloom, F. E. (1997). Child development and neuroscience. *Child Development, 68*(5), 970–987.

Rakic, P., Bourgeois, J.-P., & Goldman-Rakic, P. S. (1994). Synaptic development of the cerebral cortex: Implications for learning, memory, and mental illness. In J. van Pelt, M. A. Corner, H. B. M. Uylings, & F. H. Lopes da Silva (Eds), *Progress in Brain Research 102* (pp. 227–243). Amsterdam: Elsevier Science BV.

POSTSCRIPT

Should Brain Science Guide Educational Practice?

Over fifty years ago initial learning opportunities were provided for children when they entered kindergarten at age five. Efforts to provide additional stimulating materials or environments to children younger than age five were not considered necessary. With the creation of the federal program, Head Start, in 1965, attention turned to preparing four-year-olds to enter school ready to learn. As time went on, it was found that age four was not quite early enough to prevent the myriad of problems and deficiencies of many young children. Nor was it early enough to build a neurological foundation for math and logic. Brain research, made possible by new technology, has led researchers to focus intervention efforts even earlier than once thought necessary. Also, the prenatal months have become the new focus of efforts to prevent life-long problems with language, motor skills, social interaction, emotional development, and learning capacity.

However, are these early efforts completely necessary? Can parents go overboard in providing stimulation and learning experiences for their young children? Are we creating an even deeper crevice between the haves and the have-nots of our society? Are parents who can afford to purchase music compact discs and computer games giving their children an advantage over children who live in homes where those items are not affordable? Are all of those items necessary for strong brain development?

Brain research has found that the window of opportunity for learning a second language is before the age of ten. Up until age ten, one can learn a second language and still develop the unique speech sounds and patterns of that language. Acquiring a second or additional language after the age of ten, when the patterns for speech have been fully embedded in the brain, generally means that a speaker will never develop the fluency and speech sound of a native speaker. In most public schools in the United States a second language is not introduced until the high school years. Should major educational reforms take place as a result of the findings of brain science? Are the findings conclusive enough to warrant what may be, in some cases, dramatic changes in our educational programming?

Suggested Readings

Berger, E. H., "Supporting Parents With Two Essential Understandings: Attachment and Brain Development," *Early Childhood Education Journal* (vol. 26, no. 4, 1999).

Kulman, L., "The Prescription for Smart Kids," *U.S. News & World Report* (vol. 122, no. 9, March 10, 1997).

Lindsey, G., "Brain Research and Implications for Early Childhood Education," *Childhood Education* (vol. 75, no. 2, 1998/1999).

Newberger, J. J., "New Brain Development Research—A Wonderful Window of Opportunity to Build Public Support for Early Childhood Education!" *Young Children* (vol. 52, no. 4, 1997).

ISSUE 3

Should Young Children Use Computers?

YES: Susan W. Haugland, from "What Role Should Technology Play in Young Children's Learning?" *Young Children* (November 1999)

NO: Alliance for Childhood, from "Fool's Gold: A Critical Look at Computers and Childhood," A Report of the Alliance for Childhood, http://www.allianceforchildhood.net/projects/computers/computers_reports_fools_gold_exec.htm (September 11, 2000)

ISSUE SUMMARY

YES: Susan W. Haugland, a professor emeritus in child development, raises many of the key issues related to the use of computers by young children. She asserts that young children should use computers as long as attention and careful consideration is given to the age of introduction, support provided, and teacher training.

NO: The Alliance for Childhood released a report that critically examines the use of computers by young children and concludes that there are many more appropriate activities for children to be involved in that will also enable them to succeed in the future.

College professors are just now encountering the first generation of students to be raised with regular access to computers. The ratio of computers to young children increased from 1:125 in 1984, to 1:22 in 1990, to 1:10 in 1997. The word *mouse* means something entirely different to today's preschoolers than to children of a generation ago. What, if any, are the benefits for children raised from infancy with computers? Are children who have not been exposed to computers in their home or school at a greater risk of school failure?

Computers have permeated our culture. They can be found everywhere from airport check-in counters to voting booths. The debate in homes and schools centers on the use of computers by children as a beneficial tool for academic success. Technology has strained the budgets for even the largest and most well funded schools. Many want to know if the use of computers can improve the academic performance of our youngest students.

Doctors have become concerned about eye strain, obesity, and poor posture related to computer use. Preschoolers generally sit in a chair adjusted for an adult body and may develop poor posture as a result of tilting their heads back to see the screen or reaching their hands to the mouse and keyboard located on an adult-sized desk. Hours spent in uncomfortable positions can result in sore wrists, neck strain, back pain, and headaches. In addition, eye strain and fatigue can be a problem for young children who may sit too close to a computer screen. A more serious concern is the physical activity in which young children are *not* engaging while they are passively sitting and looking at a computer screen. Can extensive computer use by young children lead to excessive television viewing and a passive lifestyle as an adult?

The concerns of parents center on the quality of the technology experience. Is the software appropriate? Are the tasks easy, yet challenging enough, to keep the child's interest? Are children *learning* when it appears that they are just playing on the computer?

While many Americans were jumping on the computer bandwagon, a group of educators, physicians, policy makers, parents, and concerned citizens started to voice their apprehension about the use of computers by young children. The result was a report published by the Alliance for Childhood that called for a moratorium on the further introduction of computers in early childhood and during elementary education. The group recommends the use of computers only for special cases of children with certain disabilities.

There is strong support for the day-to-day learning activities available when children use computers, including the opportunity for them to control the learning experiences, collaborate with teachers and other children as they learn, and explore new areas not possible without the use of a computer. Will children who do not have access to a computer in early years be at risk of failure in school? Are two- and three-year-old children too young to be sitting in front of a computer screen? If children do not start using a computer when they are preschoolers will they be left behind when they enter elementary school?

Another issue to consider is the need for ongoing teacher instruction and support. Teachers who have confidence in their use of computers are better able to instruct children. School administrators would therefore need to secure the funding for ongoing teacher training and the support of technology. This is as critical as the acquisition of the hardware and software for the program.

In the following selections, Susan W. Haugland discusses many of the issues related to the use of computers in an early childhood setting and concludes that, with proper guidance, computers can be a beneficial early learning tool. The Alliance for Childhood issues a cautionary note against early sedentariness and calls for a moratorium on the use of computers by young children.

Susan W. Haugland

 **YES**

What Role Should Technology Play in Young Children's Learning?

We face an important crossroads regarding the role of computers in young children's lives. Over the past 10 years, significant improvements have been made in technology. Whether we use technology with young children—and if so, *how*—is a critical issue facing early childhood educators and parents.

Computers and Children— Starting at the Right Age

Many of my colleagues (Elkind 1998; Hohman 1998) and I do not recommend computer use for children younger than three. Computers simply do not match their learning style. Children younger than age three learn through their bodies: their eyes, ears, mouths, hands, and legs. While they may return over and over again to an activity, they are full of movement, changing focus frequently.

Furthermore, computers are not a good choice for the developmental skills these children are learning to master: crawling, walking, babbling, talking, toilet training, and making friends, to name just a few. Children under three are active doers, gaining control of their bodies and making things happen in a fascinating world of possibilities. They are busy manipulating a wide variety of objects, such as digging in the sandbox or finger painting with pudding, and in the process learning about themselves and their environment. Frequently it is a challenge for adults just to keep up with them!

Thus, it is my recommendation that computers be introduced to young children when they are about three years of age.

Developmentally Appropriate Computer Activities

Developmentally appropriate ways we use computers with threes and fours are different from the ways we use computers in kindergarten and the primary grades. Unfortunately, computers are used all too often in ways that are developmentally inappropriate.

In 1995 a comprehensive federal study, *Teachers and Technology: Making the Connection* (Congress 1995), found that while "schools are steadily increasing their access to new technologies... most teachers use these technologies in traditional ways, including drills in basic skills and instructional games" (p. 103). Clements (1994) makes a similar point, noting, "Children use mostly drill and practice software; their teachers state that their goal for using computers is to increase basic skills rather than to develop problem-solving or creative skills.... What we as early childhood educators are presently doing most often with computers is what research and NAEYC [National Association for the Education of Young Children] guidelines say we should be doing least often" (p. 33).

Thus it should come as no surprise that computer use by children is often attacked based upon whether computers really increase learning and if we can justify the cost of technology (Oppenheimer 1997; Healy 1998). As Papert (1998) explains, computers are being criticized because of *how* they are being used. Computers are at their "weakest doing a job that is not what [they] can do most powerfully" (p. 3). Papert stresses that computers have an impact on children when they provide concrete experiences, children have free access, children and teachers learn together, peer tutoring is encouraged, children control the learning experience, and the computers are used to teach powerful ideas. (For a more detailed description of developmentally appropriate and inappropriate computer experiences, see *Young Children and Technology: A World of Discovery* [Haugland & Wright 1997].)

Parents Support Computers in the Classroom

In contrast to the critics of children using computers, most parents believe that computers can have a positive effect on children's learning, as dramatically illustrated in a national study done by the Milken Exchange on Education Technology and Peter D. Hart (1999). When asked to rate the importance of computers for learning, 87% of parents in the study gave computers a strong rating. "The perception that computers are important in education does not vary much by occupation, income, or education, though fully 91% of [the] African American [parents in the study] think that computers will make a significant difference in the quality of [their children's] education" (Milken Exchange & Hart 1999).

In 1996 NAEYC published the "NAEYC Position Statement: Technology and Young Children—Ages Three through Eight." The position statement provides important guidelines regarding appropriate use of technology with young children. Yet, many teachers still struggle: Should I use computers with young children? Do computers teach children important cognitive, physical, language, social, and emotional skills? What is my role in the computer-integrated classroom?

Models for Computer Integration

It is important to realize that using computers with young children is a process of exploration and discovery for both you and the children. How you use computers the first year in your classroom will probably be very different from how you use them five years later.

I would like to share with you one model for using computers with three- and four-year-olds and another for children five to eight. These models are just one approach; there are alternative methods. But these models may provide a vision of how technology can offer unique opportunities for you to enhance children's development.

Computers and Preschoolers

Children three and four years of age are developmentally ready to explore computers, and most early childhood educators see the computer center as a valuable activity center for learning.

Why include a computer center for children this young? Because research has shown that three- and four-year-old children who use computers with supporting activities that reinforce the major objectives of the programs have significantly greater developmental gains when compared to children without computer experiences in similar classrooms—gains in intelligence (mean score increases were 6 points), nonverbal skills, structural knowledge, long-term memory, manual dexterity, verbal skills, problem solving, abstraction, and conceptual skills (Haugland 1992).

From September through April the children in the study used developmentally appropriate software whenever they desired. The computers were given no more importance than any other activity in the classroom. Some children were more fascinated by the computers than others. Yet even children who rarely used the computers visited with children using the computers, sometimes standing behind them to discuss a program, solve problems cooperatively, or just watch the action!

Timing is crucial. Give children plenty of time to experiment and explore. Young children are really comfortable clicking various options to see what is going to happen next. Intervene when children appear frustrated or nothing seems to be happening. Frequently, just a quick word or two, even from across the room, reminds children what they need to do next to reach their desired goal. Providing children with minimal help teaches them they can operate the computer successfully. In addition, because the teacher observes what children are doing, he can ask probing questions or propose problems to enhance and expand children's computer experiences.

Computers for Kindergartners and Early Primary Children

As children enter kindergarten and the primary grades, it is important that they continue to have a computer center with a library of developmentally appropriate software. Children need opportunities to make choices about some of their computer experiences. In addition, you as a kindergarten or primary-grade teacher will use the computer for more directed activities that match your learning objectives. For example, to enhance keyboard and language skills, children can compose a letter to a friend or relative using the template provided in Claris Works for Kids (Claris Works 1997).

In another example, you may ask children to work in small groups using Scholastic's Magic School Bus Explores the Rainforest (1997) to compare two of the seven ecozones in the program by listing how they are alike and different. Using Kids' Desk: Internet Safe (1998), other small groups can investigate these two ecozones on Internet websites selected by the teacher. The groups then merge to share their discoveries and write a report on the ecozones, illustrating each with pictures drawn by members of the group or downloaded from the Internet sites.

Through exploring computer experiences, these children build memory skills, learn how to seek out information, use knowledge until they have a clear understanding from multiple sources, and integrate their knowledge of how each ecosystem functions. In the process they learn to delegate responsibility, interact with others, problem solve, and cooperate to reach a goal.

Benefits   What are the benefits of providing computers to kindergarten and primary-grade children? The answer to this question varies depending upon the kind of computer experiences offered and how frequently children have access to computers.

The potential gains for kindergarten and primary children are tremendous, including improved motor skills, enhanced mathematical thinking, increased creativity, higher scores on tests of critical thinking and problem solving, higher levels of what Nastasi and Clements (1994) term *effectance motivation* (believing they can change or affect their environment), and increased scores on standardized language assessments.

In addition, computers enhance children's self-concept, and children demonstrate increased levels of spoken communication and cooperation. Children share leadership roles more frequently and develop positive attitudes toward learning (Clements 1994; Cardelle Elawar & Wetzel 1995; Adams 1996; Denning & Smith 1997; Haugland & Wright 1997; Matthews 1997).

Making the Connection

Research has clearly demonstrated that computers provide children with some unique and important avenues for learning. As adults committed to the development of young children, finding ways to connect children to computers is an essential goal for all centers and schools.

How children connect with computers, and the goals for children's use of computers, need to come from the teachers, parents, and administrators working in your center or school. Early childhood programs serve diverse populations and have different schedules, curriculums, staffing patterns, resources, and so on. Goals and the steps that centers or schools take to integrate computers into their classrooms may be completely different but equally successful.

An important first step, however, is provoking the interest and increasing the knowledge of administrators, teachers, and parents.

Enlisting Support From the School Community

As we all know, teachers are busy—supervising children, developing lesson plans, arranging activities, implementing activities in the classroom. Yet all teachers, no matter what their philosophy, share a common goal: to do what is best for every child in their classroom. I believe that administrators, teachers, and parents, when they recognize the dramatic learning opportunities computers can provide young children and the unique developmental gains children demonstrate from computer exposure, will not be able to turn their backs on this valuable learning resource....

Summary

Using computers with young children is a journey. It begins with being receptive to learning about a unique new resource that provides children significant opportunities for growth and learning. The path then leads to obtaining computers, providing teachers with hands-on computer experiences, sharing knowledge of research and teaching strategies, and hopefully finding mentors to aid in the process. From that point on, the journey travels in different directions as teachers create unique ways to use computers with young children. Ideally, this last part of the journey never ends as teachers continue to search for and implement new ideas and products that can enhance young children's learning.

Fool's Gold: A Critical Look at Computers and Childhood

Executive Summary

Computers are reshaping children's lives, at home and at school, in profound and unexpected ways. Common sense suggests that we consider the potential harm, as well as the promised benefits, of this change.

Computers pose serious health hazards to children. The risks include repetitive stress injuries, eyestrain, obesity, social isolation, and, for some, long-term physical, emotional, or intellectual developmental damage. Our children, the Surgeon General warns, are the most sedentary generation ever. Will they thrive spending even more time staring at screens?

Children need stronger personal bonds with caring adults. Yet powerful technologies are distracting children and adults from each other.

Children also need time for active, physical play; hands-on lessons of all kinds, especially in the arts; and direct experience of the natural world. Research shows these are not frills but are essential for healthy child development. Yet many schools have cut already minimal offerings in these areas to shift time and money to expensive, unproven technology. The emphasis on technology is diverting us from the urgent social and educational needs of low-income children. M.I.T. Professor Sherry Turkle has asked: "Are we using computer technology not because it teaches best but because we have lost the political will to fund education adequately?"

Let's examine the claims about computers and children more closely:

Do computers really motivate children to learn faster and better?

Children must start learning on computers as early as possible, we are told, to get a jump-start on success. But 30 years of research on educational technology has produced just one clear link between computers and children's learning. Drill-and-practice programs appear to improve scores modestly—though not as much or as cheaply as one-on-one tutoring—on some standardized tests in narrow skill areas, notes Larry Cuban of Stanford University.

"Other than that," says Cuban, former president of the American Educational Research Association, "there is no clear, commanding body of evidence that students' sustained use of multimedia machines, the Internet, word processing, spreadsheets, and other popular applications has any impact on academic achievement."

What is good for adults and older students is often inappropriate for youngsters. The sheer power of information technologies may actually hamper young children's intellectual growth. Face-to-face conversation with more competent language users, for example, is the one constant factor in studies of how children become expert speakers, readers, and writers. Time for real talk with parents and teachers is critical. Similarly, academic success requires focused attention, listening, and persistence.

The computer—like the TV—can be a mesmerizing babysitter. But many children, overwhelmed by the volume of data and flashy special effects of the World Wide Web and much software, have trouble focusing on any one task. And a new study from the American Association of University Women Educational Foundation casts doubt on the claim that computers automatically motivate learning. Many girls, it found, are bored by computers. And many boys seem more interested in violence and video games than educational software.

Must five-year-olds be trained on computers today to get the high-paying jobs of tomorrow?

For a relatively small number of children with certain disabilities, technology offers benefits. But for the majority, computers pose health hazards and potentially serious developmental problems. Of particular concern is the growing incidence of disabling repetitive stress injuries among students who began using computers in childhood.

The technology in schools today will be obsolete long before five-year-olds graduate. Creativity and imagination are prerequisites for innovative thinking, which will never be obsolete in the workplace. Yet a heavy diet of ready-made computer images and programmed toys appears to stunt imaginative thinking. Teachers report that children in our electronic society are becoming alarmingly deficient in generating their own images and ideas.

Do computers really "connect" children to the world?

Too often, what computers actually connect children to are trivial games, inappropriate adult material, and aggressive advertising. They can also isolate children, emotionally and physically, from direct experience of the natural world. The "distance" education they promote is the opposite of what all children, and especially children at risk, need most—close relationships with caring adults.

Research shows that strengthening bonds between teachers, students, and families is a powerful remedy for troubled students and struggling schools. Overemphasizing technology can weaken those bonds. The National Science Board reported in 1998 that prolonged exposure to computing environments may create "individuals incapable of dealing with the messiness of reality, the needs of community building, and the demands of personal commitments."

In the early grades, children need live lessons that engage their hands, hearts, bodies, and minds—not computer simulations. Even in high school, where the benefits of computers are more clear, too few technology classes emphasize the ethics or dangers of online research and communication. Too few help students develop the critical skills to make independent judgments about the potential for the Internet—or any other technology— to have negative as well as positive social consequences.

Those who place their faith in technology to solve the problems of education should look more deeply into the needs of children. The renewal of education requires personal attention to students from good teachers and active parents, strongly supported by their communities. It requires commitment to developmentally appropriate education and attention to the full range of children's real low-tech needs—physical, emotional, and social, as well as cognitive.

POSTSCRIPT

Should Young Children Use Computers?

The Alliance for Childhood asks us to consider whether children must be introduced to computers at a young age in order to be successful in the future. Are there other alternative ways in which children could be challenged to learn without being dependent on computer technology during the preschool years? The panel that reviewed the findings wondered what childhood activities, such as playing with friends, creating, and gross motor activities, the children would miss when they spend long hours in front of a computer. Haugland contends that there are appropriate ways in which computers can be introduced to young children. She argues that with parental support, knowledgeable teachers, and ready access to computers, young children can begin using a tool that will be a major part of their life-long learning.

The term *user-friendly* was not a part of our daily vocabulary until computers came into our lives. That term has great meaning when computers are used by young children. Is this experience indeed friendly for the children? Will they become more frustrated by using a computer than by trying to find information another way? Is it better for them to wait to be introduced to computers, so that they may spend the early childhood years engaged in other, more active forms of learning? What other learning opportunities are they missing out on while spending time in front of a computer screen? Preschool teachers with a computer in their classroom might consider engaging in some action research. They would chart the use of the various centers or areas of the room when the computer is available for use versus when the computer is not available for use. In what areas of the room do children gravitate when the computer area is closed? Many parents might try to remember what play activities they participated in when they were young and did not have access to computers. Do their children participate in the same activities today? Is free-choice play, involving opportunities to create and socialize with friends, a part of their children's daily schedule?

When interviewed for a national study conducted by the Milken Exchange on Education Technology and Peter D. Hart, 87 percent of parents gave computers high marks for their importance to learning. These findings were found to be consistent across all educational levels, occupations, and incomes. This seems to be a case where even though access to computers was not something parents had when they were in school, they want to make sure they are available for their children. Many parents are willing to support school fund-raising efforts if the money earned will be used to purchase additional computers or software.

One of the key questions that has been posed by many educators and parents centers on the developmental appropriateness of computers for young children. What are the principles of a truly developmentally appropriate computer program? While some educators advocate children as young as age two being introduced to computers, others suggest that children should not interact with a computer until they are at least age three. The research on the effectiveness of computers in the classrooms of young children is varied in its results. The computer industry sends the message that all computer use is positive and that schools are falling behind the times in the availability and use of technology. However, some would say that the computer industry has yet to prove the value of computers in education and is quick to exploit the fears that children in the United States will fall behind the rest of the world if they do not have access to vast amounts of technology. Who is right? Do the potential benefits of computer usage by young children outweigh the potential risks?

Suggested Readings

Anderson, G. T., "Computers in a Developmentally Appropriate Curriculum," *Young Children* (vol. 55, no. 2, 2000).

Davis, B. C. and Shade, D. D., "Integrating Computers Into the Early Childhood Curriculum," *Principal* (vol. 76, 1997).

Elkind, D., "Young Children and Technology: A Cautionary Note," *Young Children* (vol. 51, no. 6, 1996).

Gatewood, T. E. and Conrad, S. H., "Is Your School's Technology Up-to-Date? A Practical Guide for Assessing Technology in Elementary Schools," *Childhood Education* (vol. 73, no. 4, 1997).

Hohmann, C., "Evaluating and Selecting Software for Children," *Child Care Information Exchange* (vol. 123, 1998).

Lane, A. and Ziviani, J., "The Suitability of the Mouse for Children's Use: A Review of the Literature," *Journal of Computing in Childhood Education* (vol. 8, no. 2–3, 1997).

"NAEYC Position Statement: Technology and Young Children Ages Three Through Eight," *Young Children* (vol. 5, no. 6, 1996).

ISSUE 4

Is Time-Out an Effective Discipline Technique?

YES: Lawrence Kutner, from "The Truth About Time-Out," *Parents* (April 1996)

NO: Mary Ellis Schreiber, from "Time-Outs for Toddlers: Is Our Goal Punishment or Education?" *Young Children* (July 1999)

ISSUE SUMMARY

YES: Psychologist Lawrence Kutner supports time-out when effectively managed by parents or teachers.

NO: Mary Ellis Schreiber, a consultant for the Early Childhood Conflict Resolution Program, argues that time-out is an ineffective tool for guiding the behavior of young children due to the fact that the children do not learn from it.

T ime out, whether it occurs during a sporting event or in the course of a day's activities at a school, is a period of time for regrouping and assessing what has happened. When referring to time-out in a school setting, it means that one or more children are removed from a situation due to inappropriate behavior. They may have been disturbing the learning environment, involved in a dangerous situation, or destroying school or personal property.

Guiding the behavior of or disciplining young children requires one to use a variety of management techniques. Teachers of young children have a more difficult time since preschool children are not able to reason. Therefore, they cannot view the situation from another person's point of view. No matter what method is used to help a child learn which behaviors are acceptable and which are unacceptable, the adult must respect the dignity and self-worth of the child at all times. The child must feel that he or she is kept safe and over time be able to come to understand that other people will not be allowed to deliberately hurt him or his property and that adults cannot allow another child to hurt anyone else. Educational settings should be safe places for both children and adults. Teachers in schools and parents in homes sometimes rely on the behavior management technique of removing a child from a situation and having the child sit in a chair for a period of time to reflect. This can be viewed as a safe and nonthreatening form of guiding behavior. There is generally not a designated amount of time, but the recommended amount of time is approximately one minute per year of the child's age. Therefore, a four-year-old would be expected to be removed from the group and sit and reflect for about four minutes. In a school setting, the child may be isolated from an activity, a particular group, or the entire class. The adult would make the decision based on the seriousness of the misbehavior and how much the child may be disturbing the group while in time-out.

How this type of discipline is executed can be controversial. School districts have been sued over the use of time-out. Children have been left in hallways, put into locked closets, or made to sit in boxes, all in an attempt to discipline for misbehavior. Why has time-out endured for so long? Can it be used effectively with young children? What are the benefits and/or drawbacks of using time-out in a home or classroom situation? If used, how long should a child be placed in time-out? Is any follow-up required after the time-out?

In the following selections, Lawrence Kutner maintains that time-out can be an effective disciplinary tool and can help young children to gain internal control. Parents and teachers, he states, simply need to know how to properly administer a time-out. Kutner provides suggestions for adults to use when implementing a time-out with a preschool child. Mary Ellis Schreiber counters that time-out is an undesirable practice that should not be used because the young child's needs are not addressed. The adult gets a few minutes of reprieve, but the child most likely did not learn anything that would prevent the same behavior from occurring in the future.

Lawrence Kutner

 **YES**

The Truth About Time-Out

About a decade or so ago, books, magazines, and courses for parents began to hail "time-out" as the ultimate, foolproof discipline technique. However, for many parents it has seemed to work better in theory than in practice. Thrilled at first to find an alternative to yelling and spanking, they soon found themselves giving their children time-outs with ever greater frequency, often for the same problem. And when the prescribed time-out didn't correct the problem, they increased the amount of time for each infraction—but that didn't work, either.

So what's going on? Is there something fundamentally wrong with time-out? Not at all. According to child psychologists who specialize in discipline issues, it remains an extremely effective and powerful tool, especially for preschoolers. The problem is that what started out as a specific technique for stopping and changing a child's behavior has, in the hands of many parents, turned into a more general approach to punishment. That's a crucial distinction, because the goal of punishment is to make the child feel bad and pay for her mistake in the hope that she won't repeat it. The goal of discipline, on the other hand, is to help a child learn better ways of handling the situation that originally got her into trouble.

"Parents have started using time-out as a means of coercion. They put a child in time-out until she does what they want," notes Edward Christophersen, Ph.D., chief of behavioral pediatrics at Children's Mercy Hospital, in Kansas City, and author of *Beyond Discipline: Parenting That Lasts a Lifetime* (Westport). But time-out was designed as a way of helping a child learn to calm down. Therefore, it's perfectly appropriate when a preschooler is hitting or screaming, but not when she pulls the dog's ear or refuses to pick up her toys.

To make time-out effective, it's necessary to act immediately and consistently—in the original spirit of the technique. Its primary objective is to teach children how to regain a grip on their runaway emotions. Preschoolers often find themselves getting so excited that they lose control: playful pushes turn into shoves, innocent giggles into screams. Time-outs remove children from whatever is overexciting them. Once they've had a chance to settle down, their behavior improves.

Another aspect of time-out that often confuses parents is the length of time a child should spend in it. This is a case in which a little goes a long way.

Children can calm down quite quickly if they're put in a calm environment. For most misbehaviors, 20 minutes of time-out is far less effective than 20 seconds," says Philip C. Kendall, Ph.D., head of the division of clinical psychology at Temple University, in Philadelphia. "It also means that if you use long time-outs, you're reducing the effectiveness of future short time-outs."

In fact, isolating a child for more than a minute is likely to backfire. It gives her a chance to shift the focus of her attention from calming down to being resentful about the punishment. The anger that accompanies that resentment can lead to future misbehaviors. So how long is long enough? As soon as the child is calm for two or three seconds, the time-out should be over," Christopher advises. "We're now using the term *chill-out* because so many children and parents tend to equate time-out with punishment."

In fact, time-out is as much an opportunity for the parent to calm down as it is for the child. If you stay calm, your child will be able to "borrow" some of your emotional control. And showing her the behavior you'd like her to exhibit makes it easier for her to get back on track.

Also, whenever possible, use time-out before your child loses control. Most preschoolers become emotionally revved up, then misbehave. You can usually predict this pattern, which may start with fidgeting or some other sign of building emotional tension. If you call a time-out at that point, you can help your child become attuned to her feelings. The longer you wait, the more difficult it will be to break the pattern.

Finally, pay attention to what psychologists call time-in. "Whenever you're upset with your child, think about reinforcing 'positive opposites,'" advises Alan E. Kazdin, Ph.D., director of the Child Conduct Clinic at Yale University. If the behavior problem involves your child screaming, praise her when she speaks calmly. If she whines, pay more attention to her when she asks for help politely.

Say you've given your four-year-old a time-out because you caught him punching his sister. That's appropriate, but the other half of the equation is to pay extra attention to the two of them when they're being nice to each other. Compliment your son on his behavior. Pat both children on the back or give them each a quick hug and tell them you're proud of them for playing without fighting.

When he sees that he gets more attention for the behavior you want than for the behavior you don't, you'll find yourself calling time out far less often. And the less you use this technique the better it's working.

GET YOUR CHILD UNDER CONTROL

Sometimes you can tell by the look in your child's eyes or the rising pitch of her voice that she's emotionally wound up and quickly heading out of control. This is when, ideally, you should call a time-out. But whether or not you catch the signs in time, here's how your behavior can help improve your child's.

Keep your cool   Be as matter-of-fact as you can. Say something like, "You're losing control and need a time-out. Let's see if you can calm yourself down." Says Edward Christophersen, Ph.D., author of *Beyond Discipline: Parenting That Lasts a Lifetime* (Westport), "During a time-out, a child should be able to see that her parent is not angry, and to see what she's missing." This is more easily said than done, especially the part about the parent not being angry. But yelling at your child only adds to the emotional heat of the moment, because in this situation, your child is more likely to pay attention to the tone of your voice than to your words. Screaming at her to be quiet sends a contradictory message: you may, in fact, make the problem worse.

Bring your child to a location that's less stimulating   This doesn't need to be the same place every time. Any environment that's peaceful will help your child regain control, but you don't have to put her in isolation—she can even be in the room with you, as long as it's quiet.

Let her go as soon as both of you think she's ready   Don't be surprised if your child is able to calm down significantly within a few seconds. (And after all, isn't that just what you're hoping for?) Let her know you see the difference in her behavior by saying something like, "You're doing a good job of calming down. Ready to go back now?" If she says yes, give her a hug, let her resume her normal activities, and wipe the slate clean.

NO

Mary Ellis Schreiber

Time-Outs for Toddlers: Is Our Goal Punishment or Education?

Two-and-half-year-old Ben runs over to giggling two-year-old Jack and pushes him. The teacher says, "Ben! I told you not to push Jack! Use your words!" Ben tries again to push Jack. The teacher shouts, "Ben! That is not okay! You need to sit in the time-out chair!" She leads Ben to the chair and sits him down.

In the time-out chair, Ben might be thinking, "I'm sitting in the chair.... What is that noise?... I'm sitting in the chair.... I want my mommy.... I'm sitting in the chair."

Ben is probably not thinking, "Wow! I guess I'll never push Jack again! I'm really sorry I did that!"

Jack might be thinking: "What happened? I was giggling and then I was pushed down!"

A *time-out* is an enforced time alone used as a consequence for unwanted behavior. Many early childhood teachers employ time-outs as a form of discipline in their classrooms; it has become a tried-and-true method of behavior management. It is thought to be a humane and sensitive means of disciplining children because there are no raised voices or corporal punishment. The technique can be deceptive because objectionable behavior is immediately controlled and extinguished.

Some early childhood experts have suggested the use of time-out as a preferred method for setting limits with preschool children. However, time-out is *not* recommended by many early childhood leaders, especially with toddlers. Time-out is usually an *undesirable* practice for several reasons:

1. An imposed, external control of behavior circumvents a child's need to build internal controls. She may come to rely on adult intervention, and the development of autonomous problem solving may be affected. The child may begin to feel ineffectual when trying to resolve her conflicts independently. Intervention that involves a time-out makes a child feel powerless, so her feelings of being ineffectual become self-fulfilling.

2. The adult's need to maintain order is met by banishing a young child to a time-out chair, but the child's needs are not addressed. Time-out does not teach the child alternative strategies.

From Mary Ellis Schreiber, "Time-Outs for Toddlers: Is Our Goal Punishment or Education?" *Young Children*, vol. 54, no. 4 (July 1999). Copyright © 1999 by The National Association for the Education of Young Children. Reprinted by permission. References omitted.

3. The repeated use of time-out can have a negative effect on a child's developing sense of self-worth and self-confidence. A child may come to believe that his own feelings and desires have little value because adults' feelings and needs consistently take precedence. There is also the danger of certain children being stigmatized as troublemakers. The same children always sitting in a time-out chair is a concrete reminder to others of the incidence of negative behavior.

4. The indirect relationship between action and consequence is confusing to young children. Lillian Katz writes:

> If the child's mental ability is reasonably normal, it is not necessary to circumvent the mind by insisting on a time-out chair. The cognitive connection between sitting on a particular chair and granting another child's request for a turn must be fairly obscure if not confusing to a four-year-old. (1984, 8–9)

Katz points out that four-year-olds do not understand the relationship between behavior and the resulting punishment. Imagine, then, the bewilderment of an even *less* experienced child, a toddler.

5. Opportunities for valuable learning experiences are forfeited during these periods of isolation.

Toddlers benefit from direct and immediate assistance while they acquire the tools to help them resolve their difficulties independently. First and foremost, *young children need a present, alert caregiver.* The presence of an adult who can break down complexities into manageable terms helps resolve problems or keeps them from occurring (Ward 1996). Adults can join children at play and suggest or demonstrate viable solutions to obstacles.

Many conflicts arise because of young children's normal experimentation with their rapidly developing independence. A basic social and emotional challenge for toddlers is learning how to resolve the conflict between their drive for autonomy and their dependence on adults (Leiberman 1993). *They need to feel they have some control.* Adults can help a young child have an appropriate amount of control by giving her frequent opportunities to make choices and decisions.

It is important, however, to remember that too many choices can confuse children. For example, "You need to wear your mittens outside, but you can take them off once we get to the store. Do you want the red or green mittens?" is too much information and the offer of a choice all at once! The options should be clear and concrete.

Self-sufficiency can be encouraged by allowing independent exploration of toys and other materials. Children should be given opportunities to negotiate challenging situations. A request such as "Move the wagon so that you can put your coat in your cubby" provides a situation that empowers a child to overcome an obstacle independently and attain a feeling of mastery and control. Generally, children feel less driven to assert their power if they are allowed to exercise it frequently.

Toddlers are also mastering the complexities of language. Their ability to verbalize their needs and desires is limited. Adults can model effective means of communication and demonstrate how to negotiate. Responsive caregivers can verbally interpret the relationship between the child's action and another person's response.

Taking toddlers by the hand, however, and demanding that they robotically "Say you're sorry!" does them little service. The concept of "sorry" is fairly complex and probably impossible for two-year-olds to understand.

Toddlers are, by nature, egocentric and are still unable (not unwilling) to see the world from another's point of view. They are *not yet able* to be truly sorry, and forcing them to say that they are contradicts and negates their true feelings. Furthermore, a child may come to believe that merely saying "I'm sorry" resolves the conflict and that he is no longer responsible for the situation.

Similarly, "Take turns!" and "Share!" can be confusing demands for most very young children. I have noticed that when a teacher automatically tells a toddler, "Use your words!" the response is usually a blank look. I think that if a child *could* use her words, she probably *would*.

What do you suppose "Use your words" means to a two-year-old? What is a word? In response to the query, "How would you feel if I took your truck?" the toddler might say, if she were able, "I'm not even sure I know what I feel right now!" Even very bright toddlers do not comprehend linguistic and cognitive abstractions such as these. Verbal guidance must be regulated by what the child is able to understand and relevant to what the child is doing.

In typical group care situations, there is usually no need for time-outs. Caregivers can physically join young children at play and be alert for learning opportunities. Observant adults recognize a young child's need to practice asserting his independence and experiment with his control over the world. Adults can demonstrate and facilitate effective language as a means for conflict resolution.

. . . [W]hat do you think about the response of the teacher in the following scenario?

> Peter and David are in the block corner with the wooden trucks. Peter has been pushing a truck over a bridge and laughing as it rolls down. David, intrigued, tries to grab the truck away from Peter to try it for himself. Peter shrieks! Beth, the caregiver, says, "David! You keep grabbing toys away from children. You have to learn to take turns! You need a time-out." She marches him over to the time-out chair. David cries and Peter drops the truck and puts his thumb in his mouth.

Although Beth has temporarily extinguished the negative behavior, very little learning has occurred. A more responsive and helpful approach, which focuses on the children's activity, might be the following:

> Beth says firmly to David, "David, you cannot take the truck away from Peter. Tell him that you want a turn with it." She says to Peter, "David said that he wants to use that truck. I know you are using it now. When you are done, I will help you give it to him. David and I will play with this car until you are finished. Tell him that you are using it right now."
>
> Then Beth acknowledges David's feelings by saying, "It is really hard to wait! You really want to use the truck! I will help you to have a turn with it when Peter is done."

After waiting a minute or two, Beth says, "Peter, David is still waiting for the truck. He will give you the car to play with when you give him the truck."

Then in another minute Beth says, "Peter, David has been waiting for a long time. You can push the truck over the bridge one more time, and then I will help you give it to him. Then you can use the car on the bridge. Great! Look, Peter, David is really smiling because you gave him the truck! Now we can roll the car and the truck on the bridge!"

In the case above, Beth helps the children maintain some control over the situation, and she models effective and appropriate language.

The following teacher responses also focus directly on the children's behaviors and promote learning:

> "I think you want more juice, Jimmy, but you may not throw your cup! You pick up the cup, and I will get you a napkin to wipe up the spill. After we clean it up, you can ask me for more juice and I will get it for you. Say, 'More juice, please!'"

> "It really looks like you want to use the doll, Jenny. Tell Angela, 'I want a turn now, please.' Angela, Jenny said that she wants to use the doll. Can we find her another doll to hold while she is waiting for that one? Oh, look, Jenny! Angela is giving you the doll with the pajamas! Maybe we can put her in the bed now. She can sleep here, next to Angela's doll."

In all these instances the adults help the children gain control by interpreting and monitoring events. They respond to the children's actions, and the consequences are directly related to the situations. The adults model effective language and take advantage of the learning opportunities, thus avoiding the repeated time-out cycle as a limit-setting strategy.

In summary, in typical situations the technique of time-out is developmentally inappropriate and limited in its effectiveness with toddlers. Constructive strategies for behavior management focus on the *child* and the *behavior* rather than on the needs of the adult. Toddlers need direct assistance as they build internalized coping skills. A present and perceptive caregiver observes children closely and actively guides their learning experiences.

POSTSCRIPT

Is Time-Out an Effective Discipline Technique?

When children get out of control and are misbehaving, who needs a break? The child or the adult? Observation of children given a time-out shows that some young children look upon time-out as a positive experience, especially if they are removed from an unpleasant task such as cleaning up. There are some children for whom the punishment is better than not being punished. Some argue that when time-out is repeatedly used, children begin to see it as an easy way out of an unpleasant situation. Teachers who use time-out should find that over the course of a school year the use decreases. Teachers who are still putting as many children in time-out in April as they did in October are probably not making progress toward helping children learn appropriate behavior and self-control.

One parent who relied on time-out for her active preschooler stated that it gave her son time to get himself in check before his behavior escalated. Kutner recommends a short period of time be used for an effective time-out. Schreiber argues that the time-out will not be a learning tool if the child simply sits for a few minutes, then continues playing. The follow-up conversations with the child are as critical as the actual time-out. Do teachers of young children have the luxury of uninterrupted time to sit and discuss the behavior with the child? Do children learn that their behavior is unacceptable and never engage in the same behavior again after one experience with time-out? Can time-out generally be administered without risk of lowering a child's self-esteem? Are there other disciplinary methods that are as effective? Are there other disciplinary methods that are more effective? Does the effectiveness of time-out need to be judged on a case-by-case basis? These questions need careful consideration by by teachers and parents.

Suggested Readings

Johnson, R., "Time-out: Can It Control Misbehavior?" *Journal of Physical Education, Recreation and Dance* (vol. 70, no. 8, 1999).

Lang, L., "Too Much Timeout," *Teacher Magazine* (May/June 1997).

Shriver, M. D. and Allen, K. D., "The Time-out Grid: A Guide to Effective Discipline," *School Psychology Quarterly* (vol. 11, no. 1, 1996).

Turner, H. S. and Watson, T. S., "Consultant's Guide for the Use of Time-out in the Preschool and Elementary Classroom," *Psychology in the Schools* (vol. 36, no. 2, 1999).

ISSUE 5

Does Television Viewing Cause Violent Behavior in Young Children?

YES: Betty Jo Simmons, Kelly Stalsworth, and Heather Wentzel, from "Television Violence and Its Effects on Young Children," *Early Childhood Education Journal* (1999)

NO: Jonathan L. Freedman, from "Violence in the Mass Media and Violence in Society: The Link Is Unproven," *Harvard Mental Health Letter* (May 1996)

ISSUE SUMMARY

YES: Professors of education Betty Jo Simmons, Kelly Stalsworth, and Heather Wentzel assert that there are many correlations between children viewing violent acts on television and displaying aggressive behavior.

NO: Professor of psychology Jonathan L. Freedman states that many of the studies done on children's television viewing were flawed and provided inaccurate findings. He does not find a strong correlation between television viewing and aggressive behavior.

Thirteen years after televisions were introduced in 1939, researchers began to study children's television viewing to determine the effects on their behavior. The first congressional hearings on television violence were held in 1952 and led to a flurry of research on content and viewing patterns. Thousands of children have been observed and their teachers and parents have been interviewed to determine to what extent children's behavior is a reflection of what they watch. The number of commercials watched, the number of violent acts seen per hour, and the average number of hours spent in front of a television have been tracked for preschool, elementary, and adolescent children. Over 98 percent of American homes have at least one television. Many wonder to what extent children's behavior is linked to the quality and quantity of television viewed.

Currently, much focus has been directed on the increasing number of violent acts children see on television. News stories that may have been censored a generation ago are now shown nightly, and scenes once reserved for movies with a PG-13 rating are now shown at 8:00 P.M. Studio audiences cheer wildly when violent behaviors are displayed on morning and afternoon talk shows. Children who watch television are able to see violent, aggressive behavior on a regular basis.

Children who live in homes with cable access have an even wider array of violent options available for viewing. On average television is watched 7.5 hours per day in American homes. Parents may feel torn between allowing their children to watch the more popular shows and the nagging fear that watching some shows may lead to more aggressive behavior. Many parents admit that the television has become an electronic babysitter for children as young as one year of age. However, constant monitoring of television viewing is extremely difficult. When children sit alone in a room with a television and a remote control device, they can flip through many different channels in a very short time. Parents are increasingly trying to find ways to limit their children's television viewing. Some limit weekday viewing, others do not allow television in a room other than a living or family room, while still others allow each child only an allotted amount of viewing time per week. But how much is too much? Is there valid reason for so much concern?

Of great interest to many researchers and parents is the inability of children under age five to distinguish between reality and fantasy. Many young children see what they view on television as fact. Children who watch excessive television without an adult nearby to interpret what they are seeing may begin to believe that if they saw it on television, it must be true. When young children see someone recover quickly from a violent act, they may interpret the recovery as confirmation that the results of violent acts are quickly and easily fixed.

Should young children be allowed to watch television programs that contain violent acts? If so, what responsibilities do adults have in interpreting the violence viewed?

In the following selections, Betty Jo Simmons, Kelly Stalsworth, and Heather Wentzel maintain that there has been strong research since the 1960s that links television viewing to aggressive behavior. Based on findings from a study done at the University of Michigan, they argue that what children watch on television is a stronger predictor of aggressive behavior than how they are being raised or their economic lifestyle. Jonathan L. Freedman asserts that the research on television violence does not support the link between viewing violence and exhibiting violent behavior. He states that even though correlations exist between television viewing and violence, they are small and correlations do not necessarily prove causality.

Betty Jo Simmons, Kelly Stalsworth,
and Heather Wentzel

 **YES**

Television Violence and Its Effects on Young Children

Introduction

After the introduction of television in 1939, E. B. White said it was "going to be the test of the modern world. We shall stand or fall by the television—of that I am quite sure." (Asamen & Berry, 1993, p. 10) These prophetic words are proving to be more accurate on a daily basis. With its ability to inform, entertain, teach, and persuade, television unquestionably has tremendous effects upon its viewers. Indeed, television has become the central activity in most homes today. Currently, in the United States, 98% of all households have at least one set. Even more astounding is the fact that it is watched an average of 7.5 hours per day (Asamen & Berry, 1993). Beckman (1997) concurs, saying that children watch more than 28 hours of television each week and in the process the average child, before the age of 12, has viewed over 8,000 murders.

Research on Television Violence

In order to clean up the airways for young audiences, the Federal Communications Commissions (FCC) enacted The Children's Television Act in 1990. Many television stations show strictly positive programs, but the negative ones are also still being aired. This point is important because preschool children are curious and easily influenced. They tend to mimic and repeat what they hear and see on television without knowledge of right and wrong.

One of the main concerns with television programming is the violence viewed by children. Berk (1993) says that because young folks cannot fully understand what they see on television, they are very much under its influence. Davidson (1996) agrees that children are extremely vulnerable to television between the ages of 2 to 8 years because of their maturational inability to separate what they view from reality. Attention to violence on television became a matter of serious consideration in the 1950s, with the first congressional hearing taking place in 1952. From 1952 to 1967, many analyses were done of the content of television programs. In the late 1960s and early 1970s, the scrutiny shifted from content alone to specifically discerning the effects of violence on viewers. The resulting findings supported the idea that a casual relationship existed between television violence and aggressive behavior (National Institutes of Mental Health, 1983).

Imitating Violence

Levin and Carlsson-Paige (1996) lament the 1984 deregulation of broadcasting, noting that subsequently teachers began to observe an escalation of violence in their classrooms. They state that "Today, U.S. crime rates are increasing most rapidly among youth who were in their formative early years when children's TV was deregulated and violent programs and toys successfully deluged childhood culture" (p. 17). Governmental investigation led to several studies about the effects of violence. Two of the most well known were done by Bandura and Berkowitz. Bandura (1973), a social learning theorist, purported that children learn primarily through social modeling. From his studies, he concluded that children went through three stages—exposure, acquisition, and acceptance (Moody, 1980). He maintained that increased exposure to aggressive models led to reduced inhibitions toward violence. For example, when a television character acts violently and the consequences are positive, then the viewer is more likely to assume this behavior. Today, unfortunately even the "good" guys feel obligated to blow away their opponents (Munson, 1996).

Berkowitz (1962) examined the effects of television on aggressive drives. He concluded that exposure to televised violence does arouse aggressive behaviors, especially if viewers believe that aggression is justified. Noble (1975) maintains that aggressive behavior is harder to inhibit if viewers have a target which is associated with a television victim. Similarly, a study involving five different countries in which children were subjected to violence through television found evidence that even brief exposures caused them to be more accepting of other aggressive behavior. This research also concluded that the more children watched television, the more accepting they became of aggressive actions (Huesmann & Eron, 1986). Davidson (1996) reports that research done by Leonard Eron of the University of Michigan shows that violence children watched as eight-year-olds became a better predictor of adult aggression than socioeconomic and childrearing factors.

Cullingford (1984) reports on a study done by Shaw and Newell in which they interviewed families about their concerns over television. One of the major findings was that violence went almost unnoticed. Even when people were shown killings and then heavily prompted, most did not think of it as violent. The frightening truth was that "objectionable content" had become so acceptable that it was invisible. Later investigations by Drabman and Thomas (Geen, 1981) used observation to determine the effects of violent films on the way children resolved conflict. They, like Geen, who used blood pressure as the indicator concluded that violence leads to desensitization (Molitor, 1994; Voojis & Voort, 1993). Thus, it is not hard to understand that Minnow, former chair of the Federal Communications Commission, meant when he said that in the 1960s, he worried that his children would not greatly benefit from television, but in the 1990s, he worries that his grandchildren may be harmed by it (Minnow, 1995).

Violence and Fear

In addition to theories that television can cause children to be more aggressive and less sensitive to the results of violence, there is also the theory that televised violence causes viewers to be afraid. According to this theory, the misconstrued world presented on television is seen as a mirror of reality and viewers become convinced they will fall victim to violence. It is reasoned that viewers absorb information without analyzing it and subsequently develop false beliefs about law enforcement and crime. Chen (1994), who found that crime during prime time is depicted 10 times greater than in reality, gives credence to the notion that television is distorted in its portrayal and resolution of crime and violence.

Levine (1996) says 3-to 5-year-old children live in a magical world that often leaves them terrified of things which completely surprise adults. On the other hand, there are those who disagree that television makes them afraid. According to Hamilton (1993), today's children are much more preoccupied with violence. Therefore, according to Dr. Daniel Koenigsberg, chief of child psychiatry at Saint Raphael hospital, it is not so much that children are scared by it, as it is that they accept it and are intrigued by it. Thus, it is easy to see that not everyone agrees about the effects that violence has; however, it is generally agreed that it does play a significant role in the children's construction of social reality (Voojis & Voort, 1993).

Children's Programs Featuring Violence

According to Kaplan (1998), the National Coalition on Television Violence has classified the Mighty Morphin Power Rangers as the most violent program "ever studied, averaging more than 200 violent acts per hour" (p. 16). Furthermore, in an experimental study involving 5- to 11-year-olds (26 boys and 26 girls with ethnically diverse backgrounds), Kaplan (1998) reports that children who watched Power Rangers committed 7 times more aggressive acts than those who did not. Recognizing that children imitate what they see, several day care centers, nursery schools, and elementary schools have outlawed Power Rangers in play.

According to Evra and Kline (1990), "One of the dangers for preschoolers or early school-age children is their lack of ability to relate actions, motives, and consequences, and they may simply imitate the action they see" (p. 83). Levin and Carlsson-Paige (1996) purport that children cannot assimilate the Power Rangers into their own naturally limited experiences. Thus, unable to devise meaningful play from what they have seen, they act out "what they are unable to understand, primarily the kicking, fighting, and shooting" (p. 18). Teachers, according to Levin and Carlsson-Paige (1996), have observed that children become so fascinated by the Power Rangers that they excuse their own aggressiveness by saying they must do as the Power Rangers do.

Another show, similar in content, is the Teenage Mutant Ninja Turtles. Violence is also the main attraction in this program. The four heroes are pumped-up turtles named after four famous artists; Michaelangelo, Donatello, Leonardo, and Raphael. Their mentor is a skilled ninja rat. Each has a distinctive personality and each fights best with specific weapons. The main "bad guy," Shredder, is so named because he has blades protruding from his clothes, which he does not hesitate to use when fighting. In one episode on the Cartoon Network, Shredder tried to use a robot to take over the world and the Turtles stopped him by fighting. At the end of the show, the characters discuss what is supposed to have been learned by the viewers. However, young children watching these shows would not necessarily learn from these messages because they can take in only so much information at a time. According to Evra and Kline (1990), the lack of understanding and well-developed behavioral control causes the main attraction to be primarily the action.

In what may be called the "Dynamic Duos" are found Bugs Bunny and Elmer Fudd, Tweetie and Sylvester, the Roadrunner and Wyle E. Coyote, and Tom and Jerry. Each pair takes turns trying to outsmart and pummel one another. The goofy and colorful characters attract children and the only message that might be sent to children is how to solve problems through fighting.

Similarly, a new wave of cartoons, such as Beavis and Butthead, The Simpsons, King of the Hill, and Daria, are aimed at an adult audience; yet many children are intrigued by these animated cartoons. Most of the themes in these shows focus on adult life, things that young children would not understand. For example, those that focus on teenage life, such as Beavis and Butthead and Daria, show lazy characters concerned only with materialistic and selfish things. These programs also use adult language that is not appropriate for small children to hear. However, since children do watch these shows, they tend to repeat certain things that they see and hear.

For example, at the beginning to Beavis and Butthead, words come across the screen saying that the cartoon is not realistic and the acts in the show should not be repeated. However, such disclaimers do not register in the minds of children who are more intrigued by action than consequences. For example, in the early 1960s, Schramm, Lyle, and Parker (1961) were pointing out the inherent danger involved in televised violence. They noted that a 6-year-old told his father he wanted real bullets because toy ones did not kill like Hopalong Cassidy's bullets. It appears that when children watch shows, they often do not remember the plot, but they do remember the actions of their favorite characters. Evra and Kline (1990) found that even 14-month-old children have a tendency toward some type of imitation of television.

Public Reaction

Even though there are shows on television that are designed for preschoolers, many American adults feel that there are still not enough programs for young children. In a press release on October 5, 1995, the Center for Media Education (CME) published the results of a national poll which showed strong public support of more educational programs. To quote from the poll:

> More than four in five American adults (82%) believe there is not enough educational children's programming on commercial broadcast television. Three in five adults surveyed (60%) support specific requirements that broadcasters air an hour of educational programming—or more—for children each day. More than a third of all parents (35%) would require two hours daily. 80% of Americans believe there are good reasons to regulate children's TV more strictly than programming intended for general or adult audiences. The two most frequently cited reasons for the lack of quality in children's broadcast programming are violent (43%) and insufficient educational programming (25%). (Poll on Children's Television, 1995, Center for Media Education)

These complaints are slowly being attended to with new educational programs and the revival of old ones, such as Schoolhouse Rock and Sesame Street. A rating system has recently been enacted. At the beginning of each show, letters and numbers, ranging from "G" to "Adult" appear at the top left-hand corner of the television screen, stating the appropriateness of the television show.

In 1997, in response to the public's demand for improvement in the quality of children's television, the Federal Communications Commission (FCC) issued stronger rules to regulate the Children's Television Act of 1990. According to the new expectations, broadcasters must produce 3 hours weekly of educational programming. These programs must make education the major focus with clearly articulated objectives, and a designated target age group. Fortunately, more stations are appearing and many of them do show programs that are, for the most part, appropriate for all audiences. Channels such as PBS, Animal Planet, The Family Channel, and the Disney channel are examples. However, there is still the question of violence on television. Especially so, since the Children's Television Act is not definitive about the meaning of educational programming. The act simply says that programs must contribute to the well-being of children "in any respect." The "in any respect" seems to be a loophole that dilutes the original intent (*U.S. News and World Report, 1997*).

Even when educational programs are produced, problems remain. One of them lies with the competition. With the availability of cable, violence continues to be prevalent. Children can and do quickly switch the channel to the Cartoon Network (*New York Times, 1997*). Furthermore, since educational programs are not big moneymakers, producers tend to schedule many of them early in the morning or in spots which are not the most normal viewing times. Another major consideration is what Zoglin contended in 1993, namely, that children are not much attracted to educational shows. He says, "The very notion of educational TV often seems to reflect narrow, school-marmish notions" (p. 64). Five years later, Mifflin (1997) pointed out that broadcasters agree because they have a hard time finding educational programs that children will watch (*New York Times, 1997*).

Recommendations

Naturally, children are easily confused when they watch the superhero beat up other characters. Therefore, recognizing and taking a proactive position against televised violence becomes a prime responsibility for all those involved in the care and nurturance of young children. With this premise in mind, the following recommendations are offered:

1. Parents, teachers, and communities must work together to combat the violence that is permeating society. They must work to build community programs to prevent violence and diffuse aggressive behavior. They must work on an individual level to teach acceptable and unacceptable standards.

2. Children must have their television viewing supervised and regulated which means that adults have to show responsible behavior themselves by refusing to watch programs that are violent in nature. If they are unwilling to abolish violent programs in their homes, they must take the time to ask questions of their children, explain the seriousness of violence to them, and help them to evaluate what they witness.

3. Parents must not let television become the dominant part of their family's life. It is imperative that drastic steps be taken to curtail the kind of socially unacceptable behavior, which is routinely and daily invited into the average home.

4. Parents and teachers must help young children develop appropriate behavior for social interactions. Children need guidance in learning to settle disagreements with verbal rather than physical skill.

5. Schools need to take television violence seriously, especially so, since it transfers to inappropriate behavior in the classroom. Thus, school personnel should take immediate steps to involve parents and the community in open dialog through newspaper articles, PTA meetings, and public forums.

6. The curriculum must be based upon the developmental needs of young children. Consideration must be given to fantasy, animism, and the inability of children to separate real from the pretend. Young children should be taught how to make decisions and how to work through problems by finding acceptable alternatives to violent acts.

Jonathan L. Freedman

NO

Violence in the Mass Media and Violence in Society

Imagine that the Food and Drug Administration (FDA) is presented with a series of studies testing the effectiveness of a new drug. There are some laboratory tests that produce fairly consistent positive effects, but the drug does not always work as expected and no attempt has been made to discover why. Most of the clinical tests are negative; there are also a few weak positive results and a few results suggesting that the drug is less effective than a placebo. Obviously the FDA would reject this application, yet the widely accepted evidence that watching television violence causes aggression is no more adequate.

In laboratory tests of this thesis, some children are shown violent programs, others are shown nonviolent programs, and their aggressiveness is measured immediately afterward. The results, although far from consistent, generally show some increase in aggression after a child watches a violent program. Like most laboratory studies of real-world conditions, however, these findings have limited value. In the first place, most of the studies have used dubious measures of aggression. In one experiment, for example, children were asked, "If I had a balloon, would you want me to prick it?" Other measures have been more plausible, but none is unimpeachable. Second, there is the problem of distinguishing effects of violence from effects of interest and excitement. In general, the violent films in these experiments are more arousing than the neutral films. Anyone who is aroused will display more of almost any behavior; there is nothing special about aggression in this respect. Finally and most important, these experiments are seriously contaminated by what psychologists call demand characteristics of the situation: the familiar fact that people try to do what the experimenter wants. Since the children know the experimenter has chosen the violent film, they may assume that they are being given permission to be aggressive.

Putting It to the Test

The simplest way to conduct a real-world study is to find out whether children who watch more violent television are also more aggressive. They are, but the

From Jonathan L. Freedman, "Violence in the Mass Media and Violence in Society: The Link Is Unproven," *Harvard Mental Health Letter*, vol. 12, no. 11 (May 1996). Copyright © 1996 by The President and Fellows of Harvard College. Reprinted by permission of Harvard Health Publications.

correlations are small, accounting for only 1% to 10% of individual differences in children's aggressiveness. In any case, correlations do not prove causality. Boys watch more TV football than girls, and they play more football than girls, but no one, so far as I know, believes that television is what makes boys more interested in football. Probably personality characteristics that make children more aggressive also make them prefer violent television programs.

To control for the child's initial aggressiveness, some studies have measured children's TV viewing and their aggression at intervals of several years, using statistical techniques to judge the effect of early television viewing on later aggression. One such study found evidence of an effect, but most have found none.

For practical reasons, there have been only a few truly controlled experiments in which some children in a real-world environment are assigned to watch violent programs for a certain period of time and others are assigned to watch non-violent programs. Two or three of these experiments indicated slight, short-lived effects of TV violence on aggression; one found a strong effect in the opposite of the expected direction, and most found no effect. All the positive results were obtained by a single research group, which conducted studies with very small numbers of children and used inappropriate statistics.

Scrutinizing the Evidence

An account of two studies will give some idea of how weak the research results are and how seriously they have been misinterpreted.

A study published by Lynette Friedrichs and Aletha Stein is often described (for example, in reports by the National Institute of Mental Health and the American Psychological Association) as having found that children who watched violent programs became more aggressive. What the study actually showed was quite different. In a first analysis the authors found that TV violence had no effect on physical aggression, verbal aggression, aggressive fantasy, or object aggression (competition for a toy or other object). Next they computed indexes statistically combining various kinds of aggression, a technique that greatly increases the likelihood of connections appearing purely by chance. Still they found nothing.

They then divided the children into two groups—those who were already aggressive and those who were not. They found that children originally lower in aggression seemed to become more aggressive and children originally higher in aggression seemed to become less aggressive no matter which type of program they watched. This is a well-known statistical artifact called regression toward the mean, and it has no substantive significance. Furthermore, the less aggressive children actually became more aggressive after watching the neutral program than after watching the violent program. The only comfort for the experimenters was that the level of aggression in highly aggressive children fell more when they watched a neutral program than when they watched a violent program. Somehow that was sufficient for the study to be widely cited as strong evidence that TV violence causes aggression.

An ambitious cross-national study was conducted by a team led by Rowell Huesmann and Leonard Eron and reported in 1986. In this widely cited research the effect of watching violent television on aggressiveness at a later age was observed in seven groups of boys and seven groups of girls in six countries. After controlling for initial aggressiveness, the researchers found no statistically significant effect for either sex in Australia, Finland, the Netherlands, Poland, or kibbutz children in Israel. The effect sought by the investigators was found only in the United States and among urban Israeli children, and the latter effect was so large, so far beyond the normal range for this kind of research and so incongruous with the results in other countries, that it must be regarded with suspicion. Nevertheless, the senior authors concluded that the pattern of results supported their position. The Netherlands researchers disagreed; they acknowledged that they had not been able to link TV violence to aggression, and they criticized the methods used by some of the other groups. The senior authors refused to include their chapter in the book that came out of the study, and they had to publish a separate report.

A Second Look

If the evidence is so inadequate, why have so many committees evaluating it concluded that the link exists? In the first place, these committees have been composed largely of people chosen with the expectation of reaching that conclusion. Furthermore, committee members who were not already familiar with the research could not possibly have read it all themselves, and must have relied on what they were told by experts who were often biased. The reports of these committees are often seriously inadequate. The National Institute of Mental Health, for example, conducted a huge study but solicited only one review of the literature, from a strong advocate of the view that television violence causes aggression. The review was sketchy—it left out many important studies— and deeply flawed.

The belief that TV violence causes aggression has seemed plausible because it is intuitively obvious that this powerful medium has effects on children. After all, children imitate and learn from what they see. The question, however, is what they see on television and what they learn. We know that children tend to imitate actions that are rewarded and avoid actions that are punished. In most violent television programs villains start the fight and are punished. The programs also show heroes using violence to fight violence, but the heroes almost always have special legal or moral authority; they are police, other government agents, or protectors of society like Batman and the Power Rangers. If children are learning anything from these programs, it is that the forces of good will overcome evil assailants who are the first to use violence. That may be overoptimistic, but it hardly encourages the children themselves to initiate aggression.

Telling the Difference

Furthermore, these programs are fiction, and children know it as early as the age of five. Children watching Power Rangers do not think they can beam up to the command center, and children watching "Aladdin" do not believe in flying carpets. Similarly, children watching the retaliatory violence of the heroes in these programs do not come to believe they themselves could successfully act in the same way. (Researchers concerned about mass media violence should be more interested in the fights that occur during hockey and football games, which are real and therefore may be imitated by children who play those sports.)

Recently I testified before a Senate committee, and one Senator told me he knew TV made children aggressive because his own son had met him at the door with a karate kick after watching the Power Rangers. The Senator was confusing aggression with rough play, and imitation of specific actions with learning to be aggressive. Children do imitate what they see on television; this has strong effects on the way they play, and it may also influence the forms their real-life aggression takes. Children who watch the Ninja Turtles or Power Rangers may practice martial arts, just as years ago they might have been wielding toy guns, and long before that, wrestling or dueling with wooden swords. If there had been no television, the Senator's son might have butted him in the stomach or poked him in the ribs with a gun. The question is not whether the boy learned his karate kick from TV, but whether TV has made him more aggressive than he would have been otherwise.

Television is an easy target for the concern about violence in our society but a misleading one. We should no longer waste time worrying about this subject. Instead let us turn our attention to the obvious major causes of violence, which include poverty, racial conflict, drug abuse, and poor parenting.

POSTSCRIPT

Does Television Viewing Cause Violent Behavior in Young Children?

One of the first things many Americans do in the morning is turn on the television, and it may stay on until well into the night. It is no wonder that young children are fascinated by this electronic device that brings movement, color, and sound into their homes.

Teachers of young children, particularly of children in full-day child care, deal with issues related to television viewing, as well. In many programs serving preschool age children, a television and VCR are used on a daily or weekly basis. In some preschool programs the television is constantly on, but in others television is not available at all. What role should television play in a school setting? How can the staff of a preschool program come to a decision about television viewing that would be acceptable to families and staff? Do children participate in more violent play acts immediately after watching television?

Freedman contends that the correlation between children viewing violent acts on television and aggression displayed is statistically small. Further, he states that in viewing violent acts on television, children are able to learn that good overpowers evil. Do all children automatically acquire this message from viewing violent television, or is it necessary to have an adult nearby to interpret what is being watched and to provide commentary on the scenes? Should adults always be present when children are watching television? How much access should children have to a remote control device?

When television programs became popular in the 1950s and 1960s, the commercialism of these programs began to be a part of young children's lives. Initially, lunch boxes sported characters from popular shows. Dolls, action figures, and games soon followed. Does the merchandise contribute to the acceptance of television violence? When everything from Halloween costumes to birthday cake candles with a television theme are available, are children inundated with the violent characters to a point where they become desensitized to their behavior? Can parents and teachers allow children to use television as a learning and entertainment tool while still developing a healthy respect for what is seen? How can this be done? What steps can be taken if adults believe that the behavior of children is being affected by what they have watched on television?

The focus of this issue question is on television viewing and its effects on young children's behavior. Can similar discussions be held concerning other forms of media, such as video games or movies? How are television programs, video games, and movies linked? What similarities or differences exist?

Suggested Readings

Boyatzis, C. J., "Of Power Rangers and V-chips," *Young Children* (vol. 52, no. 7, 1997).

Groebal, J., "Media Violence and Children," *Educational Media International* (vol. 35, no. 3, 1998).

Hannaford, C., "How T.V. Violence Affects Children," *Principal* (vol. 75, 1996).

Hepburn, M. A., "T.V. Violence! A Medium's Effect Under Scrutiny," *Social Education* (vol. 61, no. 5, 1997).

Levin, D. E. and Carlsson-Paige, N., "The Mighty Morphin Power Rangers: Teachers Voice Concern," *Young Children* (vol. 50, no. 6, 1995).

ISSUE 6

Is Spanking an Effective Method of Discipline?

YES: Lynn Rosellini, from "When to Spank," *U.S. News & World Report* (April 13, 1998)

NO: Nadine Block, from "Abandon the Rod and Save the Child," *The Humanist* (March/April 2000)

ISSUE SUMMARY

YES: Lynn Rosellini, a writer for *U.S. News & World Report,* explores the dilemma many parents face related to widespread disapproval of spanking. Rosellini maintains that spanking is the most viable option for disciplining children.

NO: Nadine Block, director of the Center for Effective Discipline, argues that parents and teachers should not legally be allowed to use the same force on children that would not be allowed against an animal. She states that adults should find more acceptable methods of discipline.

The spanking debate is thrust into the spotlight every few years due to proposed legislation, reports of out-of-control children, or the spanking of a child by a prominent parent. The future king of England received a smack on his bottom from his mother, Princess Diana, and the incident was photographed and published worldwide. In the wake of numerous school shootings, attention has been turned to the need for more stringent discipline methods, including corporal punishment or spanking, to control wayward youth. In 1999, Oklahoma and Nevada lawmakers passed bills allowing parents to "spank, switch, or paddle" their children without fear of prosecution. Does spanking work? Is spanking the correct method for helping a child develop a sense of what is right and wrong and how to conduct oneself in society?

Many national polls have been conducted on spanking. Even though spankings may have been conducted behind closed doors in homes, many parents are hesitant to publicly admit that they have spanked their children. For some it means admitting that they could not control their children in a more socially acceptable way such as reasoning with the child or withholding privileges. For many parents, doing something to one's own children that would be illegal to do to a spouse, a neighbor child, or an animal causes conflict in their minds.

Why is spanking used as a form of discipline for children? There are a number of reasons, but many state that among the most important is that it is quick. The message for the child to change his or her behavior is sent and received immediately. Most other forms of discipline take time and effort on the part of the adult. A spanking can be administered in less than ten seconds. A spanking also allows the adult to be in total control. When a spanking is administered the adult determines what tool is used, how many swats will be administered, and the force to be applied. A spanking can range from one or two light taps with the adult's hand on the diapered bottom of a 2-year-old, to a board being used with great force 10 times to the bare buttocks of a 12-year-old. Can the same notions of appropriateness be applied to all types of spanking?

School administrators face frustrations in dealing with children who do not respect teachers and who disrupt the learning environment for other students. Teachers are stressed as they work to find acceptable methods of discipline that will allow order to be restored to the learning environment. Corporal punishment is legal in schools in 23 states. However, it is banned in 27 states and among those 19 enacted bans from 1985–1994. The states that allow corporal punishment in schools also allow local school boards of education to set policy. In states where corporal punishment is allowed, an adult witness must be present while the physical punishment is being administered.

Another reason why spanking is accepted by some is that it is deeply rooted in the Scriptures. There are religious leaders who strongly encourage their followers to heed the words of the Old Testament in the Bible regarding the use of spankings. It is believed by some that young children are born bad and must be taught the correct way to live their lives. Breaking their spirit and will through physical punishment is the way to raise children to follow the word of God, some assert. Some parents express frustration by what they perceive as weak or ineffective forms of discipline, such as talking to the child, removing privileges, or giving the child a time-out. Parents want to send a strong message that a certain behavior must be changed. Are there methods that are more effective than spanking that should be used? Does a child who received one spanking learn how to behave properly?

In the following selections, Lynn Rosellini describes the frustrations many adults are facing related to discipline and how they are turning to spanking to control unruly children. Nadine Block counters that teaching children to be respectful cannot be achieved by spanking and that there are other, more appropriate, forms of punishment that should be used instead.

Lynn Rosellini  **YES**

When to Spank

Dad and Mom are no fools: They know their '90s parenting manuals. So when 4-year-old Jason screams, "No!" and darts under the dining room table when it's time to leave Grandma's, Dad patiently crouches down. "Remember, Jason," he says soothingly, "when we talked earlier about leaving?" Jason, scowling, doesn't budge. His mother shifts uneasily and riffles through her mental Rolodex of tips garnered from all those child-rearing books. She offers Jason choices ("Would you like to come out by yourself, or shall I get you?"), then rewards ("I've got a cookie for you to eat in the car"), and finally consequences ("Get out or no *Arthur* tomorrow!"). Jason retreats further and cries, "I don't want to!" His parents look at each other wearily. Jason is a bright, cheerful child who, like most spirited kids, is gifted at pushing limits. He is often well-behaved, but lately, when his parents ask him to do something, he seems to melt down entirely, screaming and even biting. Now he sticks out his tongue and announces, "I hate you!" His father hauls the tiny tyrant, kicking and flailing, out from under the table. Jason lets loose an earsplitting yell. Dad, red-faced, finally loses it, raising his hand over his son's rear end.

Now stop the action. If Jason's father reads the newspapers and listens to TV news, he knows spanking is one of the more destructive things he can do to his kid, that it could turn Jason into an angry, violent child—and perhaps, some day, a depressed, abusive adult. He may even have heard the familiar refrain of child-development specialists, who contend that a parent who uses corporal punishment "is a parent who has failed." Yet he also feels instinctively that a mild pop on the rear might get Jason's attention in a way negotiating won't. Besides, *his* dad spanked *him* occasionally, and he didn't turn into an ax-wielding monster.

In fact, the notion advanced by a slew of American child-raising authorities that a couple of well-placed swats on the rear of your beloved preschooler irreparably harms him or her is essentially a myth. Antispanking crusaders relied on inconclusive studies to make sweeping overgeneralizations about spanking's dangers. ... [E]ven the American Academy of Pediatrics [AAP] is expected to tone down its blanket injunction against spanking, though it still takes a dim view of the practice and encourages parents to develop discipline alternatives. An AAP conference on corporal punishment in 1996 concluded that in certain circumstances, spanking may be an effective backup to other forms of discipline. "There's no evidence that a child who is spanked moderately is going to grow up to be a criminal or antisocial or violent," says S. Kenneth Schonberg, a pediatrics professor who co-chaired the conference. In fact, the reverse may be true: A few studies suggest that when used appropriately, spanking makes small children less likely to fight with others and more likely to obey their parents.

Some caveats are in order. By "spanking," the AAP and other authorities mean one or two flat-handed swats on a child's wrist or rear end, *not* a sustained whipping with Dad's belt. Neither the AAP nor any other child-development specialists believe that spanking should be the sole or preferred means of child discipline, or that it should be administered when a parent is very angry, or that it should be used with adolescents or children under 2 years old. Most experts who approve of spanking suggest it be used sparingly, as an adjunct to other discipline techniques.

Children are people   The origins of the antispanking prohibition have a lot to do with two social phenomena of postwar America: the rise of popular psychology and the breakup of the extended family. In years past, grandparents used to inundate a new mother with child-raising tips on everything from burping to bed-wetting. One of them was likely to be "spare the rod and spoil the child," an adage some adults used to justify repeated spankings as the only form of discipline—and not just in the home. Half a century ago, corporal punishment in schools was legal in all but one state. But by the early 1950s, young couples increasingly began to look to child-rearing "experts"—authors like Benjamin Spock, whose manual *Baby and Child Care* counseled against the punitive child-raising practices of earlier generations. Spock, a believer in firm and consistent parenting, did not rule out spanking in his book's early editions. But he salted his manual with concepts borrowed from Freudian theory, stressed the impact that parents have on their kids' development, and introduced what at the time was a radical notion: Children are individual little people, with a host of psychic needs.

The psychologists and child-development authorities who churned out parenting guides in the 1970s and 1980s took Spock one step further, advocating a new, child-centered view of family. The locus of power should shift, these experts seemed to suggest, so that kids are equal members of the household. Many writers, such as T. Berry Brazelton, warned that strict parenting, and particularly punishments like spanking, could promote aggression and discourage children from cooperating with others. One of the most popular of the new crop of books was Thomas Gordon's 1970 million-plus seller, *Parent Effectiveness Training,* which advised parents to stop punishing kids and to start treating them "much as we treat a friend or a spouse." More recently, writers like Nancy Samalin and Barbara Coloroso counseled an end to punishment altogether. And while such books helped open parents' eyes to the importance of listening to children and respecting their individuality, some warm, fuzzy—and not very reasonable—ideas about discipline also began to gain popularity. (One author suggested that if a child refused to get dressed in the morning, parents should send him to school in pajamas.)

This onslaught of advice did not, on the surface, appear to alter parents' attitudes toward spanking very much. [In 1997], 65 percent of Americans approved of spanking, not much less than the 74 percent who did so in 1946. But the modest overall shift in numbers concealed a marked change in opinion among the American elite. By the 1990s, the refusal to spank had, in some quarters, become a sign of enlightened parenting. In a 1997 poll, 41 percent of college-educated Americans disapproved of spanking children, compared with only 20 percent of those who didn't complete high school. Whites were more than twice as likely to disapprove of spanking as blacks, and the rich were less likely to favor the practice than the poor.

"Parents became intimidated by expertise," argues Kevin Ryan, director of the Center for the Advancement of Ethics and Character at Boston University, who thinks the antispanking movement has become too absolutist. "Psychologists and educators corrupted parents, saying that all it takes are rational appeals to a child's better side." Danielle Crittenden, a mother of two and editor of the *Women's Quarterly,* a conservative journal, adds that "if you say you swat your kid, people now look at you like you're a child abuser. You can't even talk about it because people are so hysterical."

Against spanking   Compounding parents' guilt were two books published in the mid-'90s by researchers Irwin A. Hyman and Murray A. Straus that seemed to solidify the antispanking consensus. In *Beating the Devil Out of Them,* Straus, a respected sociologist at the University of New Hampshire who has done groundbreaking research on child and spouse abuse, concluded that spanking children is a "major psychological and social problem" that can doom a child to a lifetime of difficulties ranging from juvenile delinquency to depression, sexual hangups, limited job prospects, and lowered earnings. Straus's 1994 book won raves from well-known child-development experts like Brazelton and Penelope Leach, who applauded him for spotlighting a link between spanking and violence in society. Hyman, a psychologist at Temple University, made much the same point in his 1997 manual, *The Case Against Spanking,* and promoted his views in numerous appearances on the talk-show circuit.

For Straus and Hyman, spanking became almost a unified field theory connecting seemingly disparate social problems. "We really want to get rid of violence," Hyman said [recently] in an interview on CNN. "And we really want to improve children's self-esteem and behavior. We should pass a law against spanking." Straus went even further, asserting that spanking helps foster punitive social attitudes, such as support for bombing raids to punish countries that support terrorists. If parents stop spanking, Straus said on ABC-TV news [recently], "we'll have . . . lower costs to deal with crime and with mental illness."

The problem with Straus and Hyman's pronouncements was that they were based on a body of research that is at best inconclusive and at worst badly flawed. It is virtually impossible to examine the effects of spanking in isolation, uncontaminated by other influences on behavior and development, such as the overall quality of parenting and the varying temperaments of the children in question. A "pure" study, in which researchers randomly assign children to one of two conditions—either spanking or discipline with nonphysical methods —and then track their behavior over a number of years, is for obvious reasons impractical: Few parents would agree to participate in such research.

As a result, the vast majority of studies on spanking have instead been carried out in one of two other ways. Some rely on retrospective interviews with adults, who are asked decades later to recall if they were spanked as children, and how often. Researchers then attempt to link the spanking with current behaviors like depression or spouse abuse. In the second type of study, mothers are interviewed about how often their kids misbehave and how often they spank them, and researchers look for a relationship between the two behaviors.

Neither type of study is very effective in teasing out exactly what is going on. In the case of the interview studies, it is impossible to tell if the spanking led to the misbehavior or the misbehavior led to the spanking. In the case of the retrospective studies, it is anyone's guess how accurate the adult subjects' memories are of their parents' discipline techniques. In some cases, the researchers also failed to adequately control for other factors that might have influenced the results. For instance, most of the studies conducted by Straus himself include many people who were spanked as teenagers, which most child-rearing experts agree is too old for corporal punishment. Other studies failed to distinguish between one or two taps on the rear end of a preschooler and, say, beating a child with a strap. One 1977 study of 427 third graders who were reinterviewed 10 years later found that those who had been punished more also were more likely than others to push, shove, or start fights over nothing. But "punishment" was defined as including everything from nonphysical disciplinary steps like reasoning with children or isolating them, to slapping their faces, washing their mouths out with soap, or spanking them until they cried.

The shortcomings in the research aren't just methodological quibbles— they go right to the heart of what worries parents about spanking. To take one example, one of parents' biggest fears is that spanking might lead to child abuse. Common sense suggests—and studies confirm—that child abuse typically starts from situations where a parent is attempting to discipline a child. But no study demonstrates that spanking a child leads to abuse indeed, it may be the other way around. Parents who end up abusing their children may misuse all forms of discipline, including spanking. Sweden, often cited as a test case, hasn't borne out the spanking prohibitionists' fears, either. After Sweden outlawed spanking by parents in 1979, reports of serious child abuse actually increased by more than 400 percent over 10 years, though the actual number of reports—583 cases in 1994—was still quite small. Sweden's experience does not prove that banning spanking creates more child abuse, but it does suggest that outlawing the practice may do little to lower the rate of child abuse.

Why take a chance?   Straus and Hyman and other parenting experts concede that much research on spanking is flawed, but they believe its collective weight supports their claims. "There's enough evidence to decide we don't need it [spanking]," says Hyman, "even if the evidence isn't that strong." Besides, he asks, given the stakes, is it worth taking a chance? "The question should be turned around. We should say, 'Give me a good reason why you *should* hurt kids.' "

Journalists, reporting on child-rearing trends, seem to have adopted a similar approach to spanking, rarely bothering to scrutinize the claims of pro-hibitionists. Consider the news media coverage of a much touted study by Straus, published [in 1997] in the *Archives of Pediatrics & Adolescent Medicine*. His research indicated that frequent spanking (three or more times a week) of children 6 to 9 years old, tracked over a period of two years, increased a child's antisocial behavior, measured in activities like cheating, bullying, or lying. The American Medical Association [AMA], which publishes *Archives of Pediatrics & Adolescent Medicine,* issued a news release headlined "Spanking Makes Children Violent, Antisocial," and Straus's findings were reported by the three major net-works and included in at least 107 newspaper and magazine stories. But neither the press release nor many of the news reports mentioned the study's gaps: that 9-year-olds who are spanked at the rate of every other day may have serious behavioral problems quite apart from their being spanked, and that the 807 mothers in the survey were just 14 to 24 years old at the time they gave birth —hardly a representative sample. Typically, news accounts reported simply that Straus's study determined that "spanking children causes [a] 'boomerang' of misbehavior," as the Associated Press put it.

Remarkably, the same issue of *Archives* carried another, longer-term study by psychologist Marjorie Lindner Gunnoe that came to quite different con-clusions. Unlike Straus, Gunnoe used data that tracked somewhat more chil-dren (just over 1,100) for five years (not two years), sampled older parents as well, and relied on reports from both children and adults. The researcher con-cluded that "for most children, claims that spanking teaches aggression seem unfounded." Gunnoe found that children ages 4 to 7 who had been spanked got in fewer, not more, fights at school. (The reverse was true with white boys ages 8 to 11 in single-mother families, who Gunnoe suggested might be less accept-ing of parental authority.) Yet there was no AMA press release on the Gunnoe study, and none of the network reports and only 15 of the 107 newspaper and magazine stories on Straus's research mentioned Gunnoe's contrary findings.

Outside the not-so-watchful eye of the media, researchers have been re-assessing the conventional wisdom on spanking for several years. In 1996, psy-chologist Robert E. Larzelere, director of residential research at Boys Town in Nebraska, which does not allow spanking, published the results of a sweeping review of spanking research, in which he examined 166 studies and came to several unexpected conclusions. Rejecting research that was not peer-reviewed, that included overly severe or abusive punishment (causing bruises or other injuries), or in which the child's behavior was not clearly preceded by the spanking, Larzelere ferreted out the 35 best studies. Among these, he failed to find any convincing evidence that nonabusive spanking, as typically used by parents, damaged children. Even more surprisingly, Larzelere's review revealed that no other discipline technique—including timeout and withdrawal of privi-leges—had *more* beneficial results for children under 13 than spanking, in terms of getting children to comply with their parents' wishes.

When Larzelere and others presented their research at the 1996 AAP conference on spanking, it prompted a quiet wave of revisionism. The two conference organizers, S. Kenneth Schonberg and Stanford B. Friedman, both pediatrics professors at Albert Einstein College of Medicine in New York, wrote afterward in *Pediatrics,* "We must confess that we had a preconceived notion that corporal punishment, including spanking, was innately and always 'bad.' " Yet by the end of the conference, the two skeptics acknowledged that "given a relatively 'healthy' family life in a supportive environment, spanking in and of itself is not detrimental to a child or predictive of later problems."

The spanking controversy may be an abstract debate among academics, but it is a real-life dilemma for parents of young children who wrestle daily —and sometimes hourly—with disciplining their small charges. A study of 90 mothers of 2-year-olds found that they interrupted them an average of every 6 to 8 minutes to induce them to change their behavior. Shellee Godfrey, a mother of two from High Point, N.C., swore she'd never spank her kids. "I figured, I'm gonna talk to my children," she says. Then came the day when she was late for work and Jake, her strong-willed 2-year-old, refused to get dressed, repeatedly ripping off his diaper. "I was desperate. I finally popped him and said, 'You're putting this diaper on!' He looked at me, and he did it. He was fine. But I felt really bad, like I had hurt him."

Naturally, no child-development specialist is about to run out to write a book called *Why You Should Spank Your Kid*—which may be one reason why the news media have buried the notion that spanking might in some cases be a useful discipline technique. After ethicist Ryan was quoted in the *New York Times* a few years ago saying, "Mild physical punishment is appropriate in extreme cases," he says, "I never got so much hate mail about anything."

One lesson of the spanking controversy is that whether parents spank or not matters less than *how* they spank. "If parents use it as an occasional backup for, say, a timeout," says Larzelere, "and as part of discipline in the context of a loving relationship, then an occasional spanking can have a beneficial role." The welter of child-raising books of the past 30 years has also provided a host of alternatives to spanking that allow children to express their feelings—a radical idea earlier in this century—while at the same time preserving firm limits on behavior. The best disciplinary approach, experts say, is to use a number of methods, including reasoning, timeouts, rewards, withdrawals of privileges, and what some experts term "natural consequences" (e.g., if a child refuses to eat his breakfast, he goes hungry that morning). Spanking seems to work best in conjunction with some of these techniques. For example, another analysis of spanking studies by Larzelere shows that when spanking is used among 2- to 6-year-olds to back up other discipline measures—such as reasoning—that have failed, it delays the next recurrence of misbehavior for twice as long as the use of reasoning alone.

For parents who choose to spank, there are appropriate and inappropriate ways to do so. Kids under 2 years old should not be spanked, because the danger of causing physical injury is too great. As for adolescents, research suggests a fairly solid correlation between spanking and increased misbehavior; grounding teens has proven more effective. The age when spanking is most useful appears to be between 2 and 6, and parents should take into account the nature of the child. A single disapproving word can bring a sensitive child to tears, while a more spirited youngster might need stronger measures. Finally, spankings should be done in private to spare children humiliation, and without anger. A parent who purposefully includes spanking as one of a range of discipline options may be less likely to use it impulsively and explosively in a moment of rage.

As for how to spank, the AAP warns against using anything other than an open hand, and only on the child's rear end or extremities. The intention should be to modify behavior, not cause pain. "A spanking is nothing more than a nonverbal way of terminating the [bad] behavior," says psychologist John Rosemond, author of *To Spank or Not To Spank*. It secures "the child's attention, so that you can send the child a clear message of disapproval and direction."

Plenty of parents feel they can deliver that message without striking their child. "Our belief is that spanking, hitting, any overt physical punishment isn't an effective technique for encouraging positive behavior," says Gerrie Nachman, a Manhattan mother of an 11-year-old son. "The last thing we want to do is model to our son physical abuse as a way of dealing with inappropriate behavior in other people."

Parental abuse   At the other extreme are parents who deliver far more than a tap on the rear. In response to a 1995 poll, almost 20 percent of parents said they had hit a child on the bottom with a brush, belt, or stick in the past year; another 10 percent said they had spanked the child with a "hard object." One valuable lesson to come out of the antispanking movement is an awareness of how many parents abuse spanking. Straus found that two thirds of mothers of children under 6, for instance, spank them at least three times a week, which most experts would say is too much.

The current state of knowledge about spanking may cut two ways: Parents who use spanking appropriately can relax and stop feeling that they are causing ineluctable harm to their child. But parents who overspank—and mistakenly believe that their firm thwacks are benefiting little Samantha—should scale back their spankings. Somewhere in between parents' guilt and parents' denial lies a happier medium.

Nadine Block

Abandon the Rod and Save the Child

Corporal punishment is the intentional infliction of physical pain for a perceived misbehavior. It includes spanking, slapping, pinching, choking, and hitting with objects. The practice is not permitted against prison or jail inmates, military personnel, or mental patients; nor is it allowed against a spouse, a neighbor, or even a neighbor's dog. Instead, in the United States, corporal punishment is legally preserved only for children.

Children have been the victims since early colonial times and today remain so with the support of the courts and a significant percentage of the citizenry. Each year at least a million children are beaten in the name of "discipline," billions of dollars are spent on child abuse prevention, and the system devised to protect children fails. Yet, the subject is a divisive one that often pits generation against generation and family member against family member.

One reason for this divisiveness is corporal punishment's roots in theology. The strongest and most enduring support for the practice comes from the Bible, particularly the Old Testament. Many fundamentalist, evangelical, and charismatic Protestants use scripture to justify their use of corporal punishment to develop obedience and character in children. Their position is that God wills and requires it in order to obtain his blessing and approval; to not physically punish children for misbehavior will incur God's wrath.

For example, in "The Correction and Salvation of Children" on the Way of Life website (wayoflife.org/~dcloud/), the Reverend Ronald E. Williams of the Believers Baptist Church in Winona Lake, Indiana, contends that the biblical "rod of correction" is a physical object, in most cases a wooden paddle for use in spanking a child's buttocks; any unwillingness to use physical correction is "child abuse." While he recognizes that using an object to hit a child increases the chance of injury, and while he cautions that bruising is not the goal of "correction," Williams counsels parents not to be overly concerned if bruising happens:

> But these opponents of God's methods may object, "What you are suggesting will hurt the child and may even bruise him!" My response would be, "That is correct." A child may in fact be bruised by a session of difficult correction. In fact, the Lord has already anticipated this objection and has

From Nadine Block, "Abandon the Rod and Save the Child," *The Humanist* (March/April 2000). Copyright © 2000 by Nadine Block. Reprinted by permission of the author.

discussed it briefly in the Scriptures. "The blueness of a wound cleanseth away evil: so do stripes the inward parts of the belly" (Proverbs 20:30). One may say, "That is talking about a child who has bruised himself in an accident at play." No, the latter part of the verse explains that God is giving this passage in the context of physical chastening for correction. God makes the point that if a child is bruised during one of these sessions of correction that a parent should not despair but realize that the blueness of the wound cleanses away the evil heart of rebellion and willful stubbornness that reside in that depraved little body.

Williams also believes that corporal punishment should begin early in life:

My wife and I have a general goal of making sure that each of our children has his will broken by the time he reaches the age of one year. To do this, a child must receive correction when he is a small infant.

However, the Reverend Thomas E. Sagendorf, a Methodist pastor and member of the advisory board of the Center for Effective Discipline's program, End Physical Punishment of Children (EPOCH)—USA, points out that Old Testament scripture can also be used to justify slavery, suppression of women, polygamy, incest, and infanticide. So, like many believers in the Bible, Sagendorf prefers to look for guidance on disciplining children in the New Testament. There, he says, children are shown great love and compassion, and violence is not tolerated.

Rutgers University historian Philip Greven, in his 1992 book *Spare the Child: The Religous Roots of Punishment and the Psychological Impact of Physical Abuse,* paints a deeply disturbing picture of religion's influence on discipline and the consequences of that influence. Examining the effects of corporal punishment on the American psyche and culture, Greven reminds us that, although some of the fundamentalist Protestant groups are most outspoken in defending corporal punishment, they have a great deal of secular support.

He says centuries of strong Protestant traditions begun in Europe have been infused into modern U.S. law, education, and the behavioral sciences. The beliefs that children are inherently bad, that their wills must be broken, that their behavior must be controlled all have theological sources. Whether it was overtly or tacitly endorsed in our individual experiences, corporal punishment is deeply rooted in our psyches and, therefore, not easily or willingly examined. The first step in changing our consciousness and behavior toward children, Greven advises, is to confront the repressed fundamentalism in ourselves.

Fortunately, a growing willingness to challenge ingrained attitudes has resulted in a waning societal acceptance of corporal punishment. For example, almost universally accepted in the 1950s, the practice has decreased each generation since. In 1985 only five states had banned it in public schools; today twenty-seven states have done so. Even in those states that still allow corporal punishment, many of the larger cities have banned it. In 1991 the American Academy of Pediatrics [AAP] called on parents, educators, legislators and other adults to seek the legal prohibition by all states of corporal punishment in schools. Unable to hush pro-spanking sentiments within in its own ranks, however, the AAP stopped short of calling for a complete ban in 1998. Instead it recommended that its members encourage and assist parents in developing nonviolent responses to misbehavior.

⋅᷇⟨◉⟩᷇⋅

The changing perception of corporal punishment is being helped along by research in the field of physical abuse. Much of it is correlational and retrospective in nature, given the difficulty of designing such experiments and the abhorrence of assigning children spanking and paddling treatment. It is, however, compelling.

Greven examines the effects of corporal punishment on children in *Spare the Child* and there finds the roots of public and domestic violence. He says the religious and authoritarian nature of the practice leads children to accept violence without question and believe it is deserved. Rage unable to be expressed by a child is repressed and denied—but doesn't go away. It can later appear in the form of destructive and aggressive behavior toward others or, turned on the self, can lead to psychological problems such as depression and melancholia. Greven says many such problems can be traced to a history of pain, abuse, and suffering in childhood, and the most common source has always been corporal punishment.

In his 1994 book *Beating the Devil Out of Them: Corporal Punishment in American Families,* University of New Hampshire Family Research Laboratory Co-director Murray Straus reviews the dozens of studies he has authored or coauthored that show corporal punishment contributes to interpersonal violence. Among his results, Straus found that children who were spanked regularly and severely have higher rates of hitting siblings, hitting their spouses as adults, and assaulting someone outside their family. Children who are frequently spanked for lying, cheating, hitting siblings, and being disobedient are more likely to display these kinds of antisocial behaviors.

Studies by Straus and others have also found that corporal punishment can escalate to the level of abuse prohibited by law. Since parents are more likely to spank when they are tired, stressed, depressed, and fatigued, and a majority of parents express moderate to high anger when spanking children, it is little surprise that parents who believe in corporal punishment are more likely to injure children than parents who do not. And children who are regularly spanked are more likely to continue the practice on the next generation and to show less remorse for wrongdoing as adults.

Even infrequent and moderate spanking in childhood can have deleterious effects in adult life, including a greater likelihood of depression and other psychological problems. Conversely, Straus found that children who are rarely or never spanked score higher on cognitive tests than those who are frequently spanked. He theorizes that parents who don't spank spend more time reasoning with and explaining to children, thus maximizing verbal ability.

A recent U.S. Department of Education [DOE] survey indicates that about 500,000 students are hit each year in the nation's public schools. Physical injuries, including hematomas and broken bones, have resulted from adults hitting children in school with boards—sometimes in anger and in unobserved and unsupervised settings. The National Coalition to Abolish Corporal Punishment in Schools, another program of the Center for Effective Discipline, estimates that 2 percent of children who are paddled need medical care. Twenty years of DOE surveys analyzed by the coalition and the center reveal that corporal punishment in schools is used more frequently on children with disabilities, poor children, boys, and minority children.

⌘

Despite the compelling research, the task of ending corporal punishment in the United States is a daunting one. All too often repeated by those who grew up with violence are comments like "My parents hit me because they loved me" and "I got hit because I deserved it." Progress is likely to be slow and incremental, but it is not impossible.

The last fifteen years have seen a great deal of progress on a state-by-state basis. For example, nineteen of the twenty-seven states that have banned corporal punishment in public schools did so between 1985 and 1994. The remaining twenty-three states without bans—primarily southern and southwestern states—allow local boards of education to determine whether corporal punishment may be used.

And there is a slow but steady increase in the number of those school boards adopting voluntary bans—frequently to avoid potential litigation resulting from paddling injuries. In Ohio, child advocates were unable to get a complete ban, but they got so many restrictions put into law that only forty-two out of 611 school districts report using corporal punishment. Each year a few more districts enact a local ban, making a statewide ban likely in the near future.

The use of corporal punishment in other child-caring settings (daycare centers, foster care, and institutions) varies from state to state. State regulatory agencies are moving toward complete bans, and a great deal of legislative and regulatory progress has been made over the past twenty years because of extensive public education campaigns.

Perhaps an easier route is to get a federal ban on corporal punishment. Schools could be prompted to comply by tying federal funding to requirements for adopting bans, as Democratic Representative Major Owens of New York attempted in the early 1990s.

In all this, the United States is taking a lesson from Europe, where corporal punishment in schools was banned long ago. Nine European countries—Austria, Croatia, Cyprus, Denmark, Finland, Italy (by court decision), Latvia, Norway, and Sweden—have banned corporal punishment in all settings, including homes.

Sweden was the first country to act. It took away parents' specific authority to use corporal punishment, then passed a comprehensive ban three years later in 1979, accompanied by a large-scale education effort. The law is generally used to require educational training of parents who hit children, but offenders can be subjected to criminal prosecution. The overall process has resulted in an overwhelming acceptance of the ban in Sweden and, more importantly, a decline in child abuse. U.S. child advocates are watching carefully as a number of countries—including Germany, Ireland, New Zealand, Switzerland, and the United Kingdom—are studying this model for possible adoption.

In Canada, an effort is underway to abolish Section 43 of the Criminal Code, which gives parents authority to use "reasonable chastisement" on children. Abolition of this section is likely to be followed by a complete ban that follows the Swedish model. Meanwhile, Susan Bitensky, a law professor and EPOCH advisory board member, has suggested criminalizing corporal punishment of children and making violators subject to the same criminal penalties imposed in adult assaults and batteries. In the winter 1998 *University of Michigan Journal of Law Reform,* Bitensky says such a law could be effective if accompanied by prosecutorial restraint and a strong public education program, such as that used in the Swedish model.

The most successful initiatives to end corporal punishment have included public education campaigns. With that in mind, EPOCH initiated SpankOut Day USA on April 30, 1998. Modeled after the Great American Smokeout, the annual observance seeks to bring widespread attention to the need to end corporal punishment of children as an important way of addressing the U.S. child abuse and neglect emergency. In the first two years, more than 400 informational events were held for parents and educators.

EPOCH emphasizes discipline as teaching rather than punishment. While its current activities are largely educational in nature, the organization also seeks legal reform. An important step forward in that effort would be the adoption of the United Nations Convention on the Rights of the Child, which provides a legal basis for improving the lives of children throughout the world. Specifically, the international agreement requires ratifying countries to take measures to protect children from abuse and neglect and strongly supports nonviolent discipline of children. The United States and Somalia are the only countries that haven't adopted the convention. Many of the nations that have are using it to support their efforts to ban corporal punishment in homes.

However, one doesn't have to have the backing of an entire nation or even an entire organization to make inroads toward abolishing corporal punishment. The following are a few guidelines that individuals can use to develop cooperative, self-disciplined children:

- Stop using corporal punishment on your own children.
- View children's misbehavior as a mistake in judgment. It will be easier to think of ways to teach better behavior.
- Teach behavior you want to see. You probably will need to do that more than once for most behaviors. Praise will increase the behavior you want to see.
- Establish behavior rules that are few in number, reasonable, and appropriate for each child's age and development. Enforce these rules consistently.

- Develop routines and consistency in important daily events, including mealtimes, study times, and bedtimes. It helps prevent discipline problems.
- Distract infants and toddlers when they are doing something you don't like or remove them from the situation. They lack understanding of right and wrong and shouldn't be hit or shaken.
- Use good manners when talking to children about behavior. Be a role model for children in speech and actions.

POSTSCRIPT

Is Spanking an Effective Method of Discipline?

There are two main conflicts that arise when discussing spanking and its appropriateness as a discipline method. The first centers on whether children who are spanked grow up to become more violent adults. Were the majority of criminals in our nation's prisons spanked when they were children, leading them in turn to pursue a violent lifestyle? The second conflict centers on whether children can effectively learn not to do something again after receiving a spanking.

The philosopher Quintilian, who lived from A.D. 35–95, stated, "I am by no means in favor of whipping children, though I know it to be a general practice. In the first place, whipping or spanking is very degrading. He will become insensitive to the blows. If a teacher is loving, there is no need to use the rod. The shame far outlives the physical pain." Does behavior improve as a result of receiving a spanking, or are future spankings needed, which may be longer, harder, and more severe? Many find it ironic that a spanking may be administered to a child in an attempt to alter the negative behavior of hitting others. Can young children internalize that they should not do something to others that is done to them? Are there times when spanking is an acceptable method of discipline, but other times when it should not be used? Should parents who spank their children do so in the privacy of their own home or is it acceptable to do in public? Will the spanking still have the same effect if administered long after the negative behavior has occurred?

Suggested Readings

Alexander, K. K., "Is Spanking Ever Okay?" *Parents* (vol. 76, no. 5, 2001).

Lemonick, M., "Spare the Rod? Maybe," *Time* (August 25, 1997).

Monaghan, P., "Sparing the Rod: A Crusader Against Corporal Punishment," *Chronicle of Higher Education* (July 3, 1997).

Ramsburg, D., "The Debate Over Spanking," *ERIC Digest* (1997).

Samalin, N. and Whitney, C., "Why Spanking Doesn't Work," *Parents* (vol. 73, no. 8, 1998).

Straus, M. A., *Beating the Devil Out of Them: Corporal Punishment in American Families and Its Effects on Children* (Lexington Books, 1994).

ISSUE 7

Should Superhero Play Be Discouraged?

YES: Marjorie Hampton, from "Limiting Superhero Play in Preschool Classrooms: A Philosophy Statement," *Texas Child Care* (Winter 1995)

NO: Brenda J. Boyd, from "Teacher Response to Superhero Play: To Ban or Not to Ban?" *Childhood Education* (Fall 1997)

ISSUE SUMMARY

YES: Marjorie Hampton, director of First Presbyterian Preschool in Arlington, Texas, asserts that if superhero play is allowed in schools, teachers are encouraging aggressive behavior in children.

NO: Assistant professor Brenda J. Boyd does not view superhero play to be aggressive and states that banning this type of play is not helpful in teaching children how to develop the social skills necessary for healthy living.

Marcia, a teacher of four-year-olds, asked three children to remove the baby blankets they had draped over their shoulders to resemble capes. The three had been pretending that they were going to save people from the "bad guys." When she talked to the children they told her that they were gong to tie up the bad guys and then kill them dead. As the day ended, Marcia was sharing the events of the morning with her colleagues and asked in frustration if she had done the right thing by discontinuing that type of play. What should she have done? Should she have ignored the attempts by the children to pretend that they were superheroes? Or should she have insisted that there be no play that resembled good guys versus bad guys or activities that promoted aggression? As a relatively new teacher she was torn between not intervening in the dramatic play going on in the class and eliminating aggressive behaviors that she considered not appropriate.

Marcia and her colleagues are not alone in their dilemma regarding superhero play. Children find numerous ways to model the behaviors they see on television, in video games, and in the movies. Just as older children may pretend they are Sammy Sosa or Mark McGwire while playing baseball, preschoolers will role-play characters they know from their television viewing. Admittedly,

Ernie, Bert, and Big Bird do not offer the excitement of the X-Men or the Power Rangers, therefore the more glamorous characters are often the first to be imitated.

There have always been children who imitate popular heroes. Even before television was invented, children would pretend that they were characters from books or radio shows. The difference between the imitating of many years ago versus the imitating of the twenty-first century is that children could not see what the character was actually doing. It was the child's imagination that fueled the play. Today children imitate everything from body slams and high kicks to the use of guns and bombs.

The effects of superhero play began to take center stage when the subject of imitating what one saw on television was used as a defense in criminal court cases. There have been a number of children accused of violent crimes whose attorneys argued that their client's violent behavior was a result of imitating what he or she saw on television. In most cases this defense has not been successful in winning acquittal. However, if we know how powerful adult role models are to children, is it possible that children are not influenced by what they see on television? At what age do children begin to judge that just because something was seen on television does not mean that it should be repeated?

Even the award-winning children's television show "Arthur," based on author Marc Brown's popular books, had an episode about superhero play. Two boys who were imitating space bots hit Arthur's sister, D. W., in the nose with a wooden swing. D. W. had to go to the emergency room. The subject of not doing everything seen on television was presented to the young "Arthur" viewers who are predominately four through eight. Are we sending children mixed messages by allowing them to participate in superhero play in their classrooms, yet discussing it as something that should not be done on television shows? If teachers allow some play from television and movies to be portrayed in the classroom, at what point do they intervene? At what point does the play become too aggressive? Are there important lessons to be learned from superhero play? How harshly should superhero play be judged? Should it be judged at all?

In the following selections, Marjorie Hampton writes about how she and her preschool staff decide to limit superhero play. They redirect play when it is aggressive and state that they have seen a decrease in aggressive play in their classrooms. Brenda J. Boyd asserts that in banning this type of play, teachers are forgoing an opportunity to teach children prosocial skills such as respect, getting along well with others, and safety.

Marjorie Hampton

 **YES**

Limiting Superhero Play in Preschool Classrooms

Our staff has chosen to limit superhero play. We have banned toy weapons, violent videos and books, superhero costumes, and all aggressive play, even when its pretend play.

We chose this policy because of the increased aggression we were seeing in children from toddlers through kindergartners. We saw this aggression expressed frequently in kicks and jabs on the playground as various groups of children re-enacted the latest episode of a popular children's television show. We also saw it expressed verbally and physically in the classroom.

We believe children need an alternative to the superhero characters they see in television shows and movies. The old adage "monkey see, monkey do" is a simplistic but realistic explanation of the way young children learn.

How Children Learn

Children learn through play. As they play, they take in information. Over time, they use this information to build ideas. One idea fits with another into an understanding of how things work.

Children take what they see and hear in the world and change it through play into something that has real meaning for them. Those meanings come from all their prior experiences and the ideas they have constructed from those experiences. In this way, play helps children learn, think, and build their own intelligence.

In playing with friends, children develop social skills such as getting along with others, sharing, taking turns, and living together in community. They have the opportunity to try out different roles and to consider the roles of others. They learn how to release feelings and express themselves in a nonthreatening atmosphere, which enhances personality and emotional development.

Erik Erikson, a renowned psychoanalyst and author of *Childhood and Society* (1950), suggested that child's play is "the infantile form of the human ability to deal with experiences by creating a model situation and to master reality by experiment and planning.... To 'play it out' in play is the most natural self-healing measure childhood affords" (Erikson, 1964).

From Marjorie Hampton, "Limiting Superhero Play in Preschool Classrooms: A Philosophy Statement," *Texas Child Care*, vol. 19, no. 3 (Winter 1995). Copyright © 1995 by Texas Department of Human Services. Reprinted by permission of *Texas Child Care*.

Erikson viewed adults as emotional bases and social mediators for children. Adults serve as interpreters of feelings, motives, and actions and help children in learning to solve social problems. That opportunity is assured when teachers provide secure environments, developmentally appropriate activities, and schedules that allow for both structured and unstructured periods of time.

In working with children, teachers allow them to take initiative, make choices, and explore. At the same time, teachers—and parents—provide clear limits so children can learn which behaviors are unacceptable to society.

In addition to behavioral guidance from parents and teachers, children learn from behaviors they see in their environment. They are intensely curious and are constantly absorbing and making sense of what they see and hear. They learn through repetition, modeling, observation, and imitation. This learning may occur in the home, at school, or from the media.

How Children Learn Violent Behavior

Violence is a learned behavior. Some 30 years ago, Albert Bandura, a behaviorist, conducted research with a "Bobo doll" that demonstrated that children imitate the aggressive behaviors of a model (Bandura, 1965).

Other research clearly links children's exposure to violence on television to aggression in real life (Hearold, 1986; Leibert and Sprafkin, 1988; Parke and Slaby, 1983). Aggressive behaviors appear more pronounced immediately after viewing violence. This is especially true of boys. In one popular children's TV show, most of the superheroes are male and use karate-type kicks and jabs. This gives little boys aggressive role models to mimic (Boyatzis, 1994).

Equally alarming is the effect of TV violence on children's sensibilities (Drabman and Thomas, 1974). With repeated exposure, a numbing process occurs, and violence and aggression come to seem normal to children. Their sensitivity is further lessened if their parents have also become callous to violence as a result of their own viewing habits.

Preschool children are extremely impressionable and have difficulty distinguishing between fantasy and reality. While watching television, they are generally passive physically, but active mentally. Like sponges, they absorb what they see and will often try out or imitate behaviors they view, including aggressive behavior.

When they try out this behavior, they may receive both positive and negative attention. The positive attention comes from their peers, who may think the behavior is "cool," and from parents, who may think it's "cute" or who may view it as training for a violent world. The negative attention comes from the victims, who may complain and cry, and from adults, who may scold or try to appease them. As most teachers know, many children crave any attention, positive or negative.

For victims, violence creates fear, anxiety, isolation, lack of trust, and anger. These feelings damage a child's self-esteem, whether the child is the victim or the aggressor.

Aggressive behavior in children consists of two types. The first is instrumental aggression: It's a means to an end. We see it in 1- and 2-year-olds when they throw a temper tantrum to get something they want. The second type is hostile aggression: It involves an intent to hurt. We see it beginning in 3- and 4-year-olds and continuing through the teen years. It is this type that characterizes superheroes and needs the intervention of parents and teachers.

In watching episodes of superhero cartoons, one quickly realizes that there is indeed intent to harm. Although the "good guy" gets the "bad guy," that message is not what most children absorb. Instead, they see the physical actions these superheroes use to resolve their differences. Despite a few positive verbal messages, violence is clearly the choice for settling conflicts.

Does Therapeutic Play Belong in the Classroom?

Many people have heard about the benefits of play therapy and believe that it can be carried into the preschool classroom. I do not share this view.

In my therapy practice, I do play therapy. Children are brought to therapy when they are experiencing stress and displaying inappropriate behaviors. This stress may be related to a divorce, death, move, school, blended family, new baby, fire, car accident, or similar event. For example, 4-year-old Sarah, whose parents are getting a divorce, may be having temper tantrums every day because she feels abandoned by a parent or guilty for "causing" a parent to leave.

In this kind of therapy, the child leads the play. Since young children have limited language ability, they will often use toys or props to show fears and concerns. Small animals, puppets, and dolls become the characters in children's own life stories as they play those stories out with them. Children may use toy weapons in this setting.

While aggression and toy weapons are sometimes appropriate in a therapeutic setting, they are not appropriate in a preschool classroom. First, the therapeutic setting involves one child, while a classroom involves a group of children. Because only one child is seen at a time in therapy, the limits are broader: "You may not hurt yourself or me, and you may not purposefully destroy the toys or damage the furniture or room."

Second, in play therapy—unlike preschool—the therapist has made a diagnosis and laid out a plan to help the child in solving the problem. The therapist sees the child on a consistent basis until the issue is resolved. The process requires that the child have a trusted person to reflect back feelings as the child expresses them. No such treatment plan exists in preschool.

How Modern Life Contributes to Violence

In recent years, society has become more hostile for families. In general, children and their parents are losing the qualities of life that contribute to well-being. These qualities include the following:

Trust and safety   On a daily basis we can pick up a newspaper or turn on a news broadcast and learn about violent events such as a drive-by shooting, a child finding an adult's gun and shooting another child, or a senseless bombing of a public building that kills 168 people. Increasingly the parents we serve in our own centers report such crimes as a home robbery that occurred while they were at work, an assault on a neighbor, or an incident of sexual abuse in a nearby high school.

Parents now tend to feel more insecure about leaving their children. They need to know that the place and people they take their children to are safe and that constant monitoring occurs. If parents feel unsafe, that feeling is conveyed to the children.

Children may hear their parents talking about a violent crime, or they may see a news flash about it on television. For example, during snack time Jamil says he hopes his school doesn't get blown up "like the building last night." When the teacher mentions it to Jamil's dad at the end of the day, he is astonished: "I didn't realize that Jamil was even in the room when the news was on."

In some cases, a child may directly witness violence—for example, hearing parents quarreling or seeing gang members fighting down the street. All of these experiences may cause children to feel less secure.

Autonomy   As parents listen to news reports and become more concerned about their children's welfare, they may react by overprotecting children and restricting their activities. Or they may feel helpless and fail to give children the comfort and support they need.

These responses are normal and natural but can lead children to doubt their ability to control themselves or their environment. Such responses isolate children from people and experiences that can empower them and help them learn to manage life tasks. They can deprive children of opportunities to try out skills at their own pace and become self-sufficient.

Sense of connectedness   Unlike in earlier years, families and extended families today often live across the country from one another. More often than not, parents work outside the home, and children are in child care. Many people today do not even know their next-door neighbors. Often people come and go, and never meet.

As a result, children and parents tend to feel less connected. Many children miss out on the sense of being cared for by several people who love them and whom they know well and can trust. They have fewer role models and fewer opportunities to learn by example. They don't get to hear stories passed from generation to generation that give them a sense of who they are.

Cooperation   The spirit of cooperation appears to be fading. The desire to help our neighbors is being replaced by the need to have more than they do and be better than they are. Competition is no stranger to preschools. Over the 25 years I have directed our center, I have seen competition grow. It is not limited to this center, this city, or this state; it is thriving across our country.

I see children being pressured to be the best at whatever activity they are involved in. Average is often unacceptable in any situation. Scheduled activities (such as ballet and gymnastics) leave little time for a child to be a child. This may be fine if it is what the child wants and the activity is age-appropriate, but often it is what the parent wants for the child. The child frequently ends up feeling stressed and overstimulated by so much outside activity. Competition breeds low self-esteem and hostility, not high self-esteem and cooperation.

Time and patience Answers today, it seems, must come quickly. We do not have time to wait patiently, to work through problems that develop. All too often we try to solve a problem with a threat, lawsuit, or weapon. How will children learn to cooperate, negotiate, mediate, and compromise when adults so often choose the quick-fix formula?

A quality early childhood program works to restore these qualities in the lives of children and their families. By minimizing violence in the classroom and helping children learn cooperation and caring, caregivers can help prepare children to interact peaceably and positively with others in later life.

How We Deal With Aggressive Behavior

Our staff has chosen to limit aggressive play by setting the following rules:

1. Children may bring small action-hero figures, but they may not bring weapons of any type to school.
2. If children want to engage in superhero play in the classroom, they must confine it to the block area where cars, trucks, action figures, and similar toys are available for play.
3. If children engage in aggressive play, even if it is pretend play, we interrupt it and redirect them to another activity.
4. Children may wear clothing with pictures of superheroes, but they may not wear superhero costumes.
5. Teachers may not use books and videos about superheroes or stories that contain violent material. We review lesson plans in advance on a weekly basis to ensure that books and videos relate directly to the unit of the week.
6. Staff must respect children's feelings and reactions even when they differ from their own. Staff must be aware of their own attitudes and feelings related to violence and not project negative attitudes onto children.

We recognize that there is no absolute way to end aggressive play in any setting. For example, when I chose not to buy a toy gun for my small son, he made one out of a piece of toast. In the classroom, children use the interlocking blocks to make buildings, cars, and sometimes rockets or guns. But this does not mean that we give in to children and let them play with guns. Blocks, clay, boxes, and other materials can become many things, but a toy gun can only be a toy gun.

Children can and will invent what they need in play. This is real play. When children are given dolls that represent characters from books, television, movies, and videos, they are deprived of opportunities to pretend, make their own dolls, and "write" their own stories. Our center has several small dolls representing people from many walks of life (including military figures), babies, and animals. Some are fantasy figures, and some are lifelike. Play with these toys is appropriate play.

Caregivers and parents can learn a great deal about children and their understanding by observing this play. It is important to reflect to a child what we observe. For example, when Vanessa hits the baby doll and says, "Bad girl," we say, "Vanessa, that hurts the baby. Tell me what's going on." This shows her not only that we're interested, but also that we understand what she's doing and that we're there for her.

It is one thing for a child to strike a doll or have a doll strike another doll, but quite another when a child kicks or hits another child. The feelings they experience in that instance are strong. The victim experiences fear, pain, frustration, and perhaps even rage. The aggressor may experience a rush from the power felt at that moment, but this child no doubt will experience guilt or shame soon, depending on how he or she is corrected. That reaction may in turn create additional anger and cause the aggression to continue or erupt again later.

The flying karate kicks common in superhero programs are often mimicked on the playground. Some people believe that you can teach children how to pretend fight—that is, to throw the punch or kick the kick, but not land it. I disagree firmly. Young children do not have full control of their muscles. Although they may not intend to do harm, it may happen because of their inability to aim or time the action precisely enough. I also believe it is not appropriate to pretend to hurt someone. That type of play is best reserved for small action figures.

Some parents choose to enroll their young children in karate and other martial arts classes. Karate can be a positive discipline when it is understood. But I believe, based on what I observe on the playground, that most children do not understand that karate is not intended to be used as a weapon. Most young children are not able to understand the intended discipline required in karate. Most children need to be physically active, for example, and find it difficult to stand in an attentive stance while another child completes a task or skill.

How We Teach Cooperation and Caring

In addition to limiting aggressive play, we set up the environment to ensure a safe place for learning and actively teach cooperation and caring. We do this in the following ways:

1. Provide a framework for play. For example, Mr. Adams notices that children in the dramatic play center are using wooden spoons as "rocket blasters" to "shoot you dead." He promptly announces that only three children can play in the center at one time. He also says, "In this spaceship, you have to learn how to help each other survive if you're going to make it back safely to earth." Appropriate limits and boundaries provide a safe, secure environment that minimizes the opportunity for aggressive play.

2. Empower children by offering choices. A caregiver may say, for example, "Would you like to play in the home center or block center?" and "Would you rather have snack in the room or on the courtyard?" Simple choices like these allow children to learn to make decisions and experience the consequences of those decisions.

   Emphasize to children that it is OK to say no to playmates, even when they are asked nicely for something and even when pressured by their peers. This practice can be difficult for caregivers, who often find it more convenient to let a demanding child take over a game from a quiet child in the name of "keeping the peace." To be able to stand up for themselves and resist pressure from gangs, children need to learn how to say no in an acceptable way and in a broad range of situations.

3. Encourage autonomy in children, but teach the importance of interdependence. This is a fine line, but one that everyone must learn in order to live successfully in relationship with others.

   For example, Ms. Mitchell allows the children to paint whatever they choose in the art center and encourages them to talk about who gets the last bit of purple paint. "Sometimes it's hard to talk things out," she says, "so let me know if you need help."

4. Model prosocial behaviors such as compassion, kindness, sharing, nurturing, cooperation, benevolence, caring, and protecting. When Antonio falls on the playground and skins his knee, instead of telling him to stop crying, a caregiver says something like, "Oh dear, that hurts a lot. Let's wash it and get a bandage strip."

   Develop activities that embrace these values, particularly group activities such as parachute play, mural painting, block building, cooking, and caring for classroom pets. Involve children in activities that allow them to focus outward from themselves such as making cards to send a sick classmate, decorating cookies to take to a nursing home, and making a book of cards or pictures to take to a children's hospital ward. Such activities help children, who are by nature egocentric, become aware of caring for others.

5. Acknowledge these prosocial behaviors as they occur: "Benjamin, I appreciate the way you asked Sharon if you could ride the tricycle now. I know it's hard to wait until she finishes."

   Send notes home to let parents know when children demonstrate these behaviors. Be as specific as possible: "When David was having trouble turning the handle on the water fountain today, Lori stopped playing and showed him how to hold it." This kind of feedback not only affirms that you value their children, but that you value what parents are teaching them as well. It builds stronger parent-teacher bonds and increases children' self-esteem.

6. Plan specific times for open-ended discussion with the children. Choose stories that address issues children may be dealing with such as injury, illness, death, divorce, grief, and loss. After reading a story, talk about the characters and situations they encountered. For example, when Pooh Bear gets stuck in Rabbit's hole, encourage children

to think about what happened and how they might feel in a similar situation.

Story stretchers and "What about it?" questions can occur during any part of the day, but after rest or nap time is excellent because children's minds are often active when they are quiet. At these times children do a great deal of their thinking about what is happening around them; their worries and fears are closest to the surface.

For Show-and-Tell, children sometimes bring action-hero figures. Use these times to discuss actions and consequences, as well as the characters' feelings. "Why were they fighting?" a caregiver might ask. "How would you have felt if you were the one who got kicked? What are some other ways they could have solved this problem?"

7. Plan special activities that encourage critical thinking skills. Encourage problem-solving through scenarios that are appropriate to the children's developmental level.

    For example, find large photos in books, magazines, and newspapers showing children involved in different situations and expressing varied emotions, such as a child on a bus waving goodbye to Dad, or a group of children eating hot soup after playing outdoors. Ask questions such as "What is happening here?" and "How are they feeling?" and "What would have happened if...?"

8. Allow children to be involved, as appropriate, in setting limits for play and deciding consequences. For example, when Rudy and Andrea crash into Albert's carefully built sand structure on the playground, gather the children around and ask if such behavior should be allowed to happen. Then ask them to set a rule for the sandbox and decide what to do if someone breaks the rule. Children will be more invested in complying with limits if they are involved in determining what those limits are and what the consequences of testing them will be.

9. Communicate your views about superhero play to parents, and invite them to share their views with you. Understand that parents may have a different perspective or act unconcerned. At our center most parents appreciate our efforts to redirect their children's interest in superheroes. Some have differed with our view, but all of us have shown respect for each other's perspective. It's important to listen carefully, build trust, and continue to share your viewpoints.

    Convey specific information to parents about their children: "Joey told a story today about shooting someone on the roof. What do you make of that?" Share such stories with that child's parents alone; always respect confidentiality by not mentioning such matters to other parents.

    Be open to hearing what parents have to say. Assume, for example, the center director sends a letter to parents questioning the appropriateness of karate lessons for preschoolers. Mr. Oakley, a parent, calls for an appointment. He is upset because he has had his child enrolled in karate for some time. The director listens and reflects back the father's views and feelings: "You feel that karate will make your son feel more confident about himself and stand up to bullies." Neither the parent nor the director changes stance, but both gain new insights about differing perspectives.

Communicating with parents in this manner may shed some light on a child's family situation and give clues to a child's behavior. It may also suggest ways for approaching others who have similar beliefs.

10. Set up training sessions for staff to help them learn about the effects of violence on children and ways to deal with aggressive behavior. As staff see aggressive play erupting, have them redirect it toward play that satisfies the children's needs but builds a constructive foundation for the future.

For example, while Samantha and Hayley are playing in the drama boat on the playground, they burst into an argument and attack each other with kicks and chops. Ms. Ames steps between them and says, "It's time to dock your boat on the beach and look for the dinosaurs on the shore." This redirection teaches them that fighting is not allowed but provides an appropriate outlet for angry feelings.

11. Be willing to advocate for what is best for children. Copy current articles related to violence from this magazine and others such as *Young Children,* and post them on your parents' bulletin board.

As you become aware of new research or new organizations in the area that advocate for better regulation of children's television programming, inform parents through your parents' newsletter or a special letter to each family.

BENEFITS OF LIMITING SUPERHERO PLAY

We have found many advantages to limiting superhero play.

1. Aggressive play has decreased. We seem to have fewer conflicts to resolve.
2. Children are learning to solve problems in ways that will serve them well throughout their lives.
3. They are learning to listen to and respect one another.
4. They are learning that they do not have to do what everyone else does to be OK.
5. Their play is more creative and imaginative.
6. They are developing critical thinking.
7. The environment is safer and more relaxed.
8. Both parents and staff have an increased awareness of the implications and seriousness of this issue. Staff, in particular, are more involved in "hearing" the play as it happens so that discussions can be more relevant in the classroom.

References

Bandura, A. "Influence of models' reinforcement contingencies on the acquisition of imitative responses," *Journal of Personality and Social Psychology,* 1, 589–595, 1965.

Boyatzis, C. J.; G. M. Matillo; and M. K. Nesbitt. "Effects of Mighty Morphin Power Rangers on children's aggression with peers," *Child Development Journal*, 25, 45–55, 1995.

Carlsson-Paige, N. and D. E. Levin. *Who's Calling the Shots? How to Respond Effectively to Children's Fascination With War Play and War Toys.* Philadelphia: New Society Publishers, 1990.

Erikson, E. H. "Toys and reasons," in M. R. Haworth (ed.), *Child Psychotherapy: Practice and Theory.* New York: Basic Books, 1964.

Hearold, S. "A synthesis of 1,043 effects of television on social behavior," in G. Comstock (ed.), *Public Communications and Behavior,* vol. 1. New York: Academic Press, 1986.

Joy, L. A.; M. M. Kimball; and M. L. Zabrack. "Television and children's aggressive behavior," in T. M. Williams (ed.), *The Impact of Television: A Natural Experiment in Three.* Orlando, Fla.: Academic Press, 1986.

Leibert, R. and J. Sprafkin. *The Early Window: Effects of Television on Children and Youth,* New York: Pergamon Press, 1988.

Levin, D. E. *Teaching Young Children in Violent Times: Building a Peaceable Classroom.* Philadelphia: New Society Publishers, 1994.

Parke, R. D. and R. G. Slaby. "The development of aggression," in E. M. Herrington (ed.), *Handbook of Child Psychology: Socialization, Personality, and Social Development,* vol. 4. New York: Wiley, 1983.

Segal, Marilyn and D. Adcock. *Feelings.* Atlanta: Humanics, 1987.

Smith, Charles A. *The Peaceful Classroom.* Mt. Rainier, Md.: Gryphon House, 1993.

Tuchscherer, P. *TV Interactive Toys: The New High Tech Threat to Children.* Bend, Ore.: Pinnaroo Publishing, 1988.

Brenda J. Boyd  **NO**

Teacher Response to Superhero Play

This kind of play is a fact of life for those of us directly responsible for young children or for the training and support of those who deal with young children. A look at a bibliographic database related to early childhood (e.g., ERIC) offers ample evidence that children's involvement in superhero play is of growing concern to early childhood educators—the number of articles classified under superhero play as a subject between 1990 and 1995 is twice that found for the years 1985–1990.

Teachers of young children have become increasingly vocal opponents of superhero play, voicing concern about the behavior in their classrooms. Articles in professional publications such as *Young Children, Child Care Information Exchange* and *Childhood Education* by such authors as Bergen (1994) and Carlsson-Paige and Levin (1995) report that more and more teachers are choosing to ban superhero play from their classrooms. Newspaper articles found in the *Seattle Times* (Henderson, 1994) and the *Wall Street Journal* (Pereira, 1994) indicate that this concern has gone beyond an academic debate about child behavior. Teachers are sincerely concerned for the safety of children and themselves; many worry about violence as children engaged in superhero play grow older.

As a former child care provider/early educator and current teacher educator, I also have concerns about reported increases in violent and aggressive behavior in preschool classrooms. I suggest, however, that banning superhero play may not be the most effective means for dealing with children's increasing exposure to inappropriate and poor quality television programming. I will suggest that 1) we do not yet have valid data on these "increases" in classroom superhero play, 2) this behavior may play some developmental function necessary for young children's healthy growth and 3) by banning superhero play, teachers may be denying themselves a powerful opportunity to teach about values, respect, safety and living in a democratic social group.

Teacher Estimates of Play and Aggression

I begin by examining the premise that aggressive, violent superhero play is on the rise in preschool classrooms. The published reports of this increase are based

From Brenda J. Boyd, "Teacher Response to Superhero Play: To Ban or Not to Ban?" *Childhood Education*, vol. 74, no. 1 (Fall 1997). Copyright © 1997 by The Association for Childhood Education International. Reprinted by permission of The Association for Childhood Education International and the author.

on anecdotal reports from teachers (Carlsson-Paige & Levin, 1991; Jennings & Gillis-Olion, 1979; Kostelnik, Whiren & Stein, 1986) and from limited surveys of teachers of young children (Carlsson-Paige & Levin, 1995). These non-random samples are often drawn from participants at conference workshops on super- hero and war play in the classroom, who may already be sensitized to and concerned about the issue of aggressive play. These reports lead us to believe that preschool children are spending the majority of their time karate chopping and pouncing on each other.

My own research, in which I collected time interval samples of preschool children's behavior, has led me to question this belief (Boyd, 1996). In one sam- ple of a group of 3- to 5-year-old children at a laboratory preschool, I found that only 2 of 17 children exhibited superhero play during a 1-month observation period. The time spent in superhero play accounted for less than 1 percent of the 300 minutes of play observed. In a second sample, in which children in a full-day child care program were observed, only 5 percent of play time, on the average, could be classified as superhero play. In this group of 16 children, only 4 children exhibited superhero play. In both samples, boys were the only su- perhero players. Furthermore, my observers and I never witnessed a child being physically hurt by another child while involved in superhero play.

Although these findings are clearly preliminary, they suggest that teacher reports of the occurrence and nature of superhero play may not be entirely ob- jective, and may lead to an inflated estimate of this behavior. Previous research about teachers' views of aggression offers two lines of evidence to support this hypothesis.

First, evidence suggests that children and teachers have differing perspec- tives on "play fighting" and "aggression." In a study published in 1985, Smith and Lewis showed videotapes of play episodes to preschool children, their teacher and the assistant teacher. The children were more likely to agree with each other or with an objective observer than with their teachers in assessing behavior as play or aggression.

These results suggest that teachers rely on some perspective not shared by children to differentiate aggression and play. This perspective is reflected in the criteria teachers reportedly used for determining aggression in this study. The assistant teacher, whose assessment of behavior was least often in agreement with the children, based her remarks on her knowledge of the children's per- sonalities, as reflected in comments such as "Well, knowing those boys, I know they can't cooperate together. Chances are it wasn't playful, it was aggressive" (Smith & Lewis, 1985, p. 180).

Second, one study (Connor, 1989) suggests that teachers' perspectives of- ten differ not only from children's perspectives, but also from other non- teaching adults', including teachers in training. That is, teachers tend to see behavior as aggressive, rather than playful, more often than non-teachers. In this study, three preschool teachers viewed video clips of child behavior; the teachers labeled all 14 clips as examples of aggressive behavior. When the clips were shown to psychology students, however, the majority rated only two incidents as aggressive, two as play and the rest were rated differentially, depending on the viewer's gender. Men were more likely to view behavior as playful, while women more often labeled behavior as aggression. Additionally, Connor reported that preservice teachers agreed more often with female college students than with inservice teachers when rating behavior as play or aggression.

These findings suggest two points. First, some aspect of working in child care/early education may lead teachers to view play as negative behavior, in general, and as aggression in particular. Perhaps teachers' sense of responsibility for children's behavior and their safety leads them to be overly sensitive to potential disruption and physical injury. Connor's study (1989) supports this hypothesis. Teachers reported concern with the potential for injury, noting that the children "were playing too rough and someone could get hurt" (p. 217).

As I discuss superhero play with teachers, however, I find that the sense of responsibility is not only limited to concern with immediate behavior, but also includes the long-term consequences of aggressive play. I am struck by the connection teachers make between preschool play behavior and that of adolescent gangs. Early childhood educators seem to be equating young children's pretend behaviors with the actual loss of life and violence on their streets. This equation seems premature. We have too little information about the importance and/or potential harm of such fantasy play.

Second, gender socialization may also influence how teachers of young children (predominantly women) view superhero play. As Connor (1989) has suggested, women may grow up with less desire and/or opportunity to be involved in superhero and other physical play than men. This lack of involvement may lead them to be less accepting of such play. Moreover, if girls are discouraged from involvement in physical activity because they may get hurt, this may lead them to believe that rough play is dangerous and should be avoided. Taken together, the research on gender and my anecdotal information from teachers suggest that early childhood educators may be overreacting to superhero play because of their fears about an increasingly violent society, and because of gender bias about play.

The Developmental Function of Superhero Play

The possibility that superhero play may serve some developmental purpose is the essence of my second concern about banning superhero play. Early childhood educators have long held that pretend play is critical for young children's healthy emotional development. This belief has been used to defend involvement in superhero play.

Specifically, scholars suggest children have a need to resolve feelings about power and control. Some have suggested that superhero play offers a sense of power to children in a world dominated by adults, thus helping children to cope with the frustrations of limited control (Carlsson-Paige & Levin, 1990; Curry, 1971; Ritchie & Johnson, 1982; Slobin, 1976; Walder, 1976). Similarly, by playing out scenarios focused on good and evil, children can work through feelings of anxiety and fear about their own safety (Peller, 1971). Additionally, such play may help children express their anger and aggression and become comfortable with these feelings, which may otherwise be frightening to the child (Carlsson-Paige & Levin, 1990; Ritchie et al., 1982).

While this theory is well-established in the child development literature, it is a weak argument for supporting the developmental function of super-hero play without empirical research that directly examines its developmental relevance. Moreover, this set of hypotheses about the role of superhero play in providing emotional security is not easily tested. Other perspectives for investigating the function of superhero play, however, are available.

Although superhero play has received limited empirical attention, a related type of play, known as "rough-and-tumble play" (R&T), has been more thoroughly researched. The term "rough-and-tumble play" is commonly used to refer to children's play fighting, wrestling and chasing behaviors, from preschool through adolescence (e.g., Costabile et al., 1991; Pellegrini,1987). I argue that superhero play is a special case of R&T and that the similarity of these types of play allows us to develop hypotheses about the potential function of superhero play. I will describe the similarities between these types of play, outline some of the hypothesized functions of R&T and consider the implications of this work for the study of superhero play.

R&T and superhero play share several characteristics. Both types of play can involve chasing, wrestling, kicking, mock battles and feigned attacks (Kostelnik et al.,1986). In addition, R&T frequently involves fantasy enactment or pretending (Smith & Connolly, 1987; Smith & Lewis, 1985), as does super-hero play. Adults often confuse both R&T and superhero play with aggression (Kostelnik et al.,1986); furthermore, R&T play is often identified as pretend play in research studies (Pellegrini,1987). Teachers' accounts of superhero play indicate that this play is routinely marked by play fighting, kicking and martial arts moves. In fact, these types of behavior seem to be the central cause for teachers' concern (Bergen,1994; Carlsson-Paige & Levin, 1995; Henderson, 1994). These similarities suggest to me that superhero play can be conceptualized as a special case of R&T play, in which children assume the role of a superhero character.

The similarity in these types of play led researchers to examine the function of superhero play. This body of research suggests that R&T play may serve some important developmental functions for young children, especially boys. R&T play serves three potential functions—specifically, affiliation, dominance and social skill facilitation (Smith & Boulton, 1990).

Affiliation   R&T play may help children form or maintain friendships. R&T's positive social nature is underscored by the presence of children laughing and smiling, and by the absence of children inflicting pain (Blurton Jones, 1972; Smith, 1982). R&T partners are consistently found to be friends (Humphreys & Smith, 1987; Smith & Lewis, 1985). While this does not directly show that R&T play builds friendships, these results nevertheless suggest that R&T play helps children develop or maintain friendships (Smith & Boulton, 1990).

Dominance   Animal researchers first used the concept of dominance to describe a hierarchical order of dominance within a species that controls access to resources such as space, food and mates (Wilson, 1975). They found that this hierarchy can reduce conflict, by clearly defining a power structure within a group (Hinde, 1974). Strayer and Strayer (1976) applied this concept to a group of children and observed a fairly stable hierarchy, with few conflicts.

Smith and Boulton (1990) suggest that through R&T play, children can maintain or improve their ranking within the hierarchy. A child can maintain her or his rank by picking worthy "opponents" who are equal in strength. Or, a child could safely improve her rank by picking a slightly stronger play partner, and suffer little if she was not successful.

Humphreys and Smith (1987) support the dominance maintenance hypothesis. When comparing class consensus rankings of 7- to 11-year-olds' strength, they found, in most cases, no consistent difference in the two participants of an R&T bout. Their findings suggest that children do select partners near to them in the dominance hierarchy.

Social skill facilitation   Some researchers have suggested that involvement in R&T offers children an opportunity to develop social skills, which consequently leads to successful peer interactions. Both parent-child play and peer play support this hypothesis. Parke, MacDonald and their colleagues report that children whose parents (especially fathers) engage in physical play with them are more likely to be popular with their peers (MacDonald, 1987; Parke, MacDonald, Beitel & Bhavnagri, 1987). Power and Parke (1981) argue that physical play with parents helps children learn to regulate and interpret emotion by serving "as context for a wide range of communicative and affectively charged social interaction" (p. 160). Indeed, in one study, physical play did correlate with girls' ability to "read" facial expressions, suggesting some relationship between physical play and skill at reading social cues (Parke et al., 1987).

While the results are more numerous in terms of peer-peer R&T, they are also more mixed. Pellegrini (1988) found that children rejected by their peers were less successful than popular children at discriminating between serious fighting and R&T. In addition, for popular children, R&T served as a precursor to rule-oriented games, yet for rejected children, it led to aggression (Pellegrini, 1991). Several other researchers' findings indicate either no relation between R&T and popularity, or a negative correlation (Dodge, 1983; Ladd, 1983; Rubin, Daniels-Bierness & Hayvren, 1982). It is difficult to compare these results, however, because there is no uniform definition of R&T (Smith, 1989).

While the connection between superhero play and R&T is clearly speculative, an examination of how R&T play functions offers a measurable perspective on superhero play's possible contribution to development. The similarity between R&T and superhero play suggests that these types of play may also serve similar developmental functions. At the very least, this examination makes clear that it is premature to deny children the opportunity for involvement in superhero play. We first need to know more about the developmental implications of such a denial.

Sending Play Underground and a Lost Opportunity

This brings us to my third and final concern about banning superhero play. As other scholars of play have noted, banning has two possible effects (Carlsson-Paige & Levin, 1995). First, banning superhero play from the classroom sends children the message that they must hide their interests from adults, and that it is wrong for them to be interested in issues of power and control, good and evil, and so on. A related consequence is that teachers may lose an important opportunity to influence children's ideas about violence and the use of power, and about managing individual needs in a social community.

My concern about children's covert involvement in superhero play stems from the observation that children have always involved themselves in play about "good guys" and "bad guys." By telling children that such play is wrong or bad, we may be communicating that it is not acceptable to be interested in issues of control, nor is it acceptable to have fears about power. At the same time, we lose an opportunity to help children feel safe in a world that may be dangerous at times. While we need not expose children to inappropriate levels of violence, danger or fear, we should not expect that young children do not share adults' fears about violence, even if it is undeveloped. Part of the human condition is to fear and to desire mastery of that fear. Should we tell children that using a natural tool to conquer that fear, such as play, is wrong?

Second, I think that if teachers are truly concerned about exposing children to televised violence and aggression (or are concerned children will likely hear about such programming from friends anyway, even if they are not allowed to watch), are they not required to help children work through these issues in their play? When we ban superhero play (or any behavior children find interesting), we ignore a powerful opportunity for helping children learn valuable lessons in a familiar and appealing context.

Resources are available for helping teachers to use superhero play effectively in the classroom. Diane Levin (1994) has published practical suggestions for helping children to learn about establishing "peaceable" classroom communities; these ideas attend to all children's safety needs without simply banning superhero play. These suggestions can help teachers address their concerns about the children who do not like to play superheroes or who are frightened by others' superhero play. In addition, Gayle Gronlund (1992) offers interesting ideas for moving children beyond the scripted narratives they see on television, which she developed from working with her kindergarten class during the Ninja Turtle days. More recently, Julie Greenberg (1995) discussed ways to "make friends with the Power Rangers." Even when teachers decide to support superhero play in their classrooms, they may not know the best way to begin. These resources offer a starting point.

I believe that banning superhero play is not the most productive manner for dealing with our concerns about increased violence in our classrooms. Instead, educators should consider the best means for making positive use of this play; some of the resources I have described can be useful in this endeavor. Be assured that I am not advocating a free-for-all without teacher input into play.

Each educator must decide, on the basis of information about their students and their needs, whether this sort of play is acceptable, at what level and with what supports in place. I encourage early childhood educators to take a broad and contextual view, as we do with all the behaviors we encounter, and to offer children the best supports we can in their daily lives.

References

Bergen, D. (1994). Should teachers permit or discourage violent play themes? *Childhood Education, 70*(5), 300–301.

Blurton Jones, N. (Ed.). (1972). *Ethological studies of child behavior* (pp. 97–129). London: Cambridge University Press.

Boyd, B. J. (1996). *Superhero play in the early childhood classroom.* Unpublished manuscript.

Carlsson-Paige, N., & Levin, D. E. (1995). Can teachers resolve the war-play dilemma? *Young Children, 50*(5), 62–63.

Carlsson-Paige, N., & Levin, D. (1991). The subversion of healthy development and play: Teachers' reactions to the Teenage Mutant Ninja Turtles. *Day Care and Early Education, 19*(2), 14–20.

Carlsson-Paige, N., & Levin, D. (1990). *Who's calling the shots? How to respond effectively to children's fascination with war play and war toys.* Philadelphia, PA: New Society Publishers.

Connor, K. (1989). Aggression: Is it in the eye of the beholder? *Play and Culture, 2,* 213–217.

Costabile, A., Smith, P. K., Matheson, L., Aston, J., Hunter, T., & Boulton, M. (1991). Cross-national comparison of how children distinguish serious and playful fighting. *Developmental Psychology, 27,* 881–887.

Curry, N. E. (1971). Five-year-old play. In N. E. Curry & S. Arnaud (Eds.), *Play: The child strives toward self-realization* (pp. 10–11). Washington, DC: National Association for the Education of Young Children.

Dodge, K. A. (1983). Behavioral antecedents of peer social status. *Child Development, 54,* 1383–1399.

Greenberg, J. (1995). Making friends with the Power Rangers. *Young Children, 50*(5), 60–61.

Gronlund, G. (1992). Coping with Ninja Turtle play in my kindergarten classroom. *Young Children, 48*(1), 21–25.

Henderson, D. (1994, December 14). No "morphing" allowed in class: Power Rangers play all the rage for kids. *The Seattle Times,* pp. Al, A21.

Hinde, R. A. (1974). *A biological basis of human social behavior.* New York: McGraw-Hill.

Humphreys, A. P., & Smith, P. K. (1987). Rough and tumble, friendship, and dominance in school children: Evidence for continuity and change with age. *Child Development, 58,* 201–212.

Jennings, C. M., & Gillis-Olion, M. (1979, November). *The impact of television cartoons on child behavior.* Paper presented at the meeting of the National Association for the Education of Young Children, Atlanta, GA.

Kostelnik, M., Whiren, A., & Stein, L. (1986). Living with He-Man: Managing superhero fantasy play. *Young Children, 41*(4), 3–9.

Ladd, G. (1983). Social networks of popular, average, and rejected children in a school setting. *Merrill-Palmer Quarterly, 29,* 283–307.

Levin, D. E. (1994). *Teaching young children in violent times: Building a peaceable classroom.* Cambridge, MA: Educators for Social Responsibility.

MacDonald, K. (1987). Parent-child physical play with rejected, neglected and popular boys. *Developmental Psychology, 23,* 705–711.

Parke, R. D., MacDonald, K. B., Beitel, A., & Bhavnagri, N. (1987). The role of the family in the development of peer relationships. In R. Peters (Ed.), *Social learning and systems approaches to marriage and the family* (pp. 17–44). New York: Bruner/Mazel.

Pellegrini, A.D. (1991). A longitudinal study of popular and rejected children's rough-and-tumble play. *Early Education and Development, 2*(3), 205–213.

Pellegrini, A. D. (1988). Elementary-school children's rough-and-tumble play and social competence. *Developmental Psychology, 24*(6), 802–806.

Pellegrini, A. D. (1987). Rough-and-tumble play: Developmental and educational significance. *Educational Psychologist, 22,* 23–43.

Peller, L. (1971). Models of children's play. In R. Herron & B. Sutton-Smith (Eds.), *Child's play* (pp. 110–125). New York: Wiley.

Pereira, J. (1994, December 7). Caution: Morphing may be hazardous to your teacher. *Wall Street Journal,* pp. A1, A8.

Power, T. G., & Parke, R. D. (1981). Play as a context for early learning. In L. M. Laosa & I. E. Sigel (Eds.), *Families as learning environments for children* (pp. 147–178). New York: Plenum.

Ritchie, K. E., & Johnson, Z. M. (1982, November). *Superman comes to preschool: Superhero TV play.* Paper presented at the meeting of the National Association for the Education of Young Children, Washington, DC.

Rubin, K. H., Daniels-Bierness, T., & Hayvren, M. (1982). Social and social-cognitive correlates of sociometric status in preschool and kindergarten children. *Canadian Journal of Behavioral Science, 14,* 338–347.

Slobin, D. (1976). The role of play in childhood. In C. Shaefer (Ed.), *Therapeutic use of child's play* (pp. 95–118). New York: Aronson.

Smith, P. K. (1989). The role of rough-and-tumble play in the development of social competence: Theoretical perspectives and empirical evidence. In B. H. Schneider, G. Attili, J. Nadel & R. P. Weissberg (Eds.), *Social competence in developmental perspective* (pp. 239–258). Dordrect: Kluwer Academic Publishers.

Smith, P. K. (1982). Does play matter? Functional and evolutionary aspects of animal and human play. *The Behavioral and Brain Sciences, 5,* 139–184.

Smith, P. K., & Boulton, M. (1990). Rough-and-tumble play, aggression, and dominance: Perceptions and behavior in children's encounters. *Human Development, 33,* 271–282.

Smith, P. K., & Connolly, K. J. (1987). *The ecology of preschool behavior.* Cambridge, England: Cambridge University Press.

Smith, P. K., & Lewis, K. (1985). Rough-and-tumble play, fighting and chasing in nursery school children. *Ethology and Sociobiology, 6,* 175–181.

Strayer, F. F., & Strayer, J. (1976). An ethological analysis of social agonism and dominance relations among preschool children. *Child Development, 47,* 980–989.

Walder, R. (1976). Psychoanalytic theory of play. In C. Shaefer (Ed.), *Therapeutic use of child's play* (pp. 79–94). New York: Aronson.

Wilson, E. O. (1975). *Sociobiology. The new synthesis.* Cambridge, MA: Belknap Press of Harvard University Press.

POSTSCRIPT

Should Superhero Play Be Discouraged?

Has our society's fear of being sued affected what we allow and do not allow in classrooms? Are there potential benefits to superhero play that some children could miss because they are not allowed to play out their fears and fantasies in the early childhood classroom setting? The need for young children to engage in rough-and-tumble play is well documented. However, parents and teachers are often torn as to whether they should allow this type of play. Is this type of play more acceptable in homes than in classrooms? Parents may allow a pretend fight to go on in their family room, but that same situation would not be commonly permitted in a school.

When animals in a zoo chase each other and wrestle on the ground, they are seen as playful. But when young children participate in the same behaviors they are seen by some as aggressive. Teachers may intervene when children participate in rough-and-tumble play. Beginning teachers especially are concerned that allowing superhero play in their classrooms will send a message to an administrator that they do not know how to control their students. Teachers are often evaluated by the level of noise and quiet activity that is being exhibited in their classrooms. In the eyes of many, a quiet, slow-paced environment fosters more learning. Teachers who understand and value the importance of superhero play for children to act out their concerns may be hesitant to allow it due to administrative repercussions.

In one study of superhero play, teachers who viewed videotapes of children engaged in that type of play were more likely to describe the play as aggressive than psychology students who watched the same videotapes. The students were more likely to describe the interactions viewed as merely playful. In the same study, men were less likely than women to view superhero play as aggressive. Boyd reports a very small incidence of superhero play in a classroom she observed. Less than one percent of the play in a 300-minute time period could have been classified as imitating superheroes. Are teachers worrying about superhero play too much? When children play at home or outside they are not under the scrutiny they are in a classroom. Are teachers in a school setting too quick to intervene in the play of young children? Should they instead allow the children to use the play to work out conflicts? Are there ample opportunities for young children who are in full-day child care to engage in the type of play that will allow them to develop the appropriate skills needed for successful learning experiences? Teachers have a responsibility to ensure that all children have opportunities to develop the life-long skills they will need to be successful members of society.

Suggested Readings

Bauer, K. L. and Dettore, E., "Superhero Play: What's a Teacher to Do?" *Early Childhood Education Journal* (vol. 25, no. 1, 1997).

Cooper, B. S. and Speakman, S. T., "Pikachu Goes to School," *Teacher Magazine* (vol. 96, no. 2, 1994).

Dyson, A. H., "The Ninjas, the X-men, and the Ladies: Playing With Power and Identity in an Urban Primary School," *Teachers College Record* (vol. 96, no. 2, 1994).

Fonville, B. and Afflerbach, S., "Superhero Play: Making It a Part of Your Curriculum," *Texas Child Care* (vol. 19, no. 2, 1995).

Levin, D. E. and Carlsson-Paige, N., "The Mighty Morphin Power Rangers: Teachers Voice Concern," *Young Children* (vol. 50, no. 6, 1995).

Marsh, J., " 'But I Want to Fly too!': Girls and Superhero Play in the Infant Classroom," *Gender and Education* (vol. 12, no. 2, 2000).

ISSUE 8

Should Parent Participation in Schools Be Required?

YES: Kathleen Kelley-Laine, from "Parents as Partners in Schooling: The Current State of Affairs," *Childhood Education* (1998)

NO: Mark J. Cooper and Mary H. Mosley, from "Warning: Parental Involvement May Be Hazardous," *Principal* (March 1999)

ISSUE SUMMARY

YES: Kathleen Kelley-Laine, project officer for the Organization for Economic Cooperation and Development in Paris, France, argues that building partnerships between parents and schools leads to higher student achievement.

NO: Assistant professor Mark J. Cooper and associate professor Mary H. Mosley, both of the College of Education at the University of Central Arkansas, urge caution when involving parents in the day-to-day operation of public schools as it may prove to be more counterproductive than helpful.

When working with young children, one would think that having an extra pair of hands to help in the classroom would inevitably lead to a positive experience. A classroom full of young children seeking the attention of the only adult in the room can mean an endless stream of tugs on a shirt sleeve or calls from across the room for assistance. As school administrators search for solutions to overcrowding and low achievement in some schools, parents are being used as volunteers in classrooms to assist teachers in the learning process. Some parents readily volunteer and are well-prepared to do so. These parents may have been former teachers or have some post-secondary education. Other parents may feel uncomfortable being in a classroom situation. School may have been an unpleasant or unsuccessful experience for them, and they may not be eager to relive those days even if it means helping their own child. There are also parents who, because of personal habits such as drinking, taking illegal drugs, or using profanity, would not be appropriate role models in a classroom of young children.

Many school administrators and teachers discuss requiring parental participation as a way to help provide individual attention to children throughout the day. Some private schools require parental participation as a way of keeping tuition lower. Other schools encourage parents to help, especially in the lower grades, but do not require parents to participate. Outside of Head Start programs for at-risk preschoolers, parental participation is not generally a requirement in public schools at the present time.

Some argue that teachers and administrators may be putting children in harmful situations when they encourage parents to participate in the educational process. They state that there can be negative effects on children from interaction with parents who have less-than-stellar parenting skills. Some of those encouraged to volunteer may be parents of the more than 3.1 million children neglected or abused each year. Some parents may be dealing with severe mental health problems, which would prevent them from making sound judgments and could lead to a child being harmed.

In many countries throughout the world parents not only assist in the classroom, they also serve on committees that make critical decisions for the day-to-day operation of the school. These parents volunteer because they want to improve the quality of the education that their children receive. Many assert that this type of participation benefits both students and parents. Can educators in the United States learn from the example set by educational systems around the world? Some believe they can. However, others argue that parental participation is not a requirement of a quality educational experience for children. To suggest that parents must be involved in the education of their children implies that private boarding schools cannot offer a quality education. Most of these schools do not have any parental involvement in the running of the school other than to receive economic support. Nevertheless, the academic achievement of students attending private boarding schools is highly regarded. What does this say about the quality of education in private schools versus the quality of education in public schools? Is the quality issue more to blame than the parental involvement issue?

How involved should parents be in their children's education? Should teachers and school administrators be able to exclude certain parents from participation in the classroom? If all parents are required to participate, does that mean that parents who are experiencing difficulty in parenting could learn from the positive role models in the classroom? Should parents have to pass a test before assisting in the classroom?

In the following selections, Kathleen Kelley-Laine contends that all parental participation should be welcomed and can serve to improve the quality of the educational experience for children. Mark J. Cooper and Mary H. Mosley question the ability of all parents to actually be of assistance when they are in the classroom.

Kathleen Kelley-Laine

YES

Parents as Partners in Schooling

P arents and other family members are children's first educators, responsible for children's early socialization, and for setting a mental and emotional foundation upon which the school and community will build. Families and school exist within a local community, and the education and socialization of most young people take place within this three-fold context.

The relationship between families and schools in member countries of the Organization for Economic Cooperation and Development (OECD) is complex and shifting. Both families and schools are intimately involved in educating young children—but how they identify, conduct and share their responsibilities varies among the countries according to societal customs, and in relation to changing economic and political climates.

As formal education becomes ever more important, its methods more diverse and its purposes more complex, there is a growing recognition that family, school and community each have a role to play in the process of educating children. This recognition dovetails with other changes that have taken place over the last decade—a general movement toward decentralization and local autonomy, and the realization that, in the future, most people will have to keep learning throughout their lives. As a result of these shifts, some parents and policymakers would like schools to become more outward-looking; they would prefer that schools' walls become more "permeable." The broad aim is for families, schools and communities to work together in partnerships that are better understood, more effectively planned and more fruitful than those of the past.

In 1997, the OECD's Center for Educational Research and Innovation conducted a cross-national study of schools and families. Nine member countries participated: Canada, Denmark, France, Germany, Ireland, Japan, Spain, the United Kingdom (England and Wales) and the United States. The study is the fourth in the OECD series, *What Works in Innovation in Education*. The studies do not categorize or exhaustively analyze each country's policies and practices, but rather compare their approaches and identify strengths and weaknesses. The Center hopes to identify useful models of innovation and good practice.

Why Involve Parents?

The importance of building partnerships in education is becoming more widely recognized, as young people must be educated to a higher standard than ever before. Families want to support their children's learning more effectively, work with teachers and have a greater choice of schools. At the same time, many countries are adopting policies to integrally involve parents in the education process. This is partly because parental involvement is associated with higher student achievement, partly because many governments want to make schools more accountable and partly because parents themselves are applying pressure.

OECD member countries are increasing parents' involvement in education for a number of different reasons—reasons that are embedded in each nation's political culture. The reasons given by officials and policy analysts in the nine countries in this study fall mainly into the following broad, interrelated categories:

Democracy: In many countries, parental involvement in education is considered a right. Some, like France, Germany and Denmark, have written such a right into law decades ago, although the nature of this right varies according to country.

Accountability: This is a more market-oriented concept than democracy, and is embraced most enthusiastically by England, Wales, Canada and the United States. Parental involvement is viewed not only or primarily as a parental right, but also as a means of making schools more accountable to the society that funds them.

Consumer choice: Some believe that parents, as consumers, should be able to choose their children's schools and influence how they operate. The underlying assumption is that if parents think of themselves as consumers, they are more likely to be clear about what they want and more critical of what they are being offered. In turn, this assumption may push schools into meeting the children's and families' needs more effectively.

Lever for raising standards: Findings from large-scale studies in Australia, the United Kingdom and the United States show that schools in which pupils do well (in terms of both academic attainment and attitudes toward learning) are characterized by good home-school relations.

Tackling disadvantages and improving equity: This reason is related to the one above, but refers more explicitly to raising individual children's performance by showing their parents how to support them more effectively at home. This is particularly important when there are cultural differences between the education system and the family.

Addressing social problems: In some countries, policymakers are turning to schools and to families for solutions to teenagers' drug and alcohol abuse, sexual promiscuity and high pregnancy rates, child abuse, violence and gang-based street cultures.

Resources: Not only can parents raise extra funds for schools, they also can be a very cost-effective way of mobilizing human resources—whether as helpers on school trips, coaches or assistants in sporting activities, or teachers' aides in the classroom.

◦◦◉◦

Parents have their own set of reasons for wanting to be involved, which do not always mesh with those of the policymakers. Parents' reasons for participating vary according to the age of the child and the type of school, but they can be broadly categorized as follows:

Student achievement: Parents wish to improve their children's performance and want to find out how best to do so.

Parental education: The need to support a child's learning compels some parents to attend classes (at the school or elsewhere) that cover aspects of the curriculum, or provide information on good parenting, or offer joint literacy activities.

Communication: Parents want to find out more about their children's progress, to find out what happens each day in school, and seek to increase the school's openness.

Influence: Parents wish to influence the curriculum, or to transmit family values and cultures in the school.

Support for the school: Parents recognize that schools often need funds and teachers are overburdened. They may offer to help by fundraising or assisting in other ways.

Support from the school: Parents sometimes need individual help and advice during a family crisis, or they may be interested in attending—with other parents—lectures or workshops on problems that challenge all families (e.g., drug abuse, health issues, the difficulties of adolescence, parenting issues, etc.).

Different Types of Involvement

Countries vary a great deal in the extent of parental involvement; most are strong in some aspects and weak in others. No one country in the study encouraged parental participation at all levels of the system. There is, of course, only a limited amount that governments can achieve through legislation, but the main ways that laws can have an impact include: giving parents more power in policymaking and governance at both the national and local levels; mandating the establishment of parents' associations; offering parents more choice of schools (although complete freedom of choice is never really possible); and requiring local authorities and schools to communicate certain information to parents.

The OECD report focuses on two main aspects of parental participation in education: *collective involvement* and *individual involvement.*

Collective involvement may occur at any level in the system—national, local or the school itself. There are four main aspects to this type of participation:

The representation of parents on policymaking or advisory bodies and in school governance. The nine countries differ substantially in the decision-making power that they give to parents at different levels in the system. At the *national* or *state* levels, Denmark, France, Germany, Ireland and Spain all allow parents, by law, to sit on key policymaking committees. A number of Canadian provinces recently have set up parent advisory committees. Similarly, some states in the United States have parental representation on district school board advisory committees. In England, Wales and Japan, however, parents are not represented on any national policymaking or advisory committees.

Parental involvement at the *school* level is similarly varied. Recent OECD research on education indicators estimated the extent to which parents are involved in decision-making processes in primary schools (OECD, 1997). Across the countries involved in the survey, about 60 percent of primary pupils are in schools that involve parents in school planning, and 57 percent are in schools that allow parents to participate in financial or organizational decisions. Less than 25 percent of students attends a school where the parents can influence the hiring or firing of educators.

Countries differ in how they view school councils. In Japan and France, for example, individual schools do not have governing bodies. In Germany, school councils—on which parents are represented—can influence, under certain circumstances, the appointment of school principals. Denmark, Ireland and Spain allow their schools to be more autonomous; hence, their school boards, on which parents sit, have real influence on decision-making. The process is probably most advanced in England and Wales, where individual school governing bodies—which include parents—make virtually all the significant non-curricular decisions.

Parents' associations and class councils. In virtually all of the countries in this study, parents are represented by national parents' associations. Most are built up through a system of parent councils or associations at the school level. Such associations are not compulsory, but most governments have encouraged them in recent years. Some parent organizations are longstanding. In France and Japan, for example, they are an accepted way for people to enter politics.

In Denmark, France, Germany, Ireland and Spain, members of national parents' associations have a right to sit on key national committees and give their opinions and advice. Class councils are a common form of participation in Denmark, France, Germany and Spain, but they are barely heard of in the other countries. The usual structure is simple: all parents of children in a particular class form a group and meet regularly with the teacher. In Denmark, where teachers often stay with the same group of children throughout nine years of *folkeskole*, parents and teachers may get to know each other very well, and parents often have a significant say.

Cooperation between school and community.   Most governments also strive to encourage closer relationships between schools and local communities. As the Education Minister of the 26 OECD countries said, "Schools are a major social asset and should become community learning centers offering a variety of programs and learning methods to a diverse range of students, and [they should] remain open for long hours throughout the year" (OECD, 1997).

In most countries the policy to open schools to the community has not moved much beyond the level of rhetoric. Virtually every country has an array of impressive pilot projects and local links between school and community, but these are rarely woven into the fabric of the system. Yet, schools can be very appropriate centers for building community spirit by offering sports facilities, meeting space and adult education classes, as well as other personal and social development services. Partnerships between schools and local employers also can be an important source of resources, energy and good will.

Recent research that examined the integration of services for children who are at risk of failing in school (estimated at between 15 and 30 percent in most OECD countries) contains numerous examples of successful cooperation between schools and a variety of community services (OECD, 1997). Ireland's Home-School-Community Liaison Scheme (which serves pupils and supports parents in disadvantaged areas), the Danish policy of designating about one in ten *folkeskoles* as local cultural centers for the community, and the French ZEPS (education priority zones) system are good examples of innovative central government initiatives to link home, school and community.

Parental influence on the curriculum.   Every country in this study, except for Canada and the United States, has a national curriculum that outlines what should be taught in schools. The extent to which these national curricula can be influenced or modified, however, varies a great deal. In Denmark, Ireland and Spain, parents are represented on national curriculum committees, which establish or revive the curriculum. In Germany, every state has a Parents' Council, which advises the Ministry of Culture on education issues. In other countries, such as England, Wales and Japan, parents have no say in the content or structure of the curriculum at the national level. In Canada and the United States, curricula are established at the state or province level, usually without any input from parents. Many Canadian provinces are currently restructuring, however, and some are setting up parent advisory committees, which will be consulted on such matters.

In addition to *collective involvement*, the OECD report focuses on *individual involvement*, which in most countries is more widespread, and has more direct impact on instruction, usually relating to three possible activities:

Psycho-social support. The support that schools provide to families may be in the form of parental education. Some of the most exciting individual projects involve offering parents short courses at the school (in subjects such as children's health, children's learning styles or parental challenges). Such courses can increase the confidence and competence of young parents, especially those who are economically disadvantaged, and encourage them to become more involved in other ways. Parents who attend workshops or courses may move on to more demanding educational programs, such as ones to improve their own literacy or numeracy. Many parents, after being empowered by this type of intervention, then earn credits at the local college or adult education center. Sometimes they also become involved in other local community initiatives.

Schools also can offer support at moments of family crisis, as well as intensive cooperative planning with parents of children who have special education needs. In many countries such partnerships represent excellent models of how joint approaches could work for *all* children.

Communication between home and school. The most widespread form of communication between the school and home is, of course, reporting to parents on their children's progress. Most countries mandate their schools to report two or three times a year, but the forms of their reports vary widely. Normally, schools can and do offer more frequent updates, and parents can request a discussion with the child's teacher. Other forms of communication include the use of two-way homework journals, newsletters and teachers' home visits. This last method is common in some countries (such as Denmark and Japan), but is rare in other countries, and tends to be seen as a sign of serious problems.

Parental involvement with school work—in the classroom and at home. The question of parents' presence in the classroom—whether as unskilled help or as teachers' aides—is often controversial. Although there is now a more widespread recognition that parents are children's first educators, not all teachers take the idea of partnership in the classroom seriously, and many parents are unaware of this new way of thinking. A number of initiatives (for example, in Canada, England, Wales, Ireland and the United States) demonstrate that both teachers and children can benefit if parents are available to support the teacher in the classroom—especially during the child's early years. This may not be true in other systems. Primary education in France, Germany and Japan, for example, is delivered very effectively with virtually no parental input of this kind. These three countries, however, are relatively homogeneous societies with a strong consensus as to the purpose and process of education. It may be that parental involvement of this type is more crucial in more pluralistic societies, especially in areas of socioeconomic disadvantage.

Regardless, the importance of parents helping their children with school work at home is now undisputed. The latest figures collected for the OECD's education indicators project suggest that about 75 percent of primary pupils (in the 12 countries surveyed) go to schools that regularly engage parents in actively supporting their children's learning at home (OECD, 1997).

Conclusions

Based on this study's findings, governments wishing to increase parents' involvement in schools should:

Develop methods to publicize and replicate successful strategies so that parents, students and teachers across the country—and in other countries, too—can learn about and benefit from them. Countries that have policies and commitments to increase parental involvement have an impressive range of successful projects or experiments. Too often, however, the lessons learned from successful innovations are not adequately disseminated or built into the system as a whole. Time and effort are wasted when parents and teachers must reinvent the wheel.

Recognize what all partners bring to the collaboration, in order to encourage mutual respect. Individual teachers and parents must learn how to negotiate with each other, handle differences of opinion, and understand the importance of each other's roles, without losing confidence in their own skills and leadership.

Provide training and present a clear legal framework setting out rights and responsibilities. Clear guidelines and training ensure that all partners understand the opportunities and limits of their collaboration. The most fruitful approaches often involve teachers and parents training together.

Identify parents' agendas in order to make best use of their energy and resources. Making assumptions about the needs and desires of parents or the wider community may lead to speedier policy formation, but can backfire. A successful agenda needs to be based on the views and experiences of a wide range of community groups and agencies, as well as a broad cross-section of parents. It should not be assumed that parents will always want what the current government thinks best.

NO  Mark J. Cooper and Mary H. Mosley

Warning: Parental Involvement May Be Hazardous

The involvement of parents in their children's lives is generally considered to be one of the most important ingredients in the recipe for successful educational programs. There is little doubt about the correlation between parental involvement in schools and students' academic achievement. However, there are also potentially negative aspects of parental involvement that are often ignored by educators.

As Lareau and Shumar (1996) assert, "Not only have the benefits of parental involvement not yet been adequately demonstrated, but ... there has been a near-complete failure to study the negative consequences of active family involvement in schooling." The presumption that *all* parental involvement provides quality support for children may be a leap of faith—a leap that may even result in negative or harmful situations for children.

Problems With Parents

While most home environments may be conducive to healthy relationships between parents and children, many are prone to problems. Consider these conditions:

Divorce   Approximately one-third of all children in the United States can expect to see their parents divorced before their eighteenth birthdays. Often, tension exists within families experiencing divorce, and parental involvement during this period may be counterproductive. Neither adults nor children may be receptive to homework requiring collaboration. In divorce situations, principals must encourage teachers to stay abreast of possible tensions among family members without being intrusive.

Abuse and neglect   The Children's Defense Fund (1997) reports that 3.1 million children are neglected or abused each year. It is critical for principals to help teachers recognize the warning signs of neglect and abuse and to walk a fine line in enforcing policies like encouraging parents to hold their children accountable for completing assignments.

Coercive family interactions   Some parents are overly authoritarian or demanding. Children cannot "just say no" to such coercive parents without the possibility of creating conflict. Therefore, teachers must be careful about recommending parental participation in some classroom-related activities, and principals must help teachers to distinguish coercive parents from parents who have high expectations. There is a difference between providing strong encouragement for children and frightening them. Where teachers suspect a coercive family environment, they can modify homework assignments that normally require parents and children to work together.

Mental health problems   Educators are finding that many children today show signs of mental health problems, including depression, anxiety, attention deficit disorder, learning problems, and hostile and defiant behavior. Students who are difficult for educators to deal with are likely to be difficult for parents, too. And if the parents have their own mental health problems, classroom-related activities that require the parent and child to collaborate may not be in the best interests of either.

Other adverse conditions that make quality parental involvement more difficult include poverty, unemployment, illiteracy, crime, single parenting, and families where both parents work outside the home. Educators must consider these social and economic conditions before encouraging collaboration between parents and children on homework and other school activities.

A Balanced Approach

A playing field is not level when only one side of an argument receives support, and principals can ill afford to automatically presume that all parental involvement is good while ignoring adverse home conditions that may interfere with *quality* parental involvement. While it is impossible to determine the number of parents who may be poor candidates for providing quality involvement in your school, even a small number is too many. There can be no one-size-fits-all approach. The benefits of parental involvement must be balanced with a warning label: "Parental involvement may be hazardous to our children's health."

Alliances among parents and educators are a cornerstone of education, but as society continues to change in the 21st century, these alliances will grow more complex. An important challenge for tomorrow's principal is to answer the question, "Is the help children receive from parents at home beneficial?" If it is not, the hazards of soliciting parents' involvement may be too great to risk until they are better prepared to provide quality involvement.

Adopting a "see no evil, hear no evil, speak no evil" protocol when developing school policies about parental involvement may result not only in a child's worst nightmare, but a principal's as well.

POSTSCRIPT

Should Parent Participation in Schools Be Required?

This debate has been occurring regularly in school board meetings as administrators deal with the shortage of classroom teachers and teaching assistants in schools nationwide. Many schools are turning to parents to fill in where trained, paid staff may have served in the past. Should parents be screened before being allowed to participate in the schools? If so, what criteria should be used in the screening process? Some schools require lunchtime parent volunteers to attend an orientation session on handling behavioral situations, and a handbook on how to interact with students in a school setting is also provided. What types of pre-volunteer orientation should be provided to volunteers?

There are situations where parents possess a skill that may be of value to a school staff, such as expertise in computer skills, knowledge of a particular field of science, or the ability to contribute to the performing or fine arts programs. Does possessing a certain skill or knowledge make one qualified to teach children on a one-to-one basis? What recourse do parents have if they find another parent volunteer unacceptable? School administrators recognize the need to augment the teaching staff with volunteers, but are also conscious of the legal issues that could result from an untrained parent interacting with groups of children. Teachers are in a unique situation in that they can do more than teach students, they can also model to the parent volunteers appropriate behaviors for interacting with children. Would more positive parenting skills result from parents observing certified teachers interacting with groups of children in a positive, effective way?

Suggested Readings

Grossman, S., "Examining the Origins of Our Beliefs About Parents," *Childhood Education* (vol. 76, no. 1, 1999).

Hoover-Dempsey, K. B. and Sandler, H. M., "Why Do Parents Become Involved in Their Children's Education?" *Review of Educational Research* (vol. 67, 1997).

Kieff, J. and Welhousen, K., "Planning Family Involvement in Early Childhood Programs," *Young Children* (vol. 55, no. 3, 2000).

Waggoner, K. and Griffith, A., "Parent Involvement in Education: Ideology and Experience," *Journal for a Just and Caring Education* (vol. 4, no. 1, 1998).

ISSUE 9

Does Homework in the Primary Grades Improve Academic Performance?

YES: Carol Huntsinger, from "Does K–5 Homework Mean Higher Test Scores?" *American Teacher* (April 1999)

NO: Romesh Ratnesar, from "The Homework Ate My Family," *Time* (January 25, 1999)

ISSUE SUMMARY

YES: Carol Huntsinger, professor of education and psychology at the College of Lake County in Grayslake, Illinois, concludes after conducting a four-year longitudinal study of 80 families that children who completed a considerable amount of homework each night were more academically competent than children who did little or no homework.

NO: Romesh Ratnesar, a writer for *Time* magazine, reports that homework, especially in the lower grades, causes a great deal of family stress and does not improve academic performance.

We've all struggled with homework, either as a student, a parent, or both. In many homes parents have replaced the traditional after-school question, "How was your day?" with, "What is the homework situation like for tonight?" Parents and children are stressed at home and teachers are frustrated by the lack of completed homework assignments brought in the next day. Does completing large amounts of homework help students to learn? Is there a correlation between academic achievement and hours spent doing homework?

Some children attend schools that have a mandatory homework policy wherein all teachers are required to assign work every night. For other students, homework is an option that may or may not be assigned by the teacher. Very few courses in teacher preparation programs address the topic of homework. Future teachers are given little guidance on the purpose of homework, what constitutes an appropriate assignment, how to assign, grade, and keep track of homework, or how to use homework assignments to improve academic performance. The beliefs teachers have about homework and its merits seem to come from personal experience. For a practice that can take up to three hours of an elementary school student's evening, some thought and debate should be given to the topic.

For many years Harris Cooper, a psychologist at the University of Missouri's Center for Research in Social Behavior, has been investigating this topic. One hundred years ago much of what was learned in school was acquired through rote memorization of facts. This could be done at home as well as in school. In the 1940s there was a shift to more divergent thinking skills, which required the student to come up with creative ways to solve a problem. It was believed that students could not memorize everything there was to know, so therefore how they used their thinking skills became more important than rote memorization. Homework was not a key focus. In the past 50 years the thinking on homework has flip-flopped many times. Teachers and parents find it difficult to judge what is best for students and the students can get caught in the middle.

The homework dilemma has been exacerbated in the past decade due to the rising number of single-parent and dual-income families as well as the increase in after-school activities. Children in many homes no longer have a full 5–6 hours of unscheduled time after school in which to do homework. Many children are cramming sports practices, music and arts classes, and community club activities into those after-school and evening hours. That leaves little time for homework or for family-centered activities. Some parents' work schedules leave little time to assist in homework assignments, and their children are often left on their own to figure out complicated math problems or to interpret questions on work sheets. These children can become frustrated and may learn little from their homework assignments. In other families, homework projects of extended duration can consume a family for weeks. Parents often object to the assigning of projects that appear to have minimal educational value. Students and parents should be aware of the goals of the homework program and know from the beginning the reason that the homework is being assigned. Teachers should also provide guidance to parents as to how much assistance they should provide their child and what to do when a child seems totally frustrated with an assignment. Teachers need to think carefully about how the time away from school should be used and if the student can actually complete the assignment with little or no assistance from an adult. Also, teachers need to consider if by completing the homework assignment the student will be better prepared to learn additional material.

In the following selections, Carol Huntsinger concludes that children who did what could be called "considerable homework" were more academically competent than their peers who did little or no homework. Huntsinger argues that the school curriculum today is very demanding and in order to cover all that is required during the school day, some work needs to be done at home each evening. Romesh Ratnesar finds a significant negative relationship between the amount of homework given and academic achievement, particularly in the lower grades. To Ratnesar, more homework does not translate into higher grades.

Carol Huntsinger

 **YES**

Does K–5 Homework Mean Higher Test Scores?

Our four-year longitudinal study of 80 families (40 Chinese-American, 40 European-American) indicates clearly that homework given in the preschool and primary grades reaps long-term benefits.

Children whose parents had given them homework in the early years and who had taught them in more formal ways performed significantly better in mathematics and English vocabulary in third and fourth grades than those children who were not given homework and whose parents relied on informal methods to teach them.

Contrary to the view that homework causes undue stress on young children, we might expect well-chosen homework to reduce stress and facilitate learning. For example, when children commit the addition, subtraction and multiplication facts to memory early, calculation becomes automatic. When faced with higher-level problems, children who have the math facts "down cold" expend less mental effort on calculation and devote more mental effort to solving the problem.

Our study showed that children who did considerable homework were more academically competent than, and as psychologically well adjusted as, children who did little or no homework in the early grades. It appears that children benefit from more practice on basic skills outside school.

Another interesting outcome of our study was a fuller understanding of Chinese-American parents' perspective on homework. They tend not to create a dichotomy between work and play. They believe that memorization and practice are essential to learning. They believe that teaching their children is an important part of the parental role. Many of the Chinese-American parents in our study believe that schools in the United States do not give enough homework to children in the primary grades. They are puzzled when American parents complain about homework to school officials at parent meetings. Rather than speak out, they quietly construct homework.

Coming from a culture that emphasizes the importance of hard work in achievement, Chinese-American parents believe that the homework habit needs to be established early. They give their children homework beginning in preschool. Chinese-American families view homework time as "family time." Often the whole family sits around the dining table and does homework together. The youngest children in the family often request homework from their parents so they can participate with their older siblings. Many parents assign their children regular summer homework. That homework not only builds their children's foundation skills and competencies but also builds the discipline, concentration and self-motivation required for academic endeavors.

The Homework Ate My Family

It's a typical Tuesday afternoon in early January for 11-year-old Molly Benedict, a sixth-grader at Presidio Middle School in San Francisco. When she gets home from school at 3:30, she heads straight for the basement of her family's two-story house, flips on her computer and bangs out a one-page book report on J. K. Rowling's *Harry Potter and the Sorcerer's Stone*. After half an hour of work, Molly takes the paper upstairs and gives it to her mother Libby for proofreading. As Molly nibbles a snack of a bagel and orange-spice tea, Mom jots some corrections. "Why don't you say, 'This is the best book I ever read,'" Libby suggests. "Teachers really like strong opinions like that."

Time to kick back, call a few friends and get ready for *Felicity,* right? Not even close. Next Molly pulls out her math assignment: more than 100 fraction and long-division problems. Once she slogs through those, Molly labels all the countries and bodies of water on a map of the Middle East. And she's not through yet: she then reviews a semester's worth of science, including the ins and outs of the circulatory system.

By 5:30, after doing two hours of homework, Molly sits down at the piano and practices for an hour. She'll barely have enough time to eat dinner and touch up that book report before crashing. "With less work I think we could learn what we're learning now," Molly says. "But I don't think it's too overwhelming." The strain of homework weighs more heavily on her mother. "I didn't feel [stressed] until I was in my 30s," says Libby, 43. "It hurts my feelings that my daughter feels that way at 11."

Most of us remember homework, if we remember it at all, as one of the minor annoyances of growing up. Sure, we dreaded the multiplication tables and those ridiculous shoe-box dioramas. But let's admit it: we finished most of our assignments on the bus ride to school—and who even bothered with the stuff until after the requisite hours had been spent alphabetizing baseball cards, gabbing on the phone or watching reruns of *Gilligan's Island*?

Kids today have scant time for such indulgences. Saddled with an out-of-school curriculum chock-full of Taekwondo lessons, ceramics workshops and bassoon practice, America's youngsters barely have time to check their e-mail before hunkering down with homework. On the whole, U.S. students come home with more schoolwork than ever before—and at a younger age. According to researchers at the University of Michigan, 6-to-9-year-olds in 1981 spent 44 min. a week on homework; in 1997 they did more than two hours' worth. The amount of time that 9-to-11-year-olds devoted to homework each week increased from 2 hr. 49 min. to more than 3½ hr.

After some historical ups and downs, homework in this country is at a high-water mark. In the early decades of the century progressive educators in many school districts banned homework in primary school in an effort to discourage rote learning. The cold war—specifically, the launch of Sputnik in 1957 —put an end to that, as lawmakers scrambled to bolster math and science education in the U.S. to counter the threat of Soviet whiz kids. Students frolicked in the late 1960s and '70s, as homework declined to near World War II levels. But fears about U.S. economic competitiveness and the publication of *A Nation at Risk,* the 1983 government report that focused attention on the failings of American schools, ratcheted up the pressure to get tough again. Other forces have kept the trend heading upward: increasing competition to get into the best colleges and the batteries of statewide standardized tests—starting in grade school in a growing number of states—for which teachers must prepare their pupils.

The homework crunch is heard loudest in the country's better middle-class school districts, where parents push their kids hard and demand that teachers deliver enough academic rigor to get students into top secondary schools and colleges. Now there's a blowback: the sheer quantity of nightly homework and the difficulty of the assignments can turn ordinary weeknights into four-hour library-research excursions, leave kids in tears and parents with migraines, and generally transform the placid refuge of home life into a tense war zone. "The atmosphere in the house gets very frustrated," says Lynne O'Callaghan, a mom in Portland, Ore., whose daughter Maeve, 8, does two hours of homework a night. "Some days it's just a struggle. Who wants it that way?" Laura Mandel, a mother of three in Warren, N.J., feels similarly embattled. "It's ironic that politicians talk so much about family values," says Mandel, "when you can't have any family time anymore because the kids are so busy keeping their nose to the grindstone."

While kids grow more frazzled, parents are increasingly torn. Just how involved should they be? Should they help a son or daughter finish that geography assignment, or stay aloof and risk having a frustrated, sleep-deprived child? Should they complain to teachers about the heavy workload or be thankful that their kids are being pushed toward higher achievement? Battles over homework have become so intense that some school districts have decided to formally prescribe the amount of homework kids at each grade level should receive. All of which leaves open the questions of just how much and what kind of homework is best. Though there's evidence that homework does improve academic performance, at least in the junior high and high school years, its true value may be more subtle. It encourages good study habits and acclimates students to self-directed work—but only when it's not so oppressive that it turns them off school altogether.

The war over homework is about even larger issues. Schools in the 1990s are expected to fill so many roles—and do so with often paltry resources and ill-qualified teachers—that it's no surprise more work gets sent home. For baby-boomer parents homework has become both a status gauge—the nightly load indicates the toughness of their child's school—and an outlet for nervy over-bearance, so that each homework assignment is practically theirs to complete too. Yet the growth in dual-income families means less energy and shorter fuses for assisting the kids. And all the swirling arguments over homework underscore the bigger questions that confound American teachers, parents and policymakers: What should we expect from our children? What do we want them to learn? How much is enough?

Erica Astrove is pretty sure she knows. She's just seven—a loquacious, blue-eyed second-grader at the public Hunnewell School in Wellesley, Mass. She plays the piano, takes skating lessons and plans to add pottery and chorus. For fun Erica reads almanacs; her parents gave her a book of world maps and flags for Christmas. "My little researcher," her mother Christina says. There's not much Erica shies away from—except homework. Recently, she told her mother she doesn't want to go to middle school, high school or college because of home-work. Asked if she might have a bit more tolerance for homework once she enters third grade, Erica shakes her head. "I'm going to keep on crying," she says.

Erica's mom has experience drying tears. Her homework agonies began when her eldest daughter Kate was in second grade. In addition to nightly spelling and reading assignments, Kate sometimes came home with math prob-lems so vexing that Christina wondered whether algebra was required to solve them. Mother and daughter pored over some problems for two hours. They once scattered 200 pennies on the kitchen table in a vain attempt to get a so-lution. "The [problems] would be so hard," Christina says, "that I would leave them for my husband to solve when he got home from work late." Those were not happy times. "It made all our time together negative," Christina says. "It was painful for all of us."

The pain caused by homework isn't just emotional. Carl Glassman, father of two girls who attend public school in New York City, reports that last year his eldest daughter missed much of her first semester in sixth grade because of pneumonia, "due to the fact that she was doing homework until 11 every night." Laura Mandel, the New Jersey mother of three, found her son Jeffrey, 6, suffering homework-related nightmares this month when she tried gently to rouse him for school. "Oh, Mom," he pleaded, half asleep, "don't tell me there's another homework sheet."

The steady flood of homework can cause chronic weariness. Holly Manges, a high-achieving fifth-grader at the public Eastern elementary school in Lexing-ton, Ohio, approached her mother earlier this school year close to tears. "Is it O.K. if I don't get all A's?" she asked. "I don't care anymore. I'm just too tired." Over time, that homework fatigue can pull at the fabric of families. As early as third grade, Rachel Heckelman, now 11, came home every day from her elemen-tary school in Houston with three hours' worth of homework. The assignments were often so dizzyingly complex—one asked her to design an entire magazine

—that Rachel looked for any way to procrastinate. Her mother Lissa tried banning TV for the night. When that didn't work, Lissa pleaded with increasing impatience. "I would get red in the face, and she would get defensive," Lissa says. Rachel's father typically removed himself from the fracas by repairing to the bedroom and shutting the door.

The frustrations that homework visits upon kids can irk their parents to the point of revolt. David Kooyman, of Covina, Calif., was so incensed about his three grade-schoolers' homework load that he exacted a pledge from their teachers not to lower his kids' grades if they didn't do assignments. When the kids found themselves lost in class discussions, Kooyman reluctantly allowed them to do the homework, but he is planning to sue the school district for violating his civil rights. "They have us hostage to homework," he grumbles. "I'm 47, and I have 25-year-old teachers telling me what to do with my home life."

Other parents are ambivalent. Many resent teachers for piling on projects that cut into unstructured family time. And yet the drive of middle- and upper-middle-class Americans to keep their children at the head of the class has never been more intense. The teachers who assign mountains of homework often believe they are bowing to the wishes of demanding parents. Says Jeana Considine, a fifth-grade teacher at Elm Elementary School in Hinsdale, Ill.: "The same parents who are complaining that they don't have enough family time would be really upset if their child didn't score well." Pepperdine University president David Davenport, father of a fourth-grader who clocks two hours of homework a night, sees a chain reaction: "The pressure to get into highly selective colleges and universities backs up into high school advanced-placement courses, which backs up to elementary schools." Anxious parents can rail about what teachers do in the classroom, but homework is still one area where parents can directly improve their child's chances.

So even those determined to remain passive observers while their kids labor over essays and science-fair projects can find themselves getting sucked in. "It's something I never wanted to do. I hated doing homework when I was a kid," says Lizanne Merrill, a New York City artist whose daughter Gracie is in second grade. But Gracie often trudges home with elaborate assignments that all but demand Merrill's involvement. A research paper assigned to be done over Christmas vacation required Gracie, 8, to do some fieldwork on sea turtles at the American Museum of Natural History. Mom went along: "I just tell myself, if I don't help out on her homework, what kind of deadbeat mother would I be?"

It's hard to blame parents like Alexis Rasley of Oak Park, Ill., if they occasionally get too involved. Last fall a homework assignment for fifth-graders at the public Horace Mann School was to build a mini–space station that accounted for food, water, waste treatment, radiation shielding and zero gravity. Rasley's son Taylor, 10, spent countless maddening hours toiling at a basement countertop surrounded by cut-open soda bottles. "He just kept sitting there saying, 'I don't know what to do,'" Rasley says. "When the frustration level gets that high, you say, 'O.K., I'm going to help,' because the situation has become so hurtful."

Being an attentive, empathetic parent is one thing; acting as a surrogate student is another. But when pressures mount, the line can get blurred. When Susan Solomon of San Francisco saw her son bogged down last year with a language-arts paper that would help his application to an élite high school, she took matters into her own hands: she did his math homework. He later copied his mother's calculations in his own handwriting. "He knew how to do it," Solomon shrugs. "It was just busywork." In the affluent Boston suburb of Sherborn, Mass., parents at the public Pine Hill School tend to talk about homework in the first-person plural; and they sometimes become more than equal partners in carrying out such third-grade projects as writing up the ownership history of their house, complete with a sketch of the floor plan. Homework has been known to arrive at school two hours after the child does.

"So much of this is about parents wanting their kids to look good," admits psychologist Kim Gatof, mother of third-grader Jake. For an "invention convention," members of Jake's class are building contraptions of their devising. Jake wants to build a better mousetrap. "I can say, 'Just build it yourself,'" says Kim. "Or we can help with it, and it can be on the same level as the others." Jake may have a hard time topping Tucker Carter, another third-grader, who has already made his presentation. Tucker whipped up a fully functioning battery-operated alarm clock that uses a windshield pump to squirt cold water at the sleeper. The kids whooped at this bit of ingenuity, but even they were suspicious. Either Tucker is a prodigiously gifted engineer, or his dad built the clock for him. Sighed David Nihill, the school's principal: "It looks like Alexander Graham Bell made it himself."

⋅◆⋅

Is all this homework really doing any good? Julian Betts, an associate professor of economics at the University of California, San Diego, examined surveys on the homework habits of 6,000 students over five years and found that students who did an extra 30 min. of nightly math homework beginning in seventh grade would, by 11th grade, see their achievement level soar by the equivalent of two grades. Betts argues that the amount of homework is a better indicator of how students perform than the size of class or the quality of teachers. But his study was limited to students in junior high and high school. What about younger children? In 1989 University of Missouri psychology professor Harris Cooper reviewed more than 100 studies on homework and concluded that while benefits from homework can be measured starting in junior high, the effect of home assignments on standardized test scores in the lower grades is negligible or nonexistent. "Piling on massive amounts of homework will not lead to gains," Cooper says, "and may be detrimental by leading children to question their abilities."

... All experts agree that weighing second-graders down with hours of homework is pointless and probably damaging to their self-esteem and desire to learn. But in reasonable amounts, homework has value for students at all grade levels. "Homework has benefits that go well beyond its immediate direct impact on what's going on in school," says Cooper. Doing homework is important for honing organizational skills, learning how to manage time and developing the ability to learn autonomously.

The question of the day, of course, is what is the right amount? Cooper recommends 10 to 20 min. nightly in first grade and an increase of 10 min. a night for each grade after that. But the point is not simply to fill up a set amount of time. For preoccupied teachers, admits Michelann Ortloff, a Portland school official and former elementary school teacher, "it's always easy to pull a few things out of the workbook, give them to students and say, 'This is your homework.'" Too many teachers send kids home with mind-numbing math worksheets that are not even reviewed the next day. Too many are enamored of those unwieldy "projects" that seem to exasperate kids more than they instruct them and that lead to excessive parent involvement. For young students, the optimal arrangement would mix skill-building drills with creative tasks closely tied to what's being taught in the classroom—such as interviewing grandparents as a social-studies lesson or using soccer standings to teach rudimentary statistics.

Educators agree that parents should be vigilant about making sure such a healthy blend is maintained. Everyone frowns on parents' doing homework for their kids, but most agree that parents should monitor homework; offer guidance, not answers, when asked for help; and give teachers regular reports on how their kids are handling it all. Gail Block, a fifth-grade language-arts instructor in San Francisco who feels that homework helps overcome the limits of time in the classroom, was nonetheless surprised to hear that her student Molly Benedict takes close to three hours a night to finish. Pepperdine president Davenport notes the amount of time his daughter spends on each assignment at the bottom of her work sheet. "Sometimes," he says, "teachers are not aware of how much time is being spent."

Parents could benefit from a little perspective too. American students on the whole still work less, play more and perform worse than many of their counterparts around the world. As Harold Stevenson and James Stigler point out in their book *The Learning Gap*, Japanese and Chinese elementary school students spend significantly more time on homework than do children in the U.S. A first-grader in Taipei does seven times as much homework as a first-grader in Minneapolis—and scores higher on tests of knowledge and skills.

But American parents should worry less about the precise number of minutes their students devote to homework and more about the uneven and poorly conceived way in which it is assigned. "What defines the homework problem in the U.S. today is variation," Cooper says. Less than one-third of U.S. school districts provide any guidelines to parents and teachers on how much homework children should receive and what purpose it's supposed to serve. In places that have instituted formal homework policies, a semblance of sanity has arrived. In Hinsdale, Ill., parents often complained that their children got too much homework from some teachers and too little from others. So a committee of teachers, parents and administrators spent several months devising a formal policy that requires "meaningful and purposeful" homework at all grade levels but limits the load according to age and mandates that some of it be optional. Besides helping students build their homework appetite over time, the policy aims to persuade the academically more eager parents that it's safe to back off.

The need for a more rational approach to homework may be one argument for establishing national standards for what all U.S. students should know. If such standards existed, teachers might assign homework with a more precise goal in mind, and parents might spend fewer nights agonizing about whether their children were overburdened or understimulated by homework. Of course, the debate over national standards is a complex one, and cramming for a national test could mean more mindless at-home drudgery for kids. But not necessarily. When Taylor Hoss, 10, of Vancouver, Wash., came home [recently] with packets of extra homework assigned in preparation for the state's new mandatory assessment exams, his parents shuddered. But as they worked through the test-prep material, the Hosses were pleased with the degree of critical thinking the questions required. "I was very impressed," says Taylor's dad Schuyler. "It makes you connect the dots."

There are other ways of soothing nerves. Both parents and students must be willing to embrace the "work" component of homework—to recognize the quiet satisfaction that comes from practice and drill, the steady application of concepts and the mastery of skills. It's a tough thing to ask of many American parents. "You want your children to be happy, and you pray for their success in the future," says Laura Mandel. "But does homework bring either of those goals? I don't think more homework will make a more successful adult." Maybe not, but wisely assigned homework may help make a more successful, well, child. "It is all about learning responsibility," says Janine Bempechat, an assistant professor at Harvard's Graduate School of Education. "When you have homework on a regular basis, you learn persistence, diligence and delayed gratification."

Molly Benedict, for one, seems to be swallowing the bad medicine with surprising equanimity. "I don't have a lot of time to do just whatever," she admits. "My friends and I think it's a lot of work. But we've adapted well." Kids like Molly have learned it's a rough world, and homework is only part of it. But who knows? If teachers and parents start approaching homework with a little less heat and a little more care, kids may still have time left to be kids. Or whatever.

POSTSCRIPT

Does Homework in the Primary Grades Improve Academic Performance?

One of the goals of homework is to assist the student in acquiring new information in class the next day. When students do not complete the homework, they make the learning process more difficult. Teachers cannot count on all students to complete the homework and to be able to move ahead at a quicker pace. When some students are prepared and others are not, classroom learning can suffer for all. Is the assigning of homework worth this risk? Do the benefits generally outweigh the negative consequences?

Some assert that the quantity of the homework assigned equals the amount of learning that will occur. However, each student works at a different pace, and what may be a ten-minute assignment for one student may take another student forty minutes to complete. Many assert that the time spent on homework is not as important as what is learned or what resources, skills, and prior knowledge the student needed to complete the assignment. In fact, some would argue that slower-paced students suffer needlessly when too much homework is assigned. Family activities and lifestyles can also make the completing of homework extremely difficult for some students. When there is only one night between the assignment being given and the homework being due, families may become stressed when that one night includes a scheduled family function, a religious observance, or an emergency. Teachers and families need to work together to find a balance between the work assigned and the responsibilities and activities of each student and his or her family.

Suggested Readings

Checkley, K., "Homework: A New Look at an Age-old Practice," *Education Update* (vol. 39, no. 7, 1997).

Chen C. and Stevenson, H., "Homework: A Cross-cultural Examination," *Child Development* (vol. 60, 1989).

Cooper, H., Lindsay, J., Nye, B., and Greathouse, S., "Relationships Among Attitudes About Homework, Amount of Homework Assigned and Completed, and Student Achievement," *Journal of Educational Psychology* (vol. 90, no. 1, 1998).

Diamond, D., "Winning the Homework Wars," *USA Weekend* (March 5–7, 1999).

ERIC Clearing House on Elementary and Early Childhood Education

The ERIC Clearing House on Elementary and Early Childhood Education site provides links to all Educational Resources Information Center (ERIC) sites, including clearinghouses, support components, and publishers of ERIC materials.

```
http://www.ericeece.org
```

Early Childhood Education Web Guide

The Early Childhood Education Web Guide is updated weekly and provides links for early childhood curricular issues such as anti-bias resources, the learning environment, guidance, health and safety, and program management.

```
http://www.ecewebguide.com
```

Awesome Library for Teachers

The Awesome Library for Teachers provides access to teacher information on everything from educational assessment to general child development topics.

```
http://www.neat-schoolhouse.org/teacher.html
```

Kathy Schrock's Guide for Educators

Kathy Schrock's Guide for Educators is a classified list of sites on the Internet found to be useful for enhancing curriculum and the professional growth of teachers. This site is updated daily.

```
http://school.discovery.com/schrockguide/
```

National Institute on the Education of At-Risk Students

The National Institute on the Education of At-Risk Students supports a range of research and development activities designed to improve the education of students at risk of educational failure due to limited English proficiency, poverty, geographic location, or economic disadvantage. Numerous links and summaries of the institute's work are also available at this site.

```
http://www.ed.gov/offices/OERI/At-Risk
```

America Reads

The America Reads Web site provides information on the phases of early literacy development. Also included are sample tutoring lessons and reading strategies.

```
http://www.bnkst.edu/americareads/early.html
```

PART 2

Children in Educational Settings

*E*ducational settings for young children vary greatly. Some children begin their educational career prior to kindergarten, while others wait until they are old enough to attend public schools. Teachers and school administrators are continuously adapting the school setting to meet the needs of all the children who attend. Many questions arise over the best way to provide high-quality education during the early childhood years. Some decisions are made based on funds available, but others are made based on what educational practices should be used in order for optimal learning to occur. The issues that follow include some of the topics discussed on a daily basis in schools across the country.

- Do At-Risk Young Children Learn Best Through Active Learning Experience?

- Should All Children Be Five Years of Age Before Starting Kindergarten?

- Is Full-Day Kindergarten Best for All Children?

- Should Recess Be Included in a School Day?

- Are Multi-Age Programs Best for Young Children?

- Is the Whole-Language Approach the Best Way to Teach Reading?

- Is Class Size Reduction the Most Effective Way to Improve Educational Performance?

- Is Grade Retention a Sound Educational Practice?

- Do Multi-Year Assignments With the Same Teacher Improve Primary Students' Learning?

ISSUE 10

Do At-Risk Young Children Learn Best Through Active Learning Experience?

YES: Lawrence J. Schweinhart and David P. Weikart, from "Why Curriculum Matters in Early Childhood Education," *Educational Leadership* (March 1998)

NO: Siegfried Engelmann, from "The Benefits of Direct Instruction: Affirmative Action for At-Risk Students," *Educational Leadership* (September 1999)

ISSUE SUMMARY

YES: Lawrence J. Schweinhart, research division chair of the High/Scope Educational Research Foundation, and David P. Weikart, founder and former president of the High/Scope Educational Research Foundation, examine three curriculum models for at-risk preschoolers and conclude that a child-initiated active learning curriculum is best.

NO: Siegfried Engelmann, director of the National Institute for Direct Instruction, states that a preschool curriculum approach that is highly structured and teacher directed can best help at-risk children catch up to affluent children in learning.

P reschool programs for at-risk children have been found to be beneficial for the children's future academic and economic success. The early results of successful programs for preschool children initiated the development of the federally funded Head Start program in 1965, as well as many other federally and privately funded programs that would improve the lives of at-risk children. Much has been learned about early school experiences for at-risk students, but one key question remains. What is the *best* type of curriculum for these students?

Lawrence J. Schweinhart and David P. Weikart examine three theoretically different curriculum models used for at-risk preschool children. The models studied were:

1. *Direct Instruction,* a scripted approach in which the teacher presents formal lessons and the children respond to the teachers' questions.
2. *High/Scope,* an open-framework curriculum approach in which children were involved in child-initiated, active learning experiences.
3. *Traditional Nursery School,* an approach in which the teacher creates themes that classroom activities are planned around so that the children may engage in free-choice play.

Sixty-eight children were randomly assigned to one of three groups and attended school for two-and-a-half-hour sessions five days a week. Each group had bi-weekly home visits. When the children were 23 years old, the High/Scope and Traditional Nursery School groups showed 10 significant advantages over the Direct Instruction group. The Direct Instruction group did not have any significant advantages over the other two groups, according to the findings of the study.

Siegfried Engelmann contends that at-risk children need more concentrated periods of time to learn than children who are not at-risk. According to Engelmann, at-risk children have huge learning gaps to fill and he asserts that the way to fill those gaps is through direct, efficient instruction in language, math, and reading skills. He advocates a highly structured, teacher-directed learning environment in which the children receive focused instruction on skills they have yet to acquire. His research shows that the group of children who attended Direct Instruction programs in France ended up being ahead in all academic areas over the comparison group.

What is the best curriculum for children who are at risk of not achieving successful learning in school? Is it possible to make up for lost time by giving at-risk children a concentrated dose of academic learning? If so, is there a point where their minds cannot accept any more learning? Schweinhart and Weikart have conducted research that strongly supports a child-initiated, active learning curriculum. Engelmann sees the path to success for at-risk children to be one of aggressive teacher intervention in direct drill-and-practice sessions. He states that this is the only way for these children to catch up to affluent children.

Lawrence J. Schweinhart and
David P. Weikart

 **YES**

Why Curriculum Matters in Early Childhood Education

A widespread consensus has developed in favor of public support for pre-school programs for young children living in poverty. Head Start and state prekindergarten programs today serve about two-thirds of U.S. 4-year-olds living in poverty. Federal Head Start spending has tripled in the past decade, and nearly two-thirds of the states provide similar programs for 4-year-olds.

Influential groups of citizens, such as the Committee for Economic Development, have lent their political clout to this development—partly because of the findings of the High/Scope Perry Preschool Study that a high-quality preschool program cuts participants' lifetime arrest rate in half, significantly improves their educational and subsequent economic success, and provides tax-payers a return equal to 716 percent of their original investment in the program, a return that outperformed the U.S. stock market during the same period of time (Schweinhart et al. 1993; Barnett 1996).

We have less consensus on the goals of preschool programs. The National Association for the Education of Young Children (Bredekamp and Copple 1997) strongly favors *developmentally appropriate practice,* but this position has found detractors. Academic critics, such as Mallory and New (1994), argue that developmentally appropriate practice is socially constructed, context-bound, and insensitive to cultural and individual differences in development. Conservative critics, such as Hirsch (1997), see it as progressive ideology without adequate research support.

Should early childhood curriculum be adult-directed or child-initiated? Or should there be a balance of these two approaches? Is there a well-defined, research-proven model we can follow? The High/Scope Preschool Curriculum Comparison Study (the study that followed the High/Scope Perry Preschool Study), which was begun in 1969 and now includes data through age 23, sheds new light on these questions (Schweinhart and Weikart 1997 a and b).

This study assesses which of three theoretically distinct preschool curriculum models works best. The study has followed the lives of 68 young people born in poverty who were randomly assigned at ages 3 and 4 to one of three groups, each experiencing a different curriculum model.

Three Curriculum Models

The Curriculum Comparison Study included the following curriculum models:

- *Direct Instruction* was a scripted approach in which the teacher presented activities and the children responded to them. Classroom activities were sequences of academic lessons, emphasizing positive reinforcements of correct responses. Teachers clearly defined academic goals in reading, arithmetic, and language. The psychological tradition was behaviorist (Bereiter and Engelmann 1966).

- *The High/Scope Curriculum* was an open-framework approach in which teacher and child planned and initiated activities and worked together. Classroom activities were partly the result of the *plan-do-review* sequence, planned by the children themselves and supported by the teachers. These activities reflected experiences intended to promote intellectual, social, and physical development. The psychological tradition was constructivist and cognitive-developmental (Hohmann and Weikart 1995).

- *The traditional Nursery School* was a child-centered approach in which children initiated activities and the teachers responded to them. The teachers created classroom themes from everyday events and encouraged children to actively engage in free play. The goal was to create an environment in which children could develop naturally, and the psychological tradition was psychoanalytic (Sears and Dowley 1963).

Program staff implemented the curriculum models independently and to high standards, in two-and-a-half-hour classes five days a week and home visits every two weeks. Because all three groups had biweekly home visits, these visits alone cannot explain the differences that were found, although they may have intensified the curriculum models' effects. All other aspects of the program were virtually identical. So, having taken into account slight differences in the groups' gender makeup, we are confident that outcome differences represent the effects of the three curriculum models.

Advantages at Age 23

Based on reports by the young people, either the High/Scope group or the Nursery School group had a total of 10 significant advantages over the Direct Instruction group, but the Direct Instruction group had no significant advantages over these groups. The High/Scope and Nursery School groups did not differ significantly from one another on any outcome variable.

By age 23, the High/Scope and Nursery School groups had two significant advantages over the Direct Instruction group:

- *Only 6 percent of either the High/Scope or the Nursery School group needed treatment for emotional impairment or disturbance during their schooling, as compared to 47 percent of the Direct Instruction group.* Because 47 percent is well above the typical rate for this population (17 percent of the comparable no-program group in the High/Scope Perry Preschool Study required such treatment), the Direct Instruction program experience appears to have left some of its participants with serious negative emotional residue.
- *Forty-three percent of the High/Scope group and 44 percent of the Nursery School group at some time up to age 23 engaged in volunteer work, as compared to 11 percent of the Direct Instruction group.* The programs that encouraged children to initiate their own activities had more graduates engaging in volunteer work in the community as young adults, suggesting greater awareness of the needs of others and their responsibility to take action to help.

The High/scope group had six additional significant advantages over the Direct Instruction group:

- *Only 10 percent of the High/Scope group had ever been arrested for a felony, as compared to 39 percent of the Direct Instruction group.* Given the intractability of crime, this fourfold reduction in felony arrests is of great importance. It parallels the finding of the High/Scope Perry Preschool Study through age 27 that only 7 percent of the program group (which used child-initiated activities) but 35 percent of the no-program group had been arrested five or more times (Schweinhart et al. 1993). These data indicate the clearly different levels of personal and social responsibility that the High/Scope and Direct Instruction groups developed.
- *None of the High/Scope group had ever been arrested for a property crime, as compared to 38 percent of the Direct Instruction group.* Property crime may be distinguished from violent and drug-related crimes by its emphasis on assaulting authority. The High/Scope model places authority (teachers) in the role of resource and support. Direct Instruction gives teachers power and control and requires children to submit. As young adults, more of the former Direct Instruction preschoolers strike out at authority.
- *Twenty-three percent of the High/Scope group reported at age 15 that they had engaged in 10 or more acts of misconduct, as compared to 56 percent of the Direct Instruction group.* Although this finding did not reappear in self-reports at age 23, it presaged the age-23 arrest findings.
- *Thirty-six percent of the High/Scope group said that various kinds of people gave them a hard time, as compared to 69 percent of the Direct Instruction group.* Apparently, the High/Scope group more willingly accepted responsibility for their own actions than did the Direct Instruction group

and had developed ways to relate positively to authorities and others, rather than to blame or attack them for their actions.

- *Thirty-one percent of the High/Scope group had married and were living with their spouses, as compared to none of the Direct Instruction group.* Marriage may be seen as a step that takes personal responsibility and a willingness to adapt to others.
- *Seventy percent of the High/Scope group planned to graduate from college, as compared to 36 percent of the Direct Instruction group.* While no differences were found in actual high school graduation rates or in the highest year of schooling, such planning by the High/Scope group reflects greater optimism, self-confidence, and aspirations for the future.

The Nursery School group had two additional significant advantages over the Direct Instruction group, both of which resemble the felony arrest difference between the High/Scope group and the Direct Instruction group.

- *Only 9 percent of the Nursery School group had been arrested for a felony at ages 22–23, as compared to 34 percent of the Direct Instruction group.*
- *None of the Nursery School group had ever been suspended from work, as compared to 27 percent of the Direct Instruction group.*

Goals of Early Childhood Education

This study through age 23 found that young people born in poverty experienced fewer emotional problems and felony arrests if they had attended a preschool program based on child-initiated learning activities focused broadly on children's development, rather than scripted direct instruction focused specifically on academics.

These findings suggest that the goals of early childhood education should not be limited to academic preparation for school, but should also include helping children learn to make decisions, solve problems, and get along with others. Scripted teacher-directed instruction, touted by some as the surest path to school readiness, may purchase a temporary improvement in academic performance at the cost of a missed opportunity for long-term improvement in personal and social behavior. On the other hand, child-initiated learning activities seem to help children develop their social responsibility and interpersonal skills so that they become more personally and socially competent, fewer of them need treatment for emotional impairment or disturbance. Fewer are arrested for felonies as young adults.

Although the High/Scope and Nursery School groups did not differ significantly on any outcome variable at age 23, the High/Scope curriculum model is easier to replicate than the Nursery School approach because of High/Scope's extensive documentation, training program, and assessment system. Well-documented, research-proven curriculum models based on child-initiated learning appear to have the best potential for supporting successful child development.

Siegfried Engelmann

 **NO**

The Benefits of Direct Instruction

Many children in the United States enter 1st grade far below the norm, and they never catch up. Their failures prevent them from ascending the ladder of academic growth on schedule. A large body of literature suggests that delinquency is highly correlated with school failure, particularly the failure to learn to read (Hodgkinson, 1992). For the school and the community, failure is costly, requiring special programs, welfare, and detention services.

School failure for at-risk students results largely from the fact that all children are expected to learn a specified battery of skills in so many years. This race is unfair for at-risk children because they have further to go in the specified time. They enter 1st grade substantially behind in prereading, language, and number skills. To finish the 1st grade performing on grade level, they would have to learn substantially more than the advantaged child must learn (Hart & Risley, 1995). At-risk children are not well equipped to meet this challenge. They are less familiar with the content and less practiced at learning from adults. They therefore learn more slowly.

Their performance in later grades provides evidence of the problems they encounter within beginning instruction. At-risk students in 4th grade often have not mastered the skills they were scheduled to learn in 1st grade. For example, some of the words that poor readers in 4th grade most frequently confuse are *a-the, what-that, when-then, of-for,* and *was-said.*

Effective Solutions

A well-designed preschool-kindergarten is an affirmative-action plan that makes the academic race fair. The plan is based on function, not form. We can't take these children back to age 2 and place them in an environment that exposes them to more sophisticated language and the thousands of hours of literacy-related activities they have missed. However, we can create a school setting that achieves some of the same functions, even though the form is quite different.

We can provide efficient instruction in necessary language, math, and reading skills. Unless at-risk children learn more than their affluent peers learn during the same period, they will remain behind. Therefore, the format must be highly structured and permit teachers to present large amounts of practice

From Siegfried Engelmann, "The Benefits of Direct Instruction: Affirmative Action for At-Risk Students," *Educational Leadership*, vol. 57, no. 1 (September 1999). Copyright © 1999 by Siegfried Engelmann. Reprinted by permission of the author. References omitted.

in a fraction of the time than would be possible through a more natural setting and incidental interactions.

The ideal goal is to accelerate at-risk children so that they leave kindergarten academically *ahead* of affluent children—reading and performing in math at around the 2nd grade level. Pre-kindergarten, kindergarten, and 1st grade provide the only reasonable window for achieving this acceleration. If we wait until after kindergarten to try accelerating at-risk children, the plan will fail because affluent children know more and are equipped to learn faster. At-risk children who are ahead after kindergarten, however, will tend to remain competitive, even though the competition tends to favor the affluent children, whose homes contribute much more strongly to the verbal skills and information needed in school (Hart & Risley, 1995). The chances of somebody at home being able to help a 5th grader in math are many times greater for an affluent student. Unless the school program compensates for this advantage, at-risk populations will continue to fail.

Focus on Skills

Ideally, the preschool provides an all-day program. Periods involving academic skills are distributed throughout the school day. Initially, the periods are quite short at 10 minutes each, but the length increases until periods are 25 minutes long by the end of kindergarten.

The daily schedule gives children direct, careful instruction in language, reading, and math. The schedule also includes singing, physical activity, and arts and crafts. Part of each school day also has children planning and working on self-initiated projects. Older children work on academic content $1\frac{1}{2}$ hours each day.

For this instruction to be effective, all skills are presented in a way that is highly oral so that children become facile at following spoken directions; answering questions; issuing directions; playing a variety of verbal games, such as rhyming; and using language as an adjunct to thought and reasoning.

Does It Work?

The main features of this plan have been used in Direct Instruction implementations. Outcomes of Project Follow Through show that children who started Direct Instruction in kindergarten were accelerated about seven months over children who started in 1st grade (Becker & Engelmann, 1978). By 3rd grade, kindergarten-starting children performed around the 50th percentile in language, math, spelling, reading, and science. In comparison, kindergarten-starting children in High/Scope did not perform above the 22nd percentile in any subject (and only at the 11th percentile in math, which is several standard deviations less than the 48th percentile for Direct Instruction students).

A large study of academic preschools for at-risk children in France confirms the benefits of early intervention (Jarousse, Mingat, & Richard, 1992). The children who received the academic preschool exhibited gains in all areas over the comparison children.

Are Academic Preschool Programs Feasible?

Because preschoolers know a lot less than 1st graders, they are harder to teach. The effective preschool teacher must be skilled at motivating children and teaching content to mastery in a way that does not smack of drudgery. Teachers therefore need extensive training, particularly in working with lower performing students. Teachers must learn a large number of organizational practices that facilitate efficiency, such as grouping children homogeneously for instruction and monitoring the children's performance to ensure that all are progressing on schedule.

The training and systems are expensive, but necessary. Without them, successful schools for at-risk children, such as Wesley elementary in Houston, could not achieve such high levels of performance (Palmaffy, 1998). Well-designed preschool programs represent sincere commitments to provide at-risk children with a headstart that can make an enormous difference in their skill level and self-esteem.

POSTSCRIPT

Do At-Risk Young Children Learn Best Through Active Learning Experience?

At issue when discussing preschool curriculum are the thousands of children who are delayed in their initial cognitive and language experiences because of the lack of early exposure in the home. Direct instruction advocates support intensive catch-up work to allow these children to be able to compete with children who are developing on target. Without this intensive effort, it is believed that they will fall further behind. However, can we force flowers to open before they are ready? Will children naturally acquire the needed skills when presented in an appropriate, engaging environment or is intensive intervention necessary through direct instruction? Will the intense direct instruction environment turn children off to learning or will it provide them with an added incentive to learn more? What types of preschool learning experiences are most beneficial to students as they move through their formal education? How is future academic performance affected by the type of preschool experience offered?

As more and more young children have a preschool experience, the quality of that experience will affect their future school success. What is the best foundation for future learning and where should the limited dollars available for preschool education be spent? How can we ensure the success of all children in their formal education?

Suggested Readings

Charlesworth, R., "Developmentally Appropriate Practice Is for Everyone," *Childhood Education* (vol. 74, no. 5, 1998).

Hohmann, M. and Weikart, D. P., *Educating Young Children: Active Learning Practices for Preschool and Child Care Programs* (High/Scope Press, 1995).

Kutnick, P., "Does Preschool Curriculum Make a Difference in Primary School Performance? Insights Into the Variety of Preschool Activities and Their Effects on School Achievement and Behaviour in the Caribbean Island of Trinidad," *Early Child Development and Care* (vol. 103, 1994).

Palmafy, T., "No Excuses: Houston Educator Thaddeus Lott Puts Failing School to Shame," *Policy Review* (January/February 1998).

Schweinhart, L. J. and Weikart, D. P., *Lasting Differences: The High/Scope Preschool Curriculum Comparison Study Through Age 23* (High/Scope Press, 1977).

ISSUE 11

Should All Children Be Five Years of Age Before Starting Kindergarten?

YES: Nancie L. Katz, from "Too Young for Kindergarten?" *The Christian Science Monitor* (July 21, 1997)

NO: Samuel J. Meisels, from "Out of the Readiness Maze," *Momentum* (April/May 1995)

ISSUE SUMMARY

YES: Nancie L. Katz, a writer for the *Christian Science Monitor,* examines families who chose to keep their children out of kindergarten for a year after they were eligible to go age-wise. Katz cites research that finds that children with October to December birthdays are retained at a higher rate and that the parents who retained their children are pleased with their decision to do so.

NO: Samuel J. Meisels, professor of early childhood education at the University of Michigan in Ann Arbor, discusses three school-readiness policy myths that are strongly held by parents and teachers. He presents arguments to dispel these myths and suggests that children should attend kindergarten when they are age-eligible.

Unlike children of New Zealand, who start school on the day of their fifth birthday, the children of the United States start kindergarden at different ages. Cutoff dates for kindergarten entry vary around the country. The earliest requires a child to be five years of age by June 1 before he or she can start kindergarten in the fall and the latest requires a child to be five years of age by January 1 of the school year in which he or she will start kindergarten. There are at least 12 different dates in between the earliest and the latest that are also used. In addition, there are six states that let individual school districts determine the entry date. There will always be children who are up to one year apart in age in any given class no matter when the cut-off date is for kindergarten entry. When parents keep children from starting kindergarten when they are age-eligible, an even wider age discrepancy among the children is created. In some classes, the age discrepancy can vary by as much as 24 months.

What determines if a child will be successful in school? One of the many factors that may determine if a child will be successful is having a preschool experience prior to starting kindergarten. In addition, children living in homes where appropriate school readiness experiences are provided have an even better chance of school success. A child's developmental readiness for learning and the developmental appropriateness of the teaching that the child receives is a strong determinate of having a positive school experience, some would say more than chronological age.

John Locke stated in the early 1600s, "Accommodate the educational program to fit the child, don't change the child to fit the program." When programs for young children are developmentally appropriate, there are experiences that will meet the ability levels of all children in the room. All children with the same birthdate are not necessarily going to be able to learn at the same rate. Teachers of young children need to provide a learning environment that can accommodate the diverse learning styles in the classroom. Teachers of preschool-age children are adept at adapting the environment since it is not uncommon to have a preschool class of children from $2\frac{1}{2}$ through 5 years of age in the same room. Good early childhood teachers are skilled in making the various learning experiences easier or more challenging based on the developmental abilities of the children in the class. Elementary educators, on the other hand, are expected by many to have all children doing approximately the same level of work in the same classroom. This can make for very challenging teaching.

Is kindergarten the only time when one's birthdate is important? Would a high school teacher take a child's birthdate into consideration when looking at the child's academic performance? Are there problems associated with being the oldest among one's peers at the secondary level?

What should parents consider when making a decision about their child's kindergarten entry? Should factors such as the height of the child at age 4, age of peers attending the same kindergarten class, or changes in the family also be considered when making the decision?

In the following selections, Nancie L. Katz asserts that parents who hold their child out of kindergarten for a year after the child is eligible to go are giving their child an academic and social boost by being older than most of their peers. Samuel J. Meisels dispels some commonly held myths about kindergarten readiness policies.

Nancie L. Katz

 **YES**

Too Young for Kindergarten?

When it came time to put her son in kindergarten, Holly Hankins faced a tough choice: Should he enter as one of the youngest in the class, or should he wait a year?

Like many other parents in 1985, she chose the latter. And she's glad she did.

"It was one of those years that everyone did that with boys [because they say they develop later than girls]," says Mrs. Hankins, mother of three in Washington. "He's been bored on and off, but I think he would have been bored regardless. At least now he's more mature."

A similar decision, however, left Cheryl Flax-Davidson with mixed feelings. "In the early grades, it seemed fine, because it gave her confidence," she says of her youngest child. "But lately, I think some of her friends are less mature and she's having trouble finding kids she can play with."

It's an age-old question: When is a child ready to start formal schooling? Kindergarten is widely viewed as key preparation for first grade, when a child needs to have mastered social skills so as to be able to concentrate on reading and math. Traditionally, school districts have dictated that any child who turns 5 before Dec. 31 should be in kindergarten.

But over the years, support has been growing for delaying entry into kindergarten. Today only four states—Maryland, Connecticut, Hawaii, Rhode Island—and the District of Columbia still have the end of the calendar year as an entrance cut-off date. In an attempt to ensure the child's readiness to learn, most of the others now require children to turn five by September, or earlier. And many parents are voluntarily holding children back.

Some consider it insurance against repeating kindergarten or future grades. But in an increasingly competitive era, many parents simply like the idea of giving their child an academic and social boost by being older. The popularity of doing so, particularly among well-educated, middle-class Americans, has some questioning whether it really produces benefits.

Nancy Elbin, a Montgomery County, Md., guidance counselor who taught first grade for 26 years and has researched retention issues, says studies have found no evidence that holding a child back is "a positive thing to do. Those who repeat don't generally outperform the others."

From Nancie L. Katz, "Too Young for Kindergarten?" *The Christian Science Monitor* (July 21, 1997). Copyright © 1997 by Nancie L. Katz.

Look Before You Leap

Indeed, experts caution parents against rash judgments.

"If you have a child on the younger side . . . don't use the child's reading or math ability [or] the child's size, if they're tall," says Stanley Greenspan, a child psychiatrist at George Washington University Medical School in Washington.

What parents should do, he says, is "look at how well the child is able to reason, how quick he is to think on his feet, his ability to read social cues, and his analytical reading and problem solving. Look at the ability to follow instructions and ideas."

If children appear "sluggish" in those areas, he notes, "you might want to buy them another year. Otherwise, they can move on."

He says parents can help children prepare for school—and gauge their readiness—by reading aloud, ensuring play with peers, and playing in inventive ways. He suggests daily "floor time," where parents follow the child's lead, "reading, imagining, and problem-solving" and helping them catch nonverbal social cues.

Is Bigger Really Better?

Ultimately, the evidence is mixed as to whether a delay can help children. In Fairfax County, Va., Douglas Holmes, the director of student services, says his state chose to hold back children who turn 5 after Sept. 30 because of "concern by educators that the kids who were most unsuccessful academically were younger kids.

"What we know is that kids who came in with October to December birthdays were retained at a higher rate," he says.

But, he notes, "What's missing in that is the many [as many as two-thirds] who were successful." Nevertheless, the view persists that children may have a cutting edge by being older, more articulate, and just plain larger. That assumption may be redefining the kindergarten year. Not only do teachers have students as much as a year apart in age, but they are facing more demands from parents, especially in more affluent areas, who want a curriculum that incorporates academics.

Timothy Welsh, a veteran teacher at Murch Elementary in Washington, says kindergarten should help children to learn to work in groups, to shed the egocentricity of earlier childhood, and gain skills to sort out conflict.

"They have to be able to share, to delay gratification, to treat each other with respect," he says. "It's being able to walk away from another child instead of knocking the blocks down. And it's laying that foundation so they're not dealing with these issues when they're buckling down to make those test scores that are so important."

Samuel J. Meisels

 **NO**

Out of the Readiness Maze

Although well-intentioned, few statements in recent years have caused more concern, commentary and gnashing of teeth in the early childhood education community than the first National Education Goal: **"By the year 2000, all children in America will start school ready to learn."** What is wrong with the picture this goal paints? Many things.

First, it is blind to biology. By virtue of their shared-species heritage, all children are ready to learn from birth. They need not wait until they are 5.

Second, the goal ignores individual differences in learning. It will never be the case that all children will attain the same level of performance at a single culturally defined point in time. Individual differences and variations in development associated with both endogenous and exogenous factors make a mockery of our chronological benchmarks when we try to apply them across the board to all children.

Third, the goal statement is conceptually confused and requires a definition of the term "ready." What is "readiness?" Is it something we wait for? Is it something we impose? Is it a within-the-child phenomenon or something outside of the child? My own view, to which I will return later, is that readiness is a relational, interactional educational construct that reflects a focus on both the child's status and the characteristics of the educational setting.

Finally, the simplistic interpretation of readiness that can be derived from the goal contains within it the potential for encouraging harmful policies for young children.... And often the least advantaged in our society are blamed when public policies intended to assist them go wrong.

I will describe here three policies that have been enacted to enhance readiness and that some believe will advance the first goal. These policies are not only inconsistent with research, but they are also potentially harmful to children and families. I will close by describing my way out of the readiness maze.

Three Myths

The three policies intended to enhance readiness are:

- Raising the age of school entry

- Retention in grade for kindergartners
- The installation of extra-year programs before kindergarten and first grade

I have previously written that all three of these policies are misguided and potentially harmful to children. While not physically deforming, the policies and their associated practices may alter the inner life of children and reduce their chances for a healthy, fulfilling future no less than the action of a severe biological or environmental hazard. In what follows, I will take the liberty of framing the policies in terms of three myths about America's kindergartens.

Myth #1: Raising the school-entry age produces smarter kindergarten classes.

Children in traditional American schools begin kindergarten at about age 5, putting the United States among those countries that send their children to school at the youngest age. This variation suggests there is no "magic age" for starting school. In fact, during the past decade school-starting ages have been moving back gradually, so that children are beginning school at older ages now than they were previously.

This attention to school-entry age is tied to the issue of school readiness. The assumption is that the older the child, the more able the child will be to negotiate the requirements of the kindergarten curriculum. Proponents of older entry ages note that elementary school curricula have changed in recent years as schools have become enmeshed in the academic spiral of "higher standards," accountability and increased academic expectations. They assume that if students are older when they begin school, they will be more competent academically.

This emphasis on chronology overlooks the fact that maturation is only one of many factors that impact development. Changing the entry age affects the overall range of ages enrolled but, because of natural variability and the impact of early experiences, it is still possible that the oldest children in any given group are developmentally less advanced than their younger classmates.

Moreover, negative effects are likely to flow from a change in the age of entry. Moving back the entry age encourages those who wish to fashion a more academic, less developmentally appropriate curriculum, since such advocates consider kindergarten-age children capable of doing what was once thought of as first-grade work.

Moving the age range also requires an additional year of preschool or day care. This represents not only an economic burden for parents of moderate and limited means, but also contributes to a potential crisis of supply because relatively few slots for older 4-year-olds and for 5-year-olds are available in the child-care market.

Given the societal and familial inequities that children may encounter in their first few years of life, age should remain a nondiscriminatory variable. Changing entry age serves little purpose in the effort to improve and may actually hinder school outcomes of young children.

Myth #2: If children aren't ready for first grade, we do them a favor by holding them back.

Retention in kindergarten and the first few grades of school has become prevalent across the country. We know from the *National Education Longitudinal Study* (NELS:88) that one in five public school students is retained at least once between kindergarten and grade eight.

Research regarding retention, however, suggests that the effects of retention are cause for great concern. Shepard and Smith note that kindergarten retention does not improve achievement, is not fundamentally different from retention in later grades in its consequences, and has harmful effects on socioemotional outcomes and the development of self-concept.

The unintended effects of retention are nothing less than startling. Research shows that retention is the single most sensitive indicator of dropout potential in high school. A study of urban high schools has shown that one year's retention can increase the dropout risk by 45% to 50%. Retaining students two grades in Detroit increases the risk to as much as 90%.

Furthermore, retention policies are not applied equally across ethnic and racial groups. In fact, studies of the NELS:88 dataset, as well as other more controlled investigations, demonstrate that no academic or socioemotional advantage is conferred by retention in grade.

In the face of this evidence, retention is virtually indefensible as a policy designed to improve the outcomes of young children. The apparent rationale—to ensure that students do not begin school unprepared—is clear. However, the data demonstrates that retention not only fails to achieve this goal, but also is potentially damaging.

Myth #3: Immature students or slow learners can benefit from two years of kindergarten.

"Developmental kindergarten" is one of the many names given to extra-year or transitional programs designed to provide children who are academically, socially, emotionally and/or physically "immature" with more time to grow and develop. However, recent studies show no differences in reading or math scores by third grade between developmental-kindergarten graduates and traditional kindergartners.

Even less encouraging, findings from a statewide study in Virginia show that developmental-kindergarten students who spent two years before reaching first grade fell behind their matched peers who had only one year of kindergarten.

These findings were more exaggerated for racial minority children enrolled in developmental kindergarten than for white children. Moreover, elementary school teachers do not seem to distinguish between children who were retained before first or second grade and those who attended developmental kindergartens.

Given all these findings, one can only speculate why extra-year programs, as well as retentions and the change in age of entry, remain so popular.

In all three instances teachers, parents and policy-makers find themselves in a situation not entirely of their own making. Because of increased academic demands brought about in part by the expectations of group-administered achievement testing in the early elementary years, teachers find their students less able to cope with curricula previously directed toward older and more experienced students. Consequently, teachers appear to be more amenable to strategies that remove children from situations in which they may fail.

However, the very alternatives selected to protect children from an inappropriate curriculum carry within them the seeds of failure, low self-esteem and reduced achievement.

Out of the Readiness Maze

The policies described here were introduced in response to nationwide pressures for "excellence," accountability and increased competitiveness. Unfortunately, compared with other possible alternatives, their negative potential far outweighs their likelihood of helping children become more ready for school.

How do we find our way out of this maze of unintended consequences and good intentions gone wrong?

Let me offer a strategy that differs dramatically from the organizational initiatives I have been criticizing. If we are to improve the academic success and lives of young children, we must change our focus from the organization of schools to the content of teaching and learning.

Specifically, I recommend that we make use of curriculum-based performance assessments as a means of helping teachers and children reach their potential in early childhood and early elementary classrooms. Performance assessments have a good chance of institutionalizing what responsive and developmentally appropriate classrooms should contain.

The essential character of the readiness definition that I am propounding is interactional, with a dual focus on the child's status and the educational setting. To obtain such a dynamic, a classroom structure must encourage individual planning, programming and evaluation. These characteristics are incorporated into curriculum-based performance assessments such as the Work Sampling System that my colleagues and I developed at the University of Michigan.

This approach offers an empirical test of the definition of readiness that I am suggesting. Based on teachers' perceptions of their students in actual classroom situations, it simultaneously informs, expands and structures those perceptions. It involves students and parents in the learning and assessment processes, instead of relying on measures external to the classroom and family context.

It also makes possible a systematic documentation of what children are learning and how teachers are teaching. In short, it draws attention to what the child brings to the learning situation and what the learning situation brings to the child.

As active constructors of knowledge, children should be expected to analyze, synthesize, evaluate and interpret facts and ideas. Performance assessment allows teachers to track these processes by documenting children's interactions with materials and peers in the classroom environment and to use this documentation to plan future approaches.

Performance assessment is a compelling strategy for enhancing children's success in school because it brings educational policy about young children back to the classroom—to the intersection of children, teachers and curricula. While performance assessment emphasizes the "nurturist" side of the nature/nurture debate, it does so in full recognition of the existence of individual differences among children and the concomitant importance of individualizing children's experiences in school.

Rather than relying on organizational solutions external to the classroom, performance assessment places in teachers' hands the responsibility to fashion a meaningful educational experience for their students.

The achievement of this experience demands a restatement of the first national goal: **By the year 2000, all children will have an opportunity to enhance their skills, knowledge and abilities by participating in classrooms that recognize children's individual differences, reinforce and extend children's strengths, and assist children in overcoming their difficulties in learning.**

POSTSCRIPT

Should All Children Be Five Years of Age Before Starting Kindergarten?

Future and current teachers and parents will want to stay informed concerning the results of the *Early Childhood Longitudinal Study: Kindergarten Class 1998–1999*, which will track 22,000 children who attended kindergarten in 1998 and will follow the children through the fifth grade. Data on age at kindergarten entrance and academic achievement will be obtained for this large sample of children. When the children were tested as they first entered kindergarten in 1998, the older children performed better on tests of general knowledge, reading, and math. At the end of the year the children who were older, as well as the younger children, made a year's gain in achievement.

The National Association for the Education of Young Children recommends that children enroll in a kindergarten when they are age-eligible. Is this the best recommendation? There is a need for teachers of young children to adapt activities to the range of developmental levels in the group. How can teachers work to ensure all children will be successful in school? What is the *purpose* of kindergarten? Is it to set a strong foundation for future learning or is to get children ready for the rigors of first grade?

Suggested Readings

Byrd, R., Weitzman, M., and Auinger, P., "Increased Behavior Problems Associated With Delayed School Entry and Delayed School Progress," *Pediatrics* (vol. 100, no. 4, 1997).

Crosser, S. L., "Enter Early or Hold Out: The Kindergarten Age Dilemma," *Early Childhood News* (vol. 13, no. 2, 2001).

Morrison, F., Griffith, E., and Alberts, D., "Nature-Nurture in the Classroom: Entrance Age, School Readiness, and Learning in Children," *Developmental Psychology* (vol. 33, no. 2, 1997).

National Association for the Education of Young Children, *NAEYC Position Statement on School Readiness*, http://www.naeyc.org/about/position/psredy98.htm (1995).

Spitzer, S., Cupp, R., and Parke, R. D., "School Entrance Age, Social Acceptance, and Self-Perceptions in Kindergarten and First Grade," *Early Childhood Research Quarterly* (vol. 10, 1995).

ISSUE 12

Is Full-Day Kindergarten Best for All Children?

YES: Patricia Clark and Elizabeth Kirk, from "All-Day Kindergarten," *Childhood Education* (Summer 2000)

NO: Deborah Olsen and Edward Zigler, from "An Assessment of the All-Day Kindergarten Movement," *Early Childhood Research Quarterly* (June 1989)

ISSUE SUMMARY

YES: Assistant professors Patricia Clark and Elizabeth Kirk present a review of the literature on full-day kindergarten and report that the majority of studies on the subject found increased academic performance along with additional benefits for children participating in full-day programs.

NO: Professors Deborah Olsen and Edward Zigler assert that there is a need for half-day programs for all children as well as a full-day program. Parents should be able to choose what is best for their children.

The early history of kindergarten programs indicates that they all started as half-day programs. Initially they were offered by philanthropic organizations for the benefit of underprivileged children. The teacher would work with a mixed-age group of children in the morning and then take on the role of a social worker in the afternoon. The early kindergarten teachers, most of whom were women, visited the homes of the children in their class and assisted the children's mothers by providing advice on parenting and also helping the family with health and social needs. Some private schools also provided kindergarten programs for children from middle- and upper-income families. When kindergartens began to be run by public schools in 1873, the practice of offering a half-day program continued and a second half-day section began to be taught in the afternoon. The family-assistance program was dropped and the teacher was no longer responsible for this aspect of the program. At various times throughout history kindergarten programs became full-time in some areas, mainly so young children could go to school with older siblings. During times of economic crisis and war, many kindergartens offered only half-day programs in order to accommodate more children. This was due to teacher shortages and a lack of classroom space. Renewed interest in full-day kindergartens began in the late 1960s and 1970s when half-day preschool programs became more popular and there was an increased push for improved academic performance for all children.

The number of single-parent families and dual-income families has forced school administrators and parents to reexamine the need for full-day kindergartens. What to do with five- and six-year-olds during the half-day that they are not is school is a dilemma for many working parents. Accountability for school funding causes school administrators to carefully examine all programs for cost effectiveness. Administrators need to know if there is a significant academic gain for children in full-day kindergartens that warrants the additional spending costs for classrooms, equipment, and personnel. If achieved, is that gain sustained over time? Are there other nonacademic gains that would be considered significant enough to justify the additional expense? Do the children who have attended full-day kindergarten perform significantly better on state-mandated tests? If so, are there other less-costly steps that could be taken that would provide similar benefits?

Parents approach the issue from two different sides. Parents needing child care struggle to find care during the half-day their child is not in a kindergarten program and often welcome a full-day of kindergarten. Families not needing full day care want those extra hours at home with their children before their child must attend twelve years of full-day school.

Many private schools offer full-day kindergarten in areas where public schools have only half-day programs available. The private schools attract clientele for at least a year and sometimes longer. Public schools then must address the need to offer full-day kindergarten to compete with the private schools that are attracting children away from the public system. This issue, like others in education, is a monetary issue in many areas and is often being decided by school districts based on transportation costs or staffing expenditures and by families based on the expense of child care. One point upon which all agree is that there is a need for kindergarten programs to be developmentally appropriate for all of the children served. The move to a full-day kindergarten program should not necessarily mean that there are now three additional hours each day for more rigorous academics to be presented to children.

In the selections that follow, Patricia Clark and Elizabeth Kirk present the results of a number of studies that have been found to highlight the benefits of full-day kindergarten. Deborah Olsen and Edward Zigler contend that half-day kindergarten programs should be available with a full-day option. Parents should be able to choose based on the benefits and drawbacks of both programs.

Patricia Clark and Elizabeth Kirk  **YES**

All-Day Kindergarten

Although many school systems still provide only half-day kindergarten programs, the trend in the United States has been toward implementation of all-day kindergarten. In the early 1980s, only about 30 percent of U.S. kindergarten children attended all-day kindergarten (Holmes & McConnell, 1990); by the early 1990s, the number had risen to nearly 50 percent (Karweit, 1992). By 1993, 54 percent of U.S. kindergarten teachers were teaching in full-day programs (Rothenberg, 1995).

This trend has grown as a result of both societal changes and educational concerns (Gullo, 1990; Holmes & McConnell, 1990; Karweit, 1992; Rothenberg, 1995; Sheehan, Cryan, Wiechel, & Bandy, 1991). With greater numbers of single parent and dual-income families in the workforce, parents increasingly need full-day programming for their young children. Researchers (e.g., Hough & Bryde, 1996; Housden & Kam, 1992; Lofthouse, 1994; Towers, 1991) have found that most teachers also prefer all-day kindergarten programs.

Early research conducted on the value of all-day kindergarten yielded mixed results. In a review of research on all-day kindergarten conducted in the 1970s and 1980s, Puleo (1988) suggested that much of the early research employed inadequate methodological standards that resulted in serious problems with internal and external validity; consequently, the results were conflicting and inconclusive. A number of studies of all-day kindergarten were conducted in the 1990s. While they also provided mixed results, some noteworthy trends appeared.

Effects of All-Day Kindergarten on Academic Achievement

Although research on the academic effects of all-day kindergarten conducted in the 1970s and 1980s showed mixed results, it did point to consistent results for students identified as being at-risk (Housden & Kam, 1992; Karweit, 1992; Puleo, 1988). Researchers found positive academic and social benefits of all-day kindergarten for children from low SES [socioeconomic status] or educationally disadvantaged backgrounds. Research reported in the past 10 years has found more consistent positive academic outcomes for children enrolled in all-day kindergarten (Cryan, Sheehan, Wiechel, & Bandy-Hedden, 1992; Elicker & Mathur, 1997; Hough & Bryde, 1996; Koopmans, 1991).

However, Holmes and McConnell (1990) conducted a study in which they found very few differences between children enrolled in half-day kindergarten and those enrolled in full-day kindergarten. The study was done during the first year of a move to full-day kindergarten programming by a large metropolitan school district. Twenty schools were selected randomly to provide either full-day or half-day kindergarten experiences. Half of the schools for each group were chosen from Chapter 1 schools and half were selected from affluent areas of the city. Researchers used scores on California Achievement Tests for 311 children enrolled in half-day programs and 326 children enrolled in full-day programs to determine whether or not there were differences in academic achievement. Only one of six achievement comparisons showed a significant difference that could be attributed to the kindergarten program: males in the full-day kindergarten program performed significantly better on the mathematics concepts and applications sub-test than did males in the half-day program.

Nunnelley (1996) investigated the impact of all-day versus half-day kindergarten programs on academic achievement levels of at-risk children. While no significant differences in academic achievement were found, only 19 children were included in the study (9 who attended full-day kindergarten and 10 who attended half-day kindergarten). Nunnelley suggested that further research with a larger sample was necessary.

A number of recent studies do show differences in academic achievement in children enrolled in half-day versus full-day programs. Cryan et al. (1992) conducted a two-phase study that examined the effects of half-day and all-day kindergarten programs on children's academic and behavioral success in school. In the first phase of the study, which was retrospective, data were collected on 8,290 children, from 27 school districts, who entered kindergarten in 1982–1984. The second phase was a longitudinal study of nearly 6,000 children who entered kindergarten in two cohorts, in 1986 and 1987. The researchers found that participation in all-day kindergarten was related positively to subsequent school performance. Children who attended full-day kindergarten scored higher on standardized tests, had fewer grade retentions, and had fewer Chapter 1 placements.

Hough and Bryde (1996) also found that students enrolled in full-day kindergarten programs benefited academically. Student achievement was examined for 511 children enrolled in half-day and all-day kindergarten programs in 25 classrooms during the 1994–95 school year. Data were collected from: 1) classroom observations; 2) focus groups with children, teachers, and parents; 3) report cards; 4) parent surveys; and 5) achievement test scores. Children in the all-day programs scored higher on the achievement test than those in half-day programs, on every item tested. The children enrolled in the all-day kindergarten program also had a higher attendance rate.

Koopmans (1991) examined the effectiveness of a full-day kindergarten program for the Newark, New Jersey, Board of Education. Koopmans looked at two cohorts of students: one in its third year of elementary school and the other in its second year of elementary school. Students' scores on the California

Test of Basic Skills (CTBS) were used for the analysis. Reading comprehension scores were somewhat higher in 2nd grade for those children in the first cohort who had attended all-day kindergarten. Comparison scores were significantly higher in both 1st and 2nd grade for those children in the second cohort who had attended all-day kindergarten. Math scores were also significantly higher for all-day kindergarten children in the second cohort, although no significant differences in math scores were found between full- and half-day students in the first cohort.

Finally, a study by Elicker and Mathur (1997) also found that academic outcomes at the end of the kindergarten year indicated slightly greater progress in kindergarten and higher levels of 1st-grade readiness for children in an all-day kindergarten program. In addition, teachers reported significantly greater progress for all-day kindergarten in literacy, math, and general learning skills.

Social and Behavioral Effects of All-Day Kindergarten

Although most studies of all-day kindergarten have focused on the effect of length of day on academic achievement, some researchers have also examined social and behavioral effects. Cryan et al. (1992) compared both academic and behavioral success of children enrolled in half-day versus full-day kindergarten programs. Results provided strong support for the effectiveness of the full-day kindergarten program on children's classroom behavior. Teachers rated 14 dimensions of children's behavior on the Hahnemann Elementary School Behavior Rating Scale (Spivack & Swift, 1975). According to the researchers, a clear relationship emerged between the kindergarten schedule and children's classroom behavior. Of the 14 dimensions, nine were more positive in all-day kindergarten: originality, independent learning, involvement in classroom activities, productivity with peers, intellectual dependency, failure/anxiety, unreflectiveness, holding back or withdrawal, and approach to teacher. No dimension of children's behavior was more positive in the half-day program when compared with the all-day program.

Other researchers who have studied social and behavioral outcomes found that children in all-day kindergarten programs were engaged in more child-to-child interactions (Hough & Bryde, 1996), and that they made significantly greater progress in learning social skills (Elicker & Mathur, 1997).

Attitudes Toward All-Day Kindergarten

While educators, policymakers, and parents are concerned with academic achievement, other aspects of children's, teachers', and families' lives are affected by all-day kindergarten. Recently, some researchers examined parents' and teachers' attitudes toward all-day kindergarten.

Parent attitudes   In general, parents of children in all-day kindergarten programs were satisfied with the programs and believed that all-day kindergarten better prepared their children for 1st grade (Hough & Bryde, 1996; Housden

& Kam, 1992; Towers, 1991). In one study (Hough & Bryde, 1996), parents reported that all-day kindergarten teachers more often gave suggestions for home activities. Parents also felt that their children benefited socially in the all-day kindergarten (Towers, 1991). In a survey conducted by Elicker and Mathur (1997), parents reported a preference for the all-day program, citing such advantages as a more relaxed atmosphere, more opportunities for children to choose activities and develop their own interests, and more time for creative activities.

Parents of children in the half-day program were divided in their opinions about the length of the kindergarten day. Some parents appreciated having their children home for part of the day; others indicated that they would have preferred a full-day program, because they felt their children were rushed in the half-day program.

Teacher attitudes   Researchers who reviewed teacher attitudes toward all-day kindergarten found that many teachers preferred all-day kindergarten because it allowed them more time for individual instruction (Greer-Smith, 1990; Housden & Kam, 1992). Teachers of all-day kindergarten noted that they were better able to get to know their children and families and, therefore, were better able to meet the children's needs (Elicker & Mathur, 1997). Teachers also cited the following advantages of all-day kindergarten: a more relaxed atmosphere, more opportunities for children to choose activities and develop their own interests, and more time for creative activities. In addition, teachers felt that all-day kindergarten programs were more effective than half-day programs in preparing children for 1st grade (Elicker & Mathur, 1997; Towers, 1991).

An interesting component of one all-day kindergarten program that both teachers and parents appreciated was an "easing in" process that allowed children to begin the year by attending half-day, then some full days; by the seventh week, these children attended full-day kindergarten every day (Towers, 1991).

Curriculum in All-Day Kindergarten

Several recent summaries of research (Housden & Kam, 1992; Karweit, 1992; Rothenberg, 1995) have suggested that the quality of the kindergarten experience and type of educational program, as well as the configuration of the school day, should be considered when kindergarten programs are evaluated. Some of the questions that have been addressed relate to what the children do while they are in the programs, how the teachers structure the programs, and how the teachers interact with children during instructional time. Full-day programs have the potential for offering more opportunities for the small-group and child-initiated activities that are recommended for early childhood classrooms (Bredekamp & Copple, 1997). Researchers have found, however, that the greatest percentage of time in both full-day and half-day programs is consumed by teacher-directed, large-group activity (Elicker & Mathur, 1997; Morrow, Strickland, & Woo, 1998).

Large-group, teacher-directed activity   Elicker and Mathur (1997) defined teacher-directed, large-group activity as a group of 10 or more children involved in teacher-led activities such as singing, movement, and physical exercise, as well as more quiet participation in such activities as listening to stories or to teacher instruction. In a study conducted over a two-year period that compared one school's daily activities in eight half-day and four full-day kindergarten programs, Elicker and Mathur (1997) found the greatest percentage of time in both kinds of classrooms was spent in large-group, teacher-directed activity. Although the average time spent on teacher-directed activity in full-day classrooms (100 minutes) was greater than in half-day classrooms (83.5 minutes), the percentage of total time consumed by teacher-directed activity was 16 percent less in full-day classrooms. This finding confirmed data collected earlier by Cryan et al. (1992) suggesting that children attending full- and alternate-day kindergarten programs spent less time in teacher-directed, large-group activity and more time in active free play.

In a study designed to determine the effects of the length of the kindergarten program on early literacy development, Morrow et al. (1998) found that the majority of the instructional time for literacy was spent in whole-group instruction. In the all-day classrooms, an average of 108 minutes was spent in whole-group literacy instruction, which represented 83 percent of the total time spent in literacy activity. The average time in half-day programs was 54 minutes, which represented 85 percent of the classroom literacy activity. The results of this study confirm the findings of earlier researchers indicating that full-day kindergarten teachers, as well as half-day kindergarten teachers, utilize primarily large-group, teacher-directed instructional techniques.

Small-group and individualized, teacher-directed activity Elicker and Mathur (1997) found very little difference in the amount of teacher-directed, small-group activity between the full-day and half-day programs. Teacher-led activities for groups of 2-10 children constituted only 2 to 3 percent of the day in both full-day and half-day kindergarten programs. Hough and Bryde (1996), however, found that full-day programs included a greater number of small-group activities, as well as more individualized instruction, than did the half-day programs; they suggested that full-day teachers, who had more time for instruction, may have felt less pressure to convey information expediently.

Morrow et al. (1998) also found that teachers offered fewer small-group and individualized literacy activities than whole-group instructional activities. All-day kindergarten teachers, however, utilized small-group instruction more frequently than did half-day teachers. All-day kindergarten teachers had 13 percent of their literacy activities taking place in small groups, while half-day teachers used only 8 percent of their literacy time in small-group settings. Individual literacy instructional time occurred somewhat less frequently in all-day programs. Only 4 percent of total literacy time in all-day classrooms and only 7 percent of total literacy time in half-day classrooms was spent in one-on-one teacher/student instruction.

Child-initiated activity Good (1996) suggested that children had more time for play and for self-directed activities when they attended an all-day, alternate-day program—for example, they were able to complete a project in the afternoon that they had started in the morning. Elicker and Mathur (1997) found that child-initiated activity increased by 7 percent in full-day classrooms; examples included more time spent in both indoor and outdoor free play, more extensive use of learning centers, and a small increase in cooperative learning. Children in full-day kindergarten programs engaged in child-initiated activity during 29 percent of the day, while children in half-day programs engaged in child-initiated activity for an average of 21 percent of their day.

By contrast, Morrow et al. (1998) compared the amount of time spent in child-initiated activity between full-day and half-day programs and found that while children in full-day programs had more total time per day engaged in free choice activity (25 minutes versus 19 minutes), the percentage of free choice time was greater in half-day programs (10 percent versus 13 percent). These researchers, however, noted that children in the full-day programs participated in more self-initiated literacy activities during their free choice time than did children in half-day programs.

Research data in both the Good (1996) and Morrow et al. (1998) studies were collected during the first year of the all-day kindergarten program. The data in the Elicker and Mathur (1997) study were collected over a two-year period. After comparing the data collected from the first and second years of the study, Elicker and Mathur concluded that many of the differences between full- and half-day kindergarten programming became stronger during the second year and that "children in the full-day classrooms were initiating more learning activity and receiving more one-to-one instruction from their teachers, while spending proportionally less time in teacher-directed groups" (p.477).

Summary

Most of the recent research on all-day kindergarten indicates positive benefits for children in terms of academic achievement and behavior. Parents and teachers seem to prefer all-day kindergarten over half-day kindergarten for a variety of reasons. However, Gullo (1990) cautions that the most important aspect of the full-day kindergarten may not be the length of the kindergarten day, but rather what occurs during that day. He notes that "all-day kindergarten has the potential of being either a blessing or a bane for young children. This will depend on which type of pressures prevail in influencing the development of the all-day kindergarten program" (p. 38). Gullo and others (Olsen & Zigler, 1989; Rothenberg, 1995) have warned educators and parents to resist the pressure to include increasingly more didactic academic instructional programming for all-day kindergarten, which, they contend, would be inappropriate for young children. Further research might help determine whether, over time, all-day kindergarten teachers can restructure the curriculum to conform to developmentally appropriate standards.

Educators, parents, and policymakers must remember that what children *do* in kindergarten may be more important than how long they are in the classroom each day. Results from recent research suggest, however, that a longer day can provide children the opportunity to spend more time engaged in active, child-initiated, small-group activities. In such classrooms, teachers seem to be less stressed by time constraints and may be better able to get to know the children. They report that they are able to work on themes in greater depth and can allow children more opportunities to choose activities and develop their own interests (Elicker & Mathur, 1997). Based on recent research, it appears that all-day kindergarten can offer children a developmentally appropriate curriculum, while at the same time providing academic benefits.

NO

Deborah Olsen and Edward Zigler

An Assessment of the All-Day Kindergarten Movement

All-Day Kindergarten and the Preschool Movement: A Critical Look

The past decade has witnessed an unprecedented growth in the number and variety of educational programs for young children. Notable among this panoply of educational approaches and schedules has been the widespread popularity of the all-day or extended-day kindergarten. All-day kindergarten, as it is commonly called, lengthens the amount of time 5-year-olds spend in school each day and allows more time for development of school-readiness skills of great concern at present to parents and educators. Although all-day programs vary in total length of day (from four to eight hours) and even in alternate-day versus every-day attendance, overall those who implement extended-day programs appear to share the overriding belief that more intensive diagnostic procedures, longer periods of instructional time, and a more diverse academic curriculum are essential to ensuring future school achievement (Adcock, 1980; Herman, 1984; Naron, 1981; Oelerich, 1979). Ten years ago Hawaii was the only state in the nation where all-day kindergarten programs could be found in significant numbers. Today it is estimated that about half of all kindergartners in the United States (i.e., about 40% to 45% of all the 5-year-olds in the country) attend some sort of extended-day program with enrollments continuing to rise (Kahn & Kamerman, 1987; Rohter, 1985).

The present trend favoring a longer school day and more academic instruction for 5-year-olds is part of a larger movement supporting the downward extension of formal schooling. In large part, enthusiasm for the earlier introduction of academics into programs for young children has been fueled by concern over the alleged failure of present educational practices and the poor performance of elementary and secondary students on tests of basic academic skills (National Commission on Excellence in Education, 1983). Worries over the scholastic deficiencies of our own students have been underscored by unflattering comparisons with students from foreign countries such as Japan, whose

From Deborah Olsen and Edward Zigler, "An Assessment of the All-Day Kindergarten Movement," *Early Childhood Research Quarterly*, vol. 4, no. 2 (June 1989). Copyright © 1989 by *Early Childhood Research Quarterly*. Reprinted by permission of Elsevier Science. Notes and references omitted.

technological and industrial competitiveness we fear—a concern not unlike that expressed about American education after Sputnik in the early 1960s.

Widespread belief in the efficacy of early instruction has actually stemmed from several sources. First, early intervention programs initiated in the 1960s and 1970s proved successful in spurring the developmental growth of low income 3- and 4-year-old children (Berrueta-Clement, Schweinhart, Barnett, Epstein, & Weikart, 1984; Deutsch, Deutsch, Jordan, & Grallo, 1983; Lazar & Darlington, 1982; Pierson, Tivnan, & Walker, 1984; Zigler & Valentine, 1979). The assumption here is that all-day kindergarten will provide the same sorts of growth opportunities for 5-year-olds. Second, popularization of Bloom's contention that 50% of intelligence is attained by age 4 (Bloom, 1964) led many to think of the preschool period as critical in determining later intellectual ability (e.g., Adcock, 1980; Herman, 1984). Third, European models such as those found in France and the Netherlands encourage almost universal full-day attendance from as early as 3 years. At the very least, European models are taken to show the practicability of all-day programs for young children.

Yet arguments that seemingly support widespread implementation of full-day programs for 5-year-olds require a closer look. As Zigler has pointed out elsewhere (1987), the effects of preschool intervention efforts, while heartening, have frequently been overstated. The beneficial effects of preschool programs tend to be restricted to children from lower socioeconomic status (SES) groups, with little or no effect on middle-class children (Adler, 1982; Caruso & Detterman, 1981; Clarke, 1984; Darlington, Royce, Snipper, Murray, & Lazar, 1980). Furthermore, the positive gains made required the support of both follow-through programs and parental involvement. Perhaps most important, the concept of school readiness employed in preschool programs such as Headstart was much broader than academic readiness, encompassing noneducational needs such as health and nutrition.

It is also fair to say that, in the process of being popularized, many of the developmental arguments for preschool education have become simplified and even distorted. While psychologists continue to debate the relative contributions of nature and nurture in cognitive development, few if any believe that the young child is simply a tabula rasa that can be filled with more and more learning (see Elkind, 1981). Recently, Bloom has described efforts to incorporate more formal instruction in the three R's in nursery school and kindergarten as "misdirected":

> What seems to me the most misdirected effort is the attempt by some parents and some preschool programs to teach children to read, write and do simple arithmetic in nursery school and kindergarten.... It is too simple to take the position that all that needs to be done in the cognitive domain is to take the curriculum of the first years of school and introduce them earlier. (Bloom, 1981, p. 69)

... Data on implementation and effects of all-day kindergarten do not always confirm the claims made for the efficacy and desirability of such programs. In particular, our review of the literature makes it clear that large-scale, systematic evaluations of all-day programs are still sorely needed. Thus, while the movement continues to grow pell-mell across the nation, it is fair to say that the jury is still out with respect to demonstrable benefits to young children.

Not only is the empirical evidence more equivocal than often suggested, but many experts in the field of early childhood education have expressed concern over the longer hours, the more demanding curriculum, and intensive screening procedures associated with all-day kindergarten (Ames, 1980, 1983; Cohen, 1975; Glazer, 1985; Nebraska State Board of Education, 1984; Seefeldt, 1985; Spodek, 1983). Even NAEYC [National Association for the Education of Young Children], which originally endorsed the concept of an all-day kindergarten, has recently made the point that "quality is not determined by the length of the program day" (NAEYC, 1987, p. 47). NAEYC's concerns focus not only on the time-on-task mentality underlying the assumption that "longer is better," but also on the formal teaching techniques and emphasis on achievement of narrowly defined skills that appear to go hand in hand in the "new" kindergarten.

Philosophy and Practice in Traditional and in All-Day Kindergartens

To understand the magnitude of the changes being proposed, it is helpful to describe briefly what has traditionally characterized education for young children. The first kindergarten was introduced into the United States more than 130 years ago. Based on the philosophy of Frederick Froebel, early kindergartens viewed education as *supporting* development and emphasized self-directed activities that fostered the child's innate curiosity and sense of social responsibility. While the Froebelian kindergarten underwent significant programmatic change over the course of the twentieth century, the spirit and philosophy remained very much intact until the 1970s. That is, although a greater range of materials and activities was incorporated into kindergarten practice, educators continued to consider children's personal and social adjustment foremost. This "whole child" approach, as it has been called, was thus for more than a century the guiding principle of early education, clearly demarcating it from the philosophy and structure of primary education proper (see Spodek, 1982, for an excellent history of kindergarten practice).

Over the past decade, there has been considerable erosion of the concern with the young child's overall development and an increased emphasis on school readiness and acquisition of specific academic skills: a shift from a concern for "continuity of development" to a concern for "continuity of achievement" (Spodek, 1982, p. 179). As already noted, the "excellence" movement in education and the more recent nationalistic interest in competitiveness have fostered this turn toward instruction of basic skills from an early age. In keeping with this trend, arguments for an extended-day schedule contend that the new, more demanding function of the kindergarten "requires more instructional time and better instructional tools than exist in the traditional half-day kindergarten programs" (Naron, 1981, p. 307). While not denying the important role that kindergarten must continue to play in the social, emotional, and physical development of young children, supporters of all-day programs maintain that the forces of TV, preschool, and even single parenthood have all made the child of the 1980s different from children a decade ago and thus in need of a more intellectually challenging curriculum (Helmich, 1985; Herman, 1984; Naron, 1981).

The change in kindergarten practice is, thus construed, simply a response to the changing needs of the children it serves: "The world of young children has changed and they have changed with it" (Herman, 1984, p. 8). Kindergarten is no longer the child's introduction to school, but part of a continuum of early childhood education that begins with prekindergarten and progresses through the primary grades. In this context, it should also be noted that, while the argument for more instructional time and better instructional tools is predicated on the assumption that a majority of children are ready for a more demanding, academically oriented experience, the emphasis on development of intellectual skills has important implications for those least ready as well. Advocates maintain that disadvantaged children at risk for later school failure should benefit even more than other children from the more intensive screening and remediation efforts possible in the longer school day.

Popularity of the All-Day Movement: Pragmatic and Pedagogical Arguments

Considered in light of recent demographic and sociocultural factors, the popularity of the all-day kindergarten is quite understandable. According to U.S. census figures, about half of the women in this country with 5-year-old children work outside the home (Chorvinsky, 1982, p. 19). This situation has led to an unprecedented demand for daycare—daycare that is not only difficult to obtain and variable in quality, but is also often prohibitively expensive. It is not surprising that working parents would want to shift some of the economic burden of daytime care to the school system. Perhaps more important, in leaving the child in kindergarten for the better part of the day, parents feel they are placing their child in a better environment than they might find in day care, an environment rich in opportunities to learn. The feeling expressed not infrequently is that all-day school is a better alternative than having children spend the day watching TV or playing in an unsupervised atmosphere (e.g., McCarthy, 1983; Smith, 1984).

If maternal employment has made the longer kindergarten schedule a more appealing option for parents, declining school enrollments and the availability of school staff and space have certainly encouraged school administrators to implement all-day programs (Herman, 1984; Humphrey, 1983; Jokubaitus, 1980; Zorn, 1983). All-day kindergartens often make better use of existing levels of staff and resources and attract a number of students who would otherwise attend nonpublic schools with full-day programs. In fact, there was a 5.6% increase in the number of 5-year-olds attending private kindergartens from 1970 to 1983 and a corresponding decrease in public school enrollments (Kahn & Kamerman, 1987, p. 130). Humphrey (1983) estimated that in Evansville, Indiana, schools lose $929 in state reimbursement for every child who enrolls in kindergarten elsewhere, and $11,612 over the period K–12. His argument, quite simply, is that school systems cannot afford not to implement a full-day schedule.

Although pragmatic constraints on parents and educators have helped provide an important impetus for adopting all-day programs in many parts of the country, the *explicit* rationale given for the longer kindergarten day is still its educational benefits. Failure to adequately recognize and articulate the role that pragmatics have played in furthering the growth of all-day kindergarten has had at least two unfortunate consequences: (1) the question of what is good for children, their development, and well-being, has not been sufficiently distinguished from the interests of adults charged with their care and education, and (2) parents' and teachers' needs have only been partly met because they have only been partly recognized.

In the case of all-day kindergarten, it is important to distinguish views based on empirical evidence from those that have surface plausibility but remain unverified assumptions. It is the authors' contention, based on both the existing literature on early childhood development and on empirical data on the effects of all-day kindergarten, that consensus about the positive effects of a full day of school for 5-year-olds is premature.

Nor do there appear to be empirical data to support the contention that children today are different from children 10 years ago. Demographics have changed, there are more working and single mothers, and children are more likely to have had a preschool experience. The fact that children have adapted and in many cases have thrived under the new conditions of early childhood, however, is not proof that their development has been altered in any fundamental way or even hastened significantly.

Furthermore, if we examine the question of length of day from the perspective of parents' needs, we find the notion of a 6- to 8-hour kindergarten day largely unsatisfactory. Parents who are home during the day often resent the long, daily separations from their child. Both Bloom (1981) and Tizard & Hughes (1984) have shown that children at this age gain marked intellectual and social advantages from the home environment and interactions with their parents, so that more hours spent at home clearly do not leave children at a disadvantage. On the other hand, families in which both parents work outside the home are still left with a day care dilemma for the hours between the end of school and the end of the workday. In a very real sense, the day care problem only has been moved back for a few hours. Unfortunately, some fairly negative consequences of this situation can be anticipated, the change in schedule leading some parents to take relatively fewer precautions for the shorter period of time before and after school.

Review of the Literature on All-Day Kindergarten

In reviewing the empirical data on all-day kindergarten, we will distinguish between: (a) process evaluations that assess the extent to which services promised were in fact delivered, and (b) outcome evaluations that seek to assess program outcomes, that is, to assess whether desired effects were achieved. Thus far, researchers' attention has focused largely on the *effects* of all-day kindergarten, with school achievement and performance on standardized tests receiving the lion's share of attention.

As an independent variable, length of day has been used as both a determinant of achievement and as a proxy variable for curriculum, philosophy, and other variables associated with the longer day. We begin our review with the scant literature that details actual implementation of all-day programs. Review of this literature suggests that length of day may prove to be an imperfect estimator of actual kindergarten practice, with instruction in academic tasks and school readiness skills varying substantially across programs as well as from proposed models.

Process Evaluations of All-Day Kindergarten

As noted, few studies have examined whether the content of full-day programs conforms to expectation, with focus centering instead on the length-of-day variable. While the evidence is sparse, however, it suggests that there are a number of troubling disparities between the model programs proposed (e.g., Connecticut Early Childhood Education Council, 1983; Ferguson-Florissant School District, 1974; Gorton & Robinson, 1969; Herman, 1984) and the actualities of full-day programs as they have been implemented to date. In particular, there appears to be some question about whether the following services are being delivered as promised: (a) more individualized instruction, (b) a broader curriculum, (c) a nutritious lunch, and (d) a higher level of parent involvement.

Significant among the proposed advantages of a full-day kindergarten program is the greater amount of time possible for individualized instruction. Contrary to expectation, however, it has been found that teachers in all-day programs, even experienced kindergarten teachers with teacher aids, overwhelmingly tend to teach children as a group rather than working with them on an individual basis (Jarvis & Molnar, 1986, Office of Educational Assessment, N.Y.C.). While New York City with its extensive investment in full-day kindergarten intends to rectify such problems through in-service training programs, it seems far less likely that smaller school districts will have the resources necessary to retrain teachers specifically for the new climate of the all-day kindergarten.

Related to the question of how teachers teach is the question of what they teach. Traditionally, kindergarten has been a place where children spend a significant part of their time engaged in nonacademic activities, with limited formal instruction in basic skills. In expanding the length of time 5-year-olds spend in school, it was assumed that teachers would be able to incorporate a broader range of subject matter into the curriculum, periods of more routine academic instruction being interspersed with work in music, art, social studies, science, special activities, and self-directed projects. Evidence indicates, however, that the full-day curriculum tends to resemble the half-day curriculum, simply extending the same activities and instruction over longer periods of time (e.g., Frey, 1979; Johnson, 1974; Levinson & Lalor, 1986; McClinton & Topping, 1981; Winter & Klein, 1970). One fairly comprehensive study did find a slightly broader range of academic subject matter covered in all-day programs, but it also found that a large amount of time was spent on recess (Finkelstein, 1983). Another large-scale study of full-day kindergarten found the bulk of the instructional time spent on reading (44%), about a quarter on language arts, and a quarter on math. Virtually no time was spent on social studies or science (Jarvis & Molnar, 1986). In addition, both studies found an emphasis in full-day on fine motor over gross motor skills.

These findings suggest that, while the amount of time spent on basic academic skills has increased, doubling or even tripling the time spent in half-day sessions, little has been done to expand the repertoire of activities related to less basic and potentially more creative academic domains such as science. In addition, there is a relative neglect of certain nonacademic activities such as gross motor "play" that may have less obvious but equally profound developmental consequences. Researchers working in the field of child development have found that young children require diverse experiences and ample opportunity for physical, social, and verbal interaction (Kohlberg, 1968). There is also research demonstrating that children need an environment that allows them to express and develop their native curiosity and intelligence through play, exploration, and fantasy, as well as through more structured activities (Bettleheim, 1987; Biber, 1984; Bruner, Jolly, & Sylva, 1976; Elkind, 1981; Zigler, 1970). It appears, in fact, that too much external structure, guidance, or stress can diminish the sense of autonomy and competence that underlies the persistence, independence, and intellectual challenge-seeking essential to success in later life (Baumrind, 1978; Baumrind & Black, 1967; Deci, 1971; Dweck & Elliot, 1983; Lepper, Green, & Nisbett, 1973; Sigel, 1987). Finally, research on social competence argues for the long-term importance of emotional and motivational factors, development of a positive self-image, and positive social relations with peers and adults (Zigler & Trickett, 1978, p. 79). In short, the admixture of activities and disciplines appropriate for a 5-year-old in a $2\frac{1}{2}$-hour day may be grossly inappropriate extended over a 6- to 8-hour day. Longer periods of academic instruction and fine motor work may prove particularly problematic.

Advocates of all-day programs also cite the opportunity for serving children a nutritious lunch as an advantage of the all-day program. Although seemingly of secondary importance, a nutritious lunch and snacks provided during the longer day help ensure that children are able to make the most of the educational opportunities afforded them. Certainly, one of the great lessons to be learned from Headstart and similar intervention efforts is that the success of any educational enterprise relies on children being healthy and well fed. However, at least one study reported problems establishing satisfactory lunchtime arrangements (Jarvis & Molnar, 1986), while another full-day program sent children home for lunch (Warjanka, 1982).

Finally, of the many school districts that assess all-day schedules, only two report even minimal parent involvement (Alper & Wright, 1979; Winter & Klein, 1970). This lack of parental involvement is very much in contrast to *proposed models* of the all-day kindergarten and conflicts with evidence showing that parent participation is critical to the efficacy of early educational treatments (Bronfenbrenner, 1974; Deutsch et al., 1983; Radin, 1969; Slater, 1971; Sparrow, Blachman, & Chauncey, 1983; Valentine & Stark, 1979; Waksman, 1980). Given the number of families with two working parents, the pragmatics of involving parents in the ongoing activities of the school is formidable. Nevertheless, the importance of establishing parent–school ties seems sufficient to warrant greater efforts than have been undertaken. . . .

Overall, much remains to be done to demonstrate the long-term efficacy of a longer school day with greater amounts of academic readiness training for 5-year-olds. While Humphrey's results with respect to the enhanced abilities and lower retention rates of second and third graders are promising, the results clearly require replication and confirmation not yet found in the literature. Moreover, complementing the differential social class effects discussed earlier, achievement gains may be best maintained over time by low SES children participating in a larger intervention effort (Neiman & Gastright, 1981; see also Mueller, 1977).

If evidence for the effect of all-day kindergarten on academic achievement across social class and across time is less than consistent, empirical data on other effects of the full-day schedule are even less clear. Advocates of the full-day schedule suggest that children's interpersonal skills will benefit from the more extensive contact with peers and that attitudes toward learning will be better in the more stimulating and individualized all-day environment. But attempts to empirically confirm these claims have been rare, and the findings that do exist are mixed. Out of the 30 or so empirical studies of all-day kindergarten reviewed in this paper, only 8 included any sort of objective measure of self-concept, social development, or motivation.

Of the eight studies including standard measures of noncognitive skills, three showed no differences between full-day and half-day groups. Hatcher and Schmidt (1980), for example, tested students on full-day and students on half-day schedules using the California Test of Personality and found the performance of the groups to be comparable. Similarly, teachers' ratings of social adjustment failed to reveal significant differences between half-day and full-day kindergartners in a study carried out by McClinton and Topping (1981). Gullo and Clements (1984) contrasted scores on the Hahnemann Elementary Behavior Rating scale given to half-day and full-day/alternate day students and found differences on only two of the fifteen subscales. Given the pattern of findings, the authors felt that even these small differences were simply a product of full-day teachers' greater familiarity with their students. . . .

Furthermore, one study suggests that at least in one regard a half-day schedule may prove more beneficial than full-day. Evans and Marken (1984) discovered that students who had attended kindergarten half-days exhibited a better attitude toward reading in first, second, and third grades than did those who had attended full-days. These findings, while certainly not definitive, would seem to provide some confirmation of the International Reading Association's (1986) concern that premature instruction of preschool children in formal prereading and reading skills may actually dampen their enthusiasm for reading.

Finally, even if we are willing to accept the present focus on intellectual "performance" as warranted, we are still faced with the problem that achievement test scores form the almost exclusive basis for judgments of the child's cognitive functioning. No assessment, for example, has been made of the effect of the longer school day on the child's underlying intellectual competence (e.g., IQ). Hatcher and Schmidt (1980, p. 16) point out that "the child's ability to observe, discover, generalize, experiment and solve problems in half-day and full-day programs" has yet to be explored.

Conclusions and Recommendations

In general, extended-day programs do seem to bring about short-term increases in standardized test scores, particularly with children who are disadvantaged, bilingual, or "least-ready" for school. There is little evidence to suggest, however, that positive change in academic performance is maintained beyond the early elementary school years or that there are changes in motivation or general intellectual ability that would be likely to support significant long-term change. On the basis of a review of the present literature, it appears that in many cases what we are seeing is relatively specific training in language, math, and reading for extensive periods of the day, which permits children to do better on tests of those specific skills (e.g., see Frey, 1979; Warjanka, 1982; Winter & Klein, 1970). There is no evidence that the curriculum is more individualized and innovative or that less time is spent on routine tasks (Finkelstein, 1983; Jarvis & Molnar, 1986). Furthermore, while educators' interest in greater parent participation in all-day programs is laudable, to date parental involvement is the exception rather than the rule.

While many of the effects of the all-day kindergarten remain in need of greater clarification, there are some immediate ramifications of the present all-day movement which, a number of experts in the field of early childhood agree, are not positive influences on children's growth (Ames, 1980, 1983; Cohen, 1975; Glazer, 1985; Seefeldt, 1985; Spodek, 1982). First, there is the assumption, which is given substantial weight in the formulation and operation of extended and day programs (e.g., Gorton & Robinson, 1969; Herman, 1984), that young children today are somehow different, more sophisticated, and better able to handle the experience of school and an academic curriculum than were children a generation ago. Although without empirical support, this assumption is already proving to have deleterious effects on children who are quite normal but who may not yet be up to the rigors of a curriculum with 3 or more hours of academic instruction a day. Concern over this situation has led the Nebraska State Board of Education (1984), in a now much heralded statement, to speak out against the inappropriate demands often being made of young children, the overemphasis on fine motor skills, and desk work with commercially produced textbook-type materials. The Early Childhood and Literacy Development Committee of the International Reading Association has echoed these sentiments in their joint statement of 1986, arguing that children's ability to read and interest in reading comes naturally from their day-to-day experiences with verbal language. Inappropriate training in reading readiness skills is, they maintain, more likely to impair than enhance children's inclination to read.

A second and perhaps more pervasive factor influencing the lives of young school children is the increased emphasis on screening, which has accompanied the more intensive demands made by the new kindergarten curriculum as well as the greater accountability of schools. While screening procedures are not associated exclusively with a longer kindergarten day, the role and potential benefit of screening and, in particular, opportunities for screening in all-day programs have been emphasized by advocates of those programs (Herman, 1984; Naron, 1981). One important result of more extensive screening has been that large numbers of children are now being identified as "deficient" both before and after kindergarten. Similarly, children who fail to cope with the year-end battery of standardized tests may fail to pass kindergarten. In one study, 31 out of 87 children (mostly boys) in a full-day program were referred to a special learning disabilities class (Evans & Marken, 1984).

Too often, the debate over what sort of preschool experience should be regularly provided for 5-year-old children has been obfuscated rather than clarified by the attention focused on the length-of-day variable. While the issue of whether children should attend school for two-and-a-half, four, six, or eight hours a day clearly needs to be addressed, any resolution of the issue that fails to involve an account of the philosophy and content that shapes and fills those hours is trivial. Children's school performance, their intellectual development, their quality of life will *not* improve simply because they spend longer hours every day in a classroom.

The issue of whether a more "child-centered" or a more "academic" approach to preschool education is preferable is complicated by the fact that it requires us to articulate fairly specifically our expectations of preschool education and how broadly we construe the meaning of "learning" and "education" with respect to the development of young children. The issue relates particularly to the question of length of day because the kind of experience provided becomes more critical the more hours a child spends in school. We contend that two recent trends in American education and child-rearing practices have begun to shape early education in ways that have led to an inappropriate emphasis on production of specific concrete skills: (1) the trend toward equating educational attainment with competence in basic academic skills and even more specifically scores on standardized tests, and (2) the trend toward young children's increasing assumption of the rights and responsibilities previously associated with older children and adults (Cohen, 1975; Elkind, 1981).

Developmental work on social competence (see Zigler & Trickett, 1978) shows that much of what differentiates efficacious, successful individuals from those who are less able to adapt, problem solve, and so on is not simply IQ or achievement on a test, but a composite of ability, motivation, ego-strength, and interpersonal awareness. To date, the evidence suggests that, if anything, the formal elementary school environment brings about a reduction in children's intrinsic motivation (Harter & Connell, 1984) and makes children more likely to focus on performance (success or failure on a particular task) than on learning and acquisition of problem-solving skills (see Dweck & Elliot, 1983).

Given such findings, we must question the value of a downward extension of elementary school methods and materials to the teaching of young children. The caveat here is simply that in our enthusiasm to enrich young children's educational experience and help them do "better," we must be careful not to trade off transient gains in test scores for more precious skills and interests that are the basis for functioning as fully developed, productive adults.

Given that at least half of the 5-year-olds in this country are from families with two working parents, an alternative to the present all-day kindergarten that may better meet the needs of parents and children is to complement a half-day of school with a half-day of high quality, in-school day care, with day care being provided by certified child development aids (CDAs) trained in the care of young children. Both day care and school would provide the child with an enriched learning environment. The kinds of experiences emphasized would vary, though, with school including more structured activities and a greater focus on academics and day care offering more opportunities for outdoor and exploratory play and for social interaction. It should be noted that this plan is not wed to any particular proportions of the day being denoted as "school" and "day care" so that, if desirable, some expansion of the traditional half-day of school is certainly feasible.

We believe that the combination of kindergarten and in-school care for 5-year-olds offers a number of advantages a 6- to 8-hour all-day kindergarten does not. First, given a school–day care arrangement, children could return home midday or stay until parents pick them up at the end of the workday. This means that working parents no longer have to worry about day care for the hours between the end of school and the end of work, while nonworking parents who prefer to have their children home after half a day can do so. Furthermore, rather than have a compulsory full-day of school for all children supported by school system tax dollars, a choice of schedules would allow schools to ask parents opting for the extra services to pay a somewhat greater share of the cost. It is critical, however, that the same school–day care option should be available (e.g., through a sliding scale) to less financially able parents whose children would benefit especially from the high quality, daylong care.

A second related advantage of the proposed school–day care arrangement is the fact that CDAs trained in early child development and working with children in a safe, well-kept, well-furnished school environment, would provide a better day care experience than many children now have in day care centers or home-based, after-school care. Using CDAs to provide care for the nonschool hours has two additional advantages: (1) CDAs are paid less than teachers so that costs for the longer day of care are kept to a minimum, and (2) teachers are not asked to assume a care-taking function outside their traditional role.

In sum, offering kindergarten and day care under the same school roof would make good use of increasingly available school space and resources, give working and nonworking parents much needed flexibility, leave teachers to their job-appropriate tasks and, most important, provide children with developmentally appropriate experiences in physical, social, and cognitive domains. The greater range of experiences possible in a day care–school schedule would diffuse some of the present emphasis on achievement of specific academic skills and provide more time for children to work on the interpersonal skills and emotional autonomy equally critical to success in the primary grades. Less of a formal academic orientation would thus allow more time for developmental differences common at this stage to "even out" without children being labeled as deficient or unable to cope with school. In fact, embedding "school" in a day-long context where cognitive and noncognitive attainments are all highly valued may possibly enhance children's self-concept and their attitudes towards school and, in turn, help build a solid motivational base for later achievement.

We must recognize both the pragmatics of the situation for working parents and educators and at the same time respect the individual differences and developmental variability of the 5-year-olds whose education is in our trust. To forge an educational program that optimizes the growth of all children, we may need to admit to some of the limitations of present "solutions" and seek new alternatives that build on what we now know as well as what we hope to accomplish for our children and ourselves.

POSTSCRIPT

Is Full-Day Kindergarten Best for All Children?

The bottom line for this issue is not necessarily the length of the school day, but what occurs when children are in school. No matter if the program is half-day or full-day, all kindergarten children need an environment that allows for some large group, small group, individual, and teacher-directed activities throughout the day. Activities should be adapted to meet the learning styles and abilities of all children in the class. School administrators, school board members, and parents need to carefully examine the reasons for choosing half-day or full-day programs.

Of interest to all early childhood educators and school administrators is the *Early Childhood Longitudinal Study: Kindergarten Class 1998–1999,* which will follow pupils through the fifth grade. The study is being conducted by the U.S. Department of Education's National Center for Education Statistics. An initial report was released in 2000 presenting a profile of the 22,000 children who will be followed for six years. Data collected includes whether the children attended full-day or half-day kindergarten. It will be important for educators to review the results of the study as it will provide data that will assist school administrators in allocating resources and providing the best possible curriculum for young children. Parents should also be eager to know what the best strategies are that they can employ to ensure success for their children.

Suggested Readings

Cryan, J. R., Sheehan, R., Wiechel, J., and Bandy-Hedden, I. G., "Success Outcomes of Full-day Kindergarten: More Positive Behavior and Increased Achievement in the Years After," *Early Childhood Research Quarterly* (vol. 7, no. 2, 1992).

Elicker, J. and Mathur, S., "What Do They Do All Day? Comprehensive Evaluation of a Full-day Kindergarten," *Early Childhood Research Quarterly* (vol. 12, no. 4, 1997).

Fusaro, J. A., "The Effect of Full-day Kindergarten on Student Achievement: A Meta-analysis," *Child Study Journal* (vol. 27, no. 4, 1997).

Wang, Y. L. and Johnstone, W. G., "Evaluation of a Full-day Kindergarten Program," ERS Spectrum (vol. 17, no. 2, 1999).

ISSUE 13

Should Recess Be Included in a School Day?

YES: Anthony D. Pellegrini and David F. Bjorklund, from "The Place of Recess in School: Issues in the Role of Recess in Children's Education and Development," *Journal of Research in Childhood Education* (Fall/Winter 1996)

NO: Kelly King Alexander, from "Playtime Is Cancelled," *Parents* (November 1999)

ISSUE SUMMARY

YES: Anthony D. Pellegrini, a professor at the University of Minnesota, and David F. Bjorklund, a professor at Florida Atlantic University, conducted numerous studies examining student behavior before and after recess as well as academic performance. They state that there is a strong correlation between recess and higher academic performance.

NO: Kelly King Alexander, a contributing editor for *Parents* magazine, asserts that many school administrators have no choice but to eliminate nonacademic time from the daily school schedule due to the need for as much educational activity as possible.

Recess has become such a part of the American education landscape that it is sometimes referred to as the 4th "R," along with "reading, riting, and rithmetic." However, that has changed in the many school districts that are implementing a no-recess policy. In the past two years, the Atlanta, Georgia, public school system reinforced a 1990 policy that states that children should engage in "uninterrupted instructional time" by building three new schools without playgrounds.

No specific studies exist on the academic disadvantages for children who have daily recess. However, some teachers argue for the need to eliminate recess by citing reasons such as difficulty in getting the students settled down after being outside, student fighting, the implementation of physical education classes, and the lack of time for activities other than learning.

When one-room schools were the norm in the United States, teachers and students used the break, or recess time, to do the chores that were necessary to keep the school in operation. Students had time to use the outhouse, restock wood for the stove, and draw water from the well, and teachers had time to gather materials for the next portion of the day. Recess provided a break for the teachers as well as the students. Schools of the twenty-first century offer the teaching staff no such break time from their teaching duties, so recess is now viewed as a luxury for the students more so than for the benefit of the teacher and the operation of the school.

School administrators in many states are concerned about the public's opinion of their schools. Administrators are also concerned about their districts receiving financial incentives to improve test scores. They worry about the time spent getting children ready to go outside, the actual recess time, and the time needed to get back into work mode after returning to the classroom. In some states additional hours of instructional time are being added to the school day. Doing away with recess time eliminates the need to renegotiate teacher contracts for longer work days since the additional hours are added without making the working day itself longer. Is this the only option? Are there curricular topics that can be eliminated in order to allow time for new material, such as computer instruction? How have changes in current society affected the need for recess? Has the need for recess increased or decreased due to the changes in society?

In some communities, recess is being eliminated due to safety reasons. Playgrounds are usually open to the general public and may harbor broken glass, used needles, and dangerous pieces of equipment. However, creative school architects are designing schools with enclosed courtyard playgrounds that can only be accessed from inside the building. But what can be done to solve this problem in older schools that are still in use? Monitoring the playground means that teachers must be outside with their students and that all students must be visible at all times. One teacher may not be able to supervise an entire playground. In some large schools serving preschool through elementary children, different playgrounds may be needed for the various age levels of students attending.

Just as adults welcome a break from their daily routine, those in support of recess argue that children need time to relax and regroup for more intense work. Many assert that by allowing children time to socially interact, to absorb the work just completed, and to exercise large muscles, the message is sent that if you work hard, you will be rewarded with a break.

In the following selections, Anthony D. Pellegrini and David F. Bjorklund examine the effect of breaks during academic tasks. They conclude that the greatest intellectual gains occur when there are breaks between learning activities. Kelly King Alexander quotes Mike Jordan, principal of the Magellan Charter School in Raleigh, Carolina. Jordan states that, "We're here to educate children. To take thirty minutes out of our instructional day just to let kids play doesn't sound good—to parents, to legislators, or to taxpayers."

**Anthony D. Pellegrini and
David F. Bjorklund**

The Place of Recess in School

I think there is far too much work done in the world, that immense harm is caused by the belief that work is virtuous, and that what needs to be preached in modern industrial countries is quite different from what always has been preached.

— Russell, 1932/1972, p. 9

This quote from Bertrand Russell is taken from the first paragraph of his essay titled "In Praise of Idleness," in which he argues that too much time is spent working. The stress on continuous hard work, Russell argues, is probably bad economically, morally, and spiritually for modern society. Society would be better served if more time were spent in "idleness" than in hard work. By idleness, Russell means leisure and play, the very stuff of children's recess behavior.

This provocative quote from one of the leading scholars of the 20th century seems an appropriate manifesto to begin this theme issue on the role of recess. It highlights at least two important things that might help improve children's lives in schools and the more general process of education. First, this quote calls into question the common assumption held by many educators, parents, and politicians that work time in school should be increased. In North America and in the U.K., one frequently hears cries that school days and years should be extended and that "fluff," such as recess and play, should be purged from schools. This argument, like that which Russell was contesting, presumes that there is a positive correspondence between increased work time and increased student learning.

At one level, this may be true. Certainly, children benefit from receiving quality instruction, and increasing the number of hours of instruction per year that a child receives may indeed increase learning. This, however, is not the same as stating that more intense, break-free hours of instruction will enhance learning. In fact, it is probably the opposite. Early childhood educators and child developmentalists would agree with Russell's objection to a "cult of efficiency" (p. 24). Their protests are based on their unbridled belief in the value of play and the practices, such as break times and recess periods, that support play and leisure activities for children in schools.

From Anthony D. Pellegrini and David F. Bjorklund, "The Place of Recess in School: Issues in the Role of Recess in Children's Education and Development," *Journal of Research in Childhood Education,* vol. 11, no. 1 (Fall/Winter 1996). Copyright © 1996 by The Association for Childhood Education International. Reprinted by permission of The Association for Childhood Education International and the authors. References omitted.

The playground offers opportunities for children to develop their social competence by their interaction with a variety of children. Recess is one of the few places in school where children can learn to cooperate with peers who are often from different backgrounds. Planning and organization on the part of teachers and policymakers is needed to encourage children to interact with peers from different cultural backgrounds.

The second valuable point about Russell's quote is that it forces educators to address an important education conundrum. On the one hand, there are calls for more play and leisure (breaks and recess) time in school. On the other hand, there is the very real problem of declining levels of school achievement. This apparent contradiction begs serious attention.

Russell suggests that leisure time results in "happy lives" instead of the "frayed nerves" associated with overwork. Happy people live better, and more productive, lives. Thus, his solution to the problem would indicate that both goals could be accomplished.

"The Cult of Efficiency" and Schooling Views of Work and Play

The cult of efficiency extols the values of work and devalues the role of leisure. This view contends that time spent in leisure could be spent more productively working. This dichotomy of work/play often mirrors the dichotomy of good/ evil. Authors supporting play point to the influence of Christianity (e.g., sloth-fulness as one of the seven deadly sins) and to Protestantism for the emphasis on valuing work over leisure (Sutton-Smith, 1995; Tawney, 1969). Explicitly anti-Christian theories, such as Marx's (1906) assertion that labor is a per-son's defining characteristic, also support this view. Similarly, in Soviet Russia and in China, especially during the Cultural Revolution, the dignity of labor and "workers" was stressed and hard work, long hours, and productivity were virtues. So, many viewpoints stressed that, whether the goal be the entrance into heaven or into some (workers') utopia, hard work typically guaranteed admittance.

The relation between efficiency and the direction and intensity of work are certainly reflected in American and British schools. One of the clearest examples of this view is the time-on-task literature in American education re-search (e.g., see Brophy & Good, 1974, for a summary). These studies empha-sized that education achievement was directly and positively related to the amount of time spent working on tasks. Calls for longer school days and school years and the elimination of recess periods from the school days are logical extensions of this practice.

More provocative is the way in which many play theories are also framed in terms of productivity! As pointed out by Sutton-Smith (1995), most play the-orists from Groos (1901) through Piaget (1962) and Vygotsky (1978) discuss play and its development in terms of its benefit for subsequent development. Many child developmentalists and educators, ourselves included (e.g., Bjorklund & Green, 1992; Pellegrini & Galda, 1993), discuss the importance of play in terms of its payoff in school-related tasks. The value of play can be judged in terms of a cost/benefit ratio. That is, play is good (in developmental terms) if its benefits outweigh associated costs.

Of course, discussions of play and school recess must be conducted in light of the world of real school policy. That is, parents, educators, and politicians are presently concerned about children's academic achievement and their safety in schools. Recess, for some parents, not only takes time away from instruction, but also is the venue for various unfortunate forms of aggression. They raise concerns that recess may interfere with safety and learning and, if so, those concerns must be addressed. Researchers note, however, that play is beneficial to immediate and later social and academic competence.

Recess and Cognitive Immaturity

Young children think differently than older children, who, in turn, think differently than adults. Regardless of the much debated underlying reasons for these differences, the result is that younger children learn most things at a slower rate than older children (see Bjorklund, 1995a; Flavell, Miller, & Miller, 1993; Kuhn & Siegler, in press; Siegler, 1991, for in-depth discussions). Despite young children's cognitive limitations, research over the past several decades has demonstrated that preschool and early school-age children can be taught skills that are usually spontaneously acquired only by older children, providing the impression that more rigorous instruction during the early grades will result in enhanced cognition, both immediately and later in development. It is from this perspective that recess is seen as a superfluous activity, perhaps necessary to some degree to combat boredom, but an essentially nonproductive part of the school day.

An alternative, and developmental, perspective holds that children's immature cognitions are often well suited to the peculiar demands of childhood —that immaturity is not just something to overcome, but that children's immature nervous systems may be adapted to deal effectively with the cognitive demands they face in their daily lives at those particular developmental periods (Bjorklund, 1995b; Bjorklund & Green, 1992; Bjorklund & Schwartz, 1996). This position is consistent with the view that behaviors and cognitions within the early childhood period have value or function inherent to that period and should not be considered "imperfect" variants of adult behavior (Bateson, 1981).

Of course, the evolution of cognition was not influenced by modern, information-age cultures, and thus is not adapted to those cultures. That is, math seat work, reading, or associating state capitals with their state names were not tasks for which human intelligence was selected. Schooling is thus "unnatural," albeit necessary for success in contemporary society. By recognizing the unnaturalness of formal education, especially for young children, educators can develop practices that optimize children's learning. Recess, particularly for young children, is such a practice.

The Immediate Benefits of Recess for School Performance

Primary school children in the industrialized world experience some sort of recess period during their school day. British children in middle and secondary schools have recess, or "breaktime." Recess usually takes the form of a "break" (either indoors or outdoors) from academic work, where children are free to choose and engage in an activity on their own terms. For primary school children, having recess outdoors usually means social interaction with peers mixed with vigorous physical behavior (Pellegrini & Smith, 1993). Although recess has been part of formal education systems since their inception, it has rarely been studied. The contributors to this theme issue represent a reasonable sample of the active researchers in this area.

Despite the paucity of empirical guidance for policy decisions, many school systems in North America and Europe are eliminating recess from the curriculum or replacing it with teacher-guided physical education, based on the belief that it detracts from school's primary mission: teaching the 3 R's. Although the intention of improving reading, writing, and arithmetic are commendable, it seems that education policy should be based on scientific findings. The current policy of minimizing recess is devoid of empirical justification. What data do exist support the beneficial role of recess in school. Additionally, educational experiences for children growing up in diverse societies should afford opportunities for children to interact with a variety of peers, such as opportunities for cross-gender and cross-ethnic interaction.

Theories on Benefits of Recess

Much of what goes on during preschool and primary school recess periods can be considered "play"; thus, the view that play has immediate benefits can be considered "metamorphic" (Bateson, 1976). In this view, play is not considered an imperfect or incomplete version of some adult behavior. Play has benefits for the unique niche of childhood. Research is now providing evidence, however, for the beneficial effects of recess on children's school performance.

Massed vs. Distributed Practice

Recess is beneficial for children in schools because it provides a break from sustained periods of work. Research conducted many years ago (e.g., Ebinghaus, 1885/1913; James, 1901) indicated that children and adults learn better and more quickly when their efforts on a task are distributed (i.e., when they are given breaks during tasks) rather than concentrated (i.e., when effort is grouped into longer periods) (Hunter, 1929). The positive effects of distributed effort have specifically addressed the ways in which children learn numerous school-like tasks, such as native and foreign language vocabulary, recall from text, and math facts (see Dempster, 1988, for a review). These laboratory studies yielded reliable and robust effects, documenting the efficacy of task spacing on learning.

Classroom studies have been less frequently undertaken, and generally have produced less impressive results. Factors associated with the nature of the task (e.g., simple vs. complex) seemed to mediate effects of distributed practice on classroom learning (Dempster, 1988). When the nature of the criterion variable is changed from material learned to attention to the task at hand, however, the results of the classroom research match those of the laboratory (Dempster, 1988). Spacing of tasks may make tasks less boring and correspondingly facilitate attention. Attention to task, in turn, may be important to subsequent learning (Dempster, 1988; Eder & Felmlee, 1984)....

Developmental Differences in Cognitive Efficiency and Its Relation to Recess

The facilitative effects of distributed practice should be greater for younger than for older children (Pellegrini & Bjorklund, in press). Young children do not process most information as effectively as older children. The immaturity of their nervous systems and their lack of experiences render them unable to perform higher level cognitive tasks with the same efficiency as older children and adults and directly influences their educability. As a result, young children are especially susceptible to the effects of interference (see Dempster, 1992, 1993) and should experience the greatest gains from breaks between focused intellectual activities, which recess provides....

From Theory to Research Evidence

A number of field experiments that examined directly the role of recess in maximizing children's attention to school tasks have been conducted by the authors. These studies involved manipulating spacing in terms of the time before recess (i.e., recess deprivation) and examining the effects on children's attention to school tasks; attention in these studies was defined as students looking at their teachers or their written work on their desks. The contention here was that recess provides the needed spacing during cognitively demanding tasks, thus facilitating children's attention to subsequent classroom tasks. In one preliminary study, Pellegrini and Davis (1993) found that 3rd-graders were less attentive to a school task during a long delay, or confinement, compared to a short delay before recess. Within each of the recess conditions, children's attention decreased as a function of time. Further, children's social interaction and physical activity at recess were positively and significantly related to their task attention after recess.

Pellegrini and colleagues conducted a series of experiments with a larger and more diverse sample and standardized attention tasks (Pellegrini et al., 1995). In the first experiment in this work, kindergarten, grade 2, and grade 4 children were studied. As in the earlier work, their recess period was experimentally manipulated such that two days per week they had recess outdoors 30 minutes later (i.e., the long confinement condition) than on another two days (i.e., the short confinement condition). For the latter two grades, children's before- and after-recess seat work was also manipulated. On alternate days they were read male- or female-preferred stories by their teachers. Their attention to the task, defined as in Pellegrini and Davis (1993), was coded for both periods.

As in the Pellegrini and Davis (1993) experiment, children were significantly less attentive during the long confinement period than the short period. In each of the three grades, children were significantly more attentive after recess than before, and the effects of recess deprivation were significantly greater for the younger than for the older children. That is, the longer confinement period was more detrimental to attention for the younger than for the older children. Additionally, older children were significantly less attentive to opposite gender stories. In two other replication experiments with second- and fourth-grade children, these results support the distributed effort claims (Dempster, 1988) that children's attention to a task is maximized when their efforts are spaced, in this case with recess separating task effort. Unlike the Pellegrini and Davis (1993) study, however, none of these experiments reported significant relations between either social interaction or physical activity at recess and subsequent attention to seat work following recess. Data from these experiments indicate that a break is what is important, not the physical activity or the social interaction....

Conclusion

In regard to the role of recess in children's development and education, the empirical record is unequivocal on the immediate benefits of recess. Children seem to "need" recess to the extent that the intensity of their physical play at recess increases when they are deprived of recess (Pellegrini et al., 1995; Smith & Hagan, 1980). Furthermore, children's attention to school tasks wanes as they are expected to work for sustained periods. Recess seems to provide a break that maximizes subsequent attention to school work.

Play may thus have beneficial consequences that are unique to childhood. Play helps juveniles adapt to the specific demand of childhood, as Bjorklund and Green (1992) have argued. In the sense, play seems to serve a "metamorphic function" (Bateson, 1976): Its immediate benefits are clear but its long-term benefits are not readily apparent.

There is still much to know about recess and play in school. For starters, researchers need to study systematically the role of different recess regimens: What is the optimum recess duration? How does this vary with children's age? How many recess periods per day are needed? What changes in the ways the playground is organized can have effects on children's play behaviors?

Another, perhaps more important, dimension of the recess period is the opportunities for social interaction. As most authors in this theme issue state, recess is one of the few school experiences where children can interact with peers on their own terms. Thus, the playground could possibly provide a "classroom for social competence." It enables children to interact with the peers with whom they usually interact as well as those with whom they might interact. Social interaction with a variety of peers certainly is an important aspect of children's education experience, if we still contend that a primary purpose of education is to develop a democratic and inclusive orientation in children.

Merely providing recess time, of course, will not accomplish these goals. As papers by Boulton and Hartle illustrate, children's social interaction habits are very stable: They choose to interact with others like themselves. Specific education interventions, of the sort suggested by Hartle and Barbour, are certainly a starting point.

Although there are many benefits of recess and the playground, playgrounds are also a primary venue of aggression, as illustrated by McNeilly-Choque and colleagues. Without proper supervision and planning, playgrounds are often feared by children because they are bullied by their classmates (Pellegrini & Smith, 1993).

Recess is an important aspect of children's education experience, in the broad sense. What is known empirically about recess, however, is very limited. It is the authors' contention that school policy should be guided by theory-driven empirical research.

Playtime Is Cancelled

At first, Julie Moorhead, of Algiers, Louisiana, was unfazed when her four children came home from elementary school complaining that they weren't having recess. "Give it a couple of days," she reassured her kids. "Things may be disorganized because it's the first week."

But Moorhead soon received a bulletin from the principal of Alice M. Harte Elementary School explaining that recess had, in fact, been cut to comply with a state mandate increasing the amount of time students must spend on academics. "No time for recess?" asked Moorhead, a former teacher. "How could this happen?"

Parents across the country have been similarly shocked by the elimination of what many fondly remember as the best part of the school day. In the scramble to improve standardized test scores, as many as 40 percent of the country's school districts are considering doing away with recess or modifying it in some way, according to an informal poll conducted by the American Association for the Child's Right to Play.

And the no-recess movement may be more than just a passing educational fad. In Atlanta, which scrapped recess in all of its 69 elementary schools more than a decade ago, at least two elementary schools have been constructed without playgrounds, and a third is on the drawing board. This makes it unlikely, if not impossible, for these schools to one day reverse their policies. "It's sad," says Rhonda Clements, Ed.D., author of *The Case for Elementary School Recess* (American Press, 1999). "An entire generation may never experience games like jump rope, hopscotch, or freeze tag."

Until recently, recess was almost the fourth "R" in American education. In colonial times, educators had a "religious duty" to give students breaks from their studies, and healthy play in fresh air was considered an essential counterbalance to the confinement of one-room schoolhouses. Recess periods were much longer—a typical lunch break might last 90 minutes—as children played in nearby woods or meadows.

By the turn of the 20th century, most American schools held 15- to 20-minute morning and afternoon recesses in addition to hour-long lunch breaks. Until the 1950s, three daily recesses were still the norm; then, as fine arts, physical education, and other specialty areas were added to the curriculum, the afternoon break began to disappear. Since the 1970s, the lunch hour has been cut in half, and the length of the periods devoted to traditional academics has increased.

All Work and No Play

In the 1990s, American students' poor showings on standardized tests have spawned a back-to-basics movement that regards recess as frivolous. Although concerns such as school-yard safety, liability for injuries, and teachers' unwillingness to supervise are sometimes cited, the overwhelming reason for the decline of recess is the intense pressure on schools to improve test scores.

"We're here to educate children," says Mike Jordan, principal of Magellan Charter School, a middle school with no formal recess, in Raleigh, North Carolina. "To take thirty minutes out of our instructional day just to let kids play doesn't sound good—to parents, to legislators, or to taxpayers."

Child-development experts, who are unanimous in their belief that play is an essential part of a child's day, don't have much say in the matter. Nor do kids themselves. Certainly no one asked Julie Moorhead's son David, 7, an active first-grader who began returning home from first grade every afternoon with a headache, or Nicholas Maxwell, 10, a straight-A fourth-grader at Ashworth Elementary, in Arlington, Texas, who often complains of being exhausted after a seven-hour recessless school day followed by two hours of homework.

But such a rigid emphasis on work, not play, along with the force-feeding of academics, could backfire, experts say, creating kids who despise school and misbehave more often. After all, if adults need coffee breaks and lunch hours, don't kids as well? "It really isn't normal for children to sit quietly in chairs all day," says Jane McGrath, M.D., school health officer for the state of New Mexico.

There is also growing evidence that the dramatic increase over the past two decades of children with attention disorders may be related to the decline in physical activity. "We have an epidemic of attention-deficit disorder (ADD) in this country," says educational psychologist Jane M. Healy, Ph.D., author of *Failure to Connect* (Simon and Schuster, 1999). "This is partly because children lack the physical and emotional outlets found in active play."

Keli Strain, of Arlington, doesn't believe that lack of recess caused her 10-year-old son Benjamin's ADD, but she's convinced that his sitting for seven hours a day without a play break has made it worse. In fact, Benjamin's ADD was not diagnosed until he was in the fourth grade, when his class suspended recess in order to buckle down for state standardized tests.

Even children who do not have attention disorders will struggle to stay focused when they go for long periods without a break, says Olga Jarrett, Ph.D., an assistant professor of early-childhood education at Georgia State University, in Atlanta. Dr. Jarrett and her colleagues found that kids who have regular recesses were less fidgety and spent more time "on task"—teacher-speak for being engaged in schoolwork—than kids who did not. "There's this misguided idea that you can just pump information into kids all day," says Dr. Jarrett. "Learning doesn't happen that way."

Let's Get Physical

In many ways, however, child burnout is the least of it. In an era when childhood obesity is at an all-time high, and many kids are enrolled in before- and after-school day-care programs (which are usually indoors and highly structured), or return home from school only to spend several latchkey hours in front of the TV or computer, Dr. McGrath believes that outdoor free play at school is more essential than ever.

Indeed, last year, the National Association for Sport and Physical Education (NASPE) released its first-ever guidelines for elementary-school children, recommending that young kids be physically active for at least one hour a day. No-recess proponents often argue that kids move round in the classroom during group work or as they change classes. But a brief episode of controlled movement, such as "walking quietly to the library, finger on your lips, does not constitute physical activity," says Judy Young, NASPE's executive director.

Similarly, some school administrators maintain that their students don't need recess because they run around in physical-education [PE] class. But even Young, whose Virginia-based group represents over 25,000 PE teachers, coaches, and sports professionals, rejects that argument. PE is to recess, she says, what phonics drills are to reading comic books at home: The former teaches a structured curriculum, while the latter gives kids a chance to practice what they've learned in ways of their own choosing.

The views of children themselves highlight another critical difference between recess and PE. In another study by Dr. Jarrett and Darlene Maxwell, of Mercer University, in Atlanta, fourth-graders said they needed a time in the day when they had choices about what to play and whom to play with. Or as Elisabeth Bayer, a freckle-faced 8-year-old, puts it, "In PE, you have to do certain things. At recess, you do whatever you want."

New research suggests that 10- to 15-minute bursts of varied activity throughout the day aren't just good for the body, they actually stimulate brain development, especially in children. Other studies suggest that aerobic exercise pumps oxygen into the brain, thereby improving alertness and memory. "We are about to see an upsurge in research about the connection between motor development and brain development that will make recess critics look even more foolish," says Dr. Healy, who also notes that in countries where students academically outperform those in the United States, recess has not been sacrificed. Even the highly rigorous Japanese system offers more outdoor recess time than the average American elementary school.

Playing to Learn

Anyone harboring doubts that play spurs learning need only listen in on a group of kindergartners engrossed in sculpting a hamlet out of pea gravel during morning recess at St. George School, in Baton Rouge. "We're reptiles, and this is our reptile village," says Bradley, 6, who will not formally study cold-blooded vertebrates for at least another two years. "This is our bridge, this is our lake, and these are our houses. We're snakes and alligators and Tasmanian devils."

"Sometimes we build a volcano and turn it into a castle," adds Paige, 5, "or pretend we're unicorns."

As important as the flights of imagination gleaned from this quarter hour of play is the socialization taking place. During the freedom of recess, children figure out how to get along. Bradley and the other kids settle a dispute over who will be the reptilian king. Paige and two other girls agree on a game without interference from their teacher, who observes from a distance.

"Recess is sort of like the sandlot of life before kids go to the major leagues," says June Lange Prewitt, state developer for the Parkway School District, in Missouri. "It allows them to develop emotional and social skills. To learn to say, 'Can I play?' is an important skill. And so is being able to handle the answer when it's no."

Ironically, kids' difficulty in getting along has been the reason for some principals' decisions to revoke recess. As many of us remember, recess is often the time when bullies hold sway. Annette Maiden, principal of Ames Elementary School, in Marrero, Louisiana, declined to talk to *Parents* but told *The Times-Picayune*, a New Orleans newspaper, that the number of fights and disciplinary infractions of her school has dropped by 80 to 90 percent since recess was cut. Many of Philadelphia's 176 public elementary schools have implemented "socialized recess" periods—a kind of cross between free play and PE class—to reduce bullying and another playground violence.

Yet most experts believe that such statistics only point to a greater, rather than lesser, need for recess. Children who have little free play lose not only a positive outlet for excess energy but also, gradually, the ability to entertain themselves. "In my neighborhood, kids don't know how to go out and organize a game," says NASPE's Young. "A fight breaks out in five minutes. We referee every minute of our children's lives, and then we wonder why they're bored and out of control when they reach adolescence."

Of course, few educators disagree with the myriad benefits of recess. But, they ask defensively, how can they fulfill all their responsibilities to the children in a six- or seven-hour day? Although the length of the American school day has changed very little in 30 years, much has been squeezed into the curriculum, including mandated courses in everything from self-esteem and sex education to character building and conflict resolution.

"Because so much has been heaped on the curriculum, teachers struggle to fit everything in," says Judy Linderman, principal of Ashworth Elementary, in Arlington. "We're constantly forced to choose what's more or less important." Linderman has left the recess decision up to the discretion of individual teachers, but recent complaints from parents whose kids miss recess have prompted her to reexamine the policy.

There has been no research to determine whether kids without recess perform better academically, but past studies have shown a link between higher scores and more time spent on schoolwork. One solution might be to lengthen the school day or year to allow time for play and rest as well as for the teaching of core courses and enrichment programs. Proponents cite the success of some

European schools with extended days and add that the change would relieve many working parents of the burden of securing child care during latchkey hours, as well as cut down on crime by unsupervised minors. Opponents include teachers' groups, which worry that longer hours will mean additional responsibilities without commensurate pay.

In the meantime, a counterrevolution is afoot. The National Education Association and the National Association of Elementary School Principals have adopted resolutions encouraging members to preserve recess at their schools. Private and parochial schools, which have traditionally put a high premium on recess, have strengthened that commitment by extending free-play periods, according to Rhonda Clements.

And some districts and individual schools have actually retracted their no-recess policies. Last year, the superintendent of elementary schools in the Evanston and Skokie, Illinois, district reinstated recess within months of its elimination because of parental outrage. Recess has also returned to Alice M. Harte Elementary—thanks to Julie Moorhead and other parents who believe so strongly in its value that they have volunteered to supervise kids during lunch and for one 15-minute recess per day. Student conduct has since improved in the cafeteria and on the playground, says principal Stacy Rockwood, because kids don't want to waste valuable free time misbehaving.

Moorhead fondly recalls the day students first got their freedom back. "One little boy was standing in line as we were preparing to leave the cafeteria," she says. 'I know what we have to do now,' he said in a monotone. 'Walk in a straight line back to class.' I looked at him and said, 'No, we don't. It's recess now. Go play.'

"I wish I'd had a video camera," Moorhead says, laughing. "The kids were whooping and running around the playground. You'd have thought I'd given them a million bucks. In fact, I gave them something better."

POSTSCRIPT

Should Recess Be Included in a School Day?

The daily schedule of young children in the twenty-first century is quite different from a that of a child a century ago. Children living then had ample opportunities to spend time outside. There were no school buses, so children walked to and from school. After-school hours might have been spent playing outside or helping the family with outside chores. There were no televisions or video games to keep children occupied indoors and safety issues related to drive-by shootings or high-traffic areas were of little or no concern. In short, children in the past had numerous opportunities to exercise large muscles and to be outside playing and socializing with peers. School children in the 2000s live a much different lifestyle. They may ride a school bus or be driven to school. After school they often come home to an empty house and are told to stay inside until an adult arrives home. The weekends may be spent grocery shopping or visiting a noncustodial parent. Free-choice activities may include indoor pastimes such as e-mailing friends or watching television. Children who live in a warm climate have more casual opportunities to be outside, but just because it is warm does not mean that it is safe for children to be out or that they will receive the proper supervision. Stray dogs, gangs of older children, and unsafe neighborhoods make being outside a dangerous activity for many children.

A recent survey by the consulting firm William M. Mercer found that 35 percent of executives say that play is included in their work environment or is included as a part of their company's mission statement. Many businesses are offering opportunities during the workday to participate in recreation. It has been found that the right kind of play will result in a marked improvement in the ability of employees to be creative, innovative, and productive. If this is the philosophy taken by many workplaces, why would the philosophy be so different in some schools? Would adults tolerate a day with no breaks, other than the 20 minutes allowed for lunch? How can the attitude in workplace environments be transferred to schools for young children? Should children receive the same types of breaks in a learning environment?

Children today are heavier than ever before, and the amount of cardiovascular activity that they receive on a daily basis is very low. Physical activity is necessary for good health, and recess is one option for implementing daily exercise. Advocates of recess support the healthy body–healthy mind philosophy. They also ask educators to use the same judgment one would use when making a medical decision. What does the research support? There is evidence to support both sides of this issue. Sound educational decisions should be made based on sound empirical evidence. What is most important to consider is what is best for children.

Suggested Readings

Chmelynski, C., "Is Recess Needed?" *Education Digest* (vol. 64, no. 4, 1998).

Jarrett, O. S. and Maxwell, D. M., "What Research Says About the Need for Recess," in Clements, R., ed., *Elementary School Recess: Selected Readings, Games, and Activities for Teachers and Parents* (American Press, 2000).

Johnson, D., "Many Schools Putting an End to Child's Play," *The New York Times* (April 7, 1998).

Pelligrini, A. D. and Smith, P., "School Recess: Implications for Educational Development," *Review of Educational Research* (vol. 63, no. 1, 1993).

Schultz, K., "On the Elimination of Recess," *Education Week* (vol. 17, 1997).

ISSUE 14

Are Multi-Age Programs Best for Young Children?

YES: Wendy C. Kasten, from "Why Does Multiage Make Sense? Compelling Arguments for Educational Change," *Primary Voices K–6* (April 1998)

NO: DeWayne A. Mason and Roland W. Doepner III, from "Principals' Views of Combination Classes," *The Journal of Educational Research* (January/February 1998)

ISSUE SUMMARY

YES: Associate professor Wendy C. Kasten argues that multi-age classrooms are stable and effective learning environments for children. Kasten asserts that students benefit from the consistency and close relationship with their fellow students and their teacher.

NO: Assistant professor DeWayne A. Mason and professor Roland W. Doepner III contend that multi-age classes contain inferior curriculum to accommodate the lower-level students in the class.

In order to explore this issue it is important to acknowledge the different terms used to signify the class groupings that occur in primary school settings. Some of the terms include: *single age groups, vertically grouped, mixed-age groups, multi-grade, multi-age, combination classes, split grades, continuous progress, non-graded,* and *ungraded.* Many students in the United States today have great-grandparents who attended a one-room schoolhouse. The teacher in this type of school accommodated the curriculum to meet the needs of all of the children in the community who attended. It was not uncommon to have children from ages five through thirteen in the same class. Some one-room schools still exist today in isolated areas in both the United States and Canada. Over the years, as the population in cities and suburbs grew, school administrators changed the classsrooms from consisting of multi-age groups to consisting of single-age groups. Administrators also became more knowledgeable about the marked differences that occur among children and worked to meet all students' needs. Parents became comfortable with the model of all children in the same class being approximately the same age. Teachers came to expect the same level of performance from all students in the class. Studies done in the 1960s and 1970s on the benefits of multi-age groupings were inconclusive and found that the levels of academic achievement were the same in single-age and multi-age classrooms. It has been reported that some teachers, parents, and children believe that multi-age classrooms are more supportive for learning. Beliefs on appropriate learning settings have affected school building design. Elementary schools built in the late 1960s and early 1970s reflected the thinking of many that multi-age classrooms were superior. Schools were built with large pod areas consisting of moveable walls that teachers could adjust to accommodate different-sized groups of students. For some teachers and children the setting worked and allowed for small learning groups that met the needs of individual learners. For other teachers and students the large, open-space classrooms, often accommodating up to 100 students, were overwhelming. Many of these schools today have some of the large pods divided into self-contained classrooms with fixed walls that keep out the noise of adjacent classrooms. Many schools built in the 1980s and 1990s were built with only self-contained classrooms. In some, two of the self-contained classrooms could be modified by removing a connecting wall, thus creating a shared multi-purpose space. This shared space would still allow teachers and students in one room to interact with teachers and students in the next room if necessary.

School administrators in some areas are looking to multi-age programs to solve class size issues. By mixing children of two or three different grade levels in one or more classrooms, class size can be adjusted without concern for keeping children in a single grade. Are multi-age programs the answer for school districts struggling with a sudden increase or decrease in enrollment?

In the following selections, Wendy C. Kasten supports multi-age programs and argues that it is important for students to develop relationships with teachers who can be supportive to them as they move through the elementary school years. She is a strong proponent of the comfort zone that she asserts is created by a consistent and stable environment. DeWayne A. Mason and Roland W. Doepner III contend that multi-age primary programs are not indicative of a progressive curriculum or innovative instructional practices and in fact may contain inferior curriculum.

Wendy C. Kasten

Why Does Multiage Make Sense? Compelling Arguments for Educational Change

O nce upon a time, according to legend, there was an innkeeper and a cruel robber named Procrustes. Travelers who sought shelter at his home were shocked to find that they would be tied to an iron bedstead for the night; furthermore, if the traveler was shorter than the bed, Procrustes would stretch him or her to fit, and if the traveler was longer than the bed, then limbs were chopped off to make the traveler fit. Thus, Procrustes shaped his guests until they were the same size, albeit dead in some cases (Goodlad & Anderson, 1987).

The structure of education as most of us have known it—formed in grade-level, age-segregated structures—not only is geared to and supportive of mediocrity and averages, it was also designed to serve the convenience of the administrators and the economy instead of the educational needs of children. Grade levels were not an invention designed to suit the needs of children; they were instituted to emulate the factory model and to be cheaper, more efficient, and easier to monitor for administrators.

Isn't it embarrassing that we still group kids in schools like cars in factories?

The industrial model is alive and well in twentieth-century school. We call those individuals who head up school districts *superintendents* as they were first called in factories. We have kids proceed through the assembly line of school we call *grade levels*. Our quality control checks for standards and uniformity are called promotion (and nonpromotion). We act upon our children along the way (as cars or refrigerators are assembled uniformly) with grade-level curriculum. We further check their place along the continuum of the finished product with standardized tests (which of course check the teachers, too) and, if we think there are any problems, we give children more tests and try to fix them. In this model, a proportion of failure is expected, and discards are made (schools call it *dropping out*).

What's wrong with this picture?

First of all, we educate children; we don't assemble combustion engines. Children are more complex, and the solutions to educating them are neither easy nor tidy. Second, our goal is to educate *everyone*, without discards. Our free public education system is predicated on the notions of equal opportunity, access, and an education that enables citizens to become literate, informed, and critically aware. Third, we know a great deal more about how to educate children than did our nineteenth-century predecessors (who were doing the best they could for the times), and yet we often fail to implement what we know.

We know there's no logic or reason for grouping students in age-segregated ways as we have been doing for the last 150 years. In the remainder of this article, I hope to present arguments that are both practically and theoretically based in order to illuminate the logic of educating students in mixed-aged groups that we call *multiage*. I'll speak to the features and attributes I have come to learn about educating children in the multiage milieu, including the academic and social advantages, the more affective potentials, and the impact on both promotion and long-term educational goals. Unlike the travelers to Procrustes' inn, I will demonstrate in theory how multiage education can serve the spectrum of diverse travelers who journey through our schools with opportunities for all to succeed; education as most of us have known it does not have a great track record for dealing with *everyone*. . . .

Let me begin by presenting to you why I believe multiage makes sense.

Long-Term Goals

The first consideration of why multiage makes sense is our goals. Before we can discuss how to educate children, we must first ask ourselves, as individuals and as communities, what do we want for our children? What are our goals for K–12 education? What outcomes do we desire?

I have asked these questions of many audiences over the years. Responses are remarkably similar, both in the United States and in other countries. Parents and teachers want their children to become good and happy adults who will earn a productive living, communicate effectively, be good citizens in their community, be critical consumers, make responsible decisions, and go on learning for their entire lives. Goodlad's survey of over 27,000 teachers, students, and parents concluded that people want more than just intellectual development from their schools; they also want attention to social, vocational, and personal emphases. They want school to be a nurturing, caring place (Goodlad, 1984).

How, then, does school contribute to these goals? We would hope that school would, in fact, help meet these goals both in the curriculum and in the learning environment it provides. In considering what goes into the school day, these long-term goals should be kept in mind. We want these things for our children—*all* our children—and all decisions henceforth about schools should help further these goals.

I like Eisner's wise words when he speaks of school goals. He says that a "culture or a school that dulls the senses by neglect or disrespect thwarts the development of human aptitude and undermines the possibilities of the human mind" (1994, p. 29). By aptitude, we aren't just talking about the "basics" here, or the raising of test scores toward some mythical view of excellence; as Howard

Gardner points out, the pursuit of basic skills may sometimes be counterproductive, and when we "cover the curriculum" we may be "undermining more crucial educational goals" (1991, p. 187). In the schools of today and tomorrow, we are looking for more than basics. We want students to be nurtured toward their own potentials, and we'd like this for all of our children, not just those with economic resources and supportive families. We want students to be respected as well as taught, and leave school understanding their own strengths and the confidence to pursue them in life. All the remarks in this article, as well as those that follow, should be viewed in terms of long-range goals and expectations for the students we teach.

Affective Benefits

Another argument for multiage education concerns some affective parts of schooling. Imagine for a moment that a youngster in an elementary school classroom changes teachers for different subjects (a practice called departmentalization, which focuses on disciplines more than on children). If this student has different teachers for art, music, physical education, and computers (and perhaps speech or special education or ESL), then how many teachers does the child have during one school year? Let's imagine further that this scene could change each year, starting with a new classroom teacher or homeroom teacher —how many teachers has such a student had by the end of his or her elementary school years?

If this student has anywhere from 6 to 40 teachers during the elementary school years, who will be the one person he or she remembers? Who will be the most responsible for that student? Who will notice when things are going wrong? Who will take action and find out what's wrong? Why do we play "musical chairs" with teachers? Would anyone think it was a good idea to change *parents* every year? Where's the continuity? Stability? Longevity? Predictability? Can we pretend all our children have these needs met at home?

One aspect of the multiage environment that I have come to understand is the comfort zone which is created by an environment which is consistent (and hopefully good), predictable, accepting, and stable. The benefits here aren't just for the students, by the way. Parents and teachers benefit from this as well.

Students benefit from the stable environment when teachers know them well. Their needs are better met. School isn't a scary place with all sorts of very new things to get used to each year. Starting a new year or semester does not produce anxiety. Some researchers and theorists don't take these features lightly. Their belief is that children learn and perform better when that work is part of a long-term relationship. Even the human brain, it is believed, works better in situations when the milieu is safe and accepting (Bruner, 1979; Forester & Reinhard, 1989; Hart, 1979; Ridgway & Lawton, 1965; Wakefield, 1979). In a multiage classroom, children report that starting a new year is a lot like going home.

Parents similarly report that vacations between school years or terms are not fraught with anxiety. They have noted the lack of concern they generally experience as new school years approach and children worry about who will be their teacher and who will be in their class. In the case of the multiage environment, these worries occur far less often. Sometimes, there's no big adjustment or change, and the transition from one term to another is seamless.

Teachers remark on the same feature when they realize a particularly smooth beginning to a new year. Many of the class members already know expectations and routines, and many need little or no assessment in order to determine their strengths. Discipline issues are also eased. One teacher described how, with students she's taught for a year or more, she need only look at them if they are off-task or misbehaving. The relationship that has been built over time with the child and the family pays off in everyday classroom life.

Perhaps one 11-year-old said it best when he was interviewed after four years in a multiage classroom and after one subsequent year in a fourth grade. "We were more like a family," he reported. "We knew each other very well. My new class (fourth grade) is okay. I like it a little, but it is not the same. If you are in a class for a long time, you will not want to leave either."

Academic and Social Benefits

A few years ago when I co-authored *The Multiage Classroom: A Family of Learners* (Kasten & Clarke, 1993), I thought of these two areas as separate and wrote about them that way. Since then, and much reading later, I have discovered that many psychologists believe that academic or cognitive development and social development are as interrelated as the reading/writing connection. In other words, they are two sides of the same coin. Social development impacts academic development, and academic or cognitive development impacts social development, in a somewhat spiraling fashion.

The implication is that the diverse multiage environment likely is more conducive to learning in several different ways, whether the difference is academic or social in origin. These benefits include interaction, role theory, and modeling; cross-aged tutoring; a decrease in aggressive and competitive behaviors; enhanced social development and self-esteem; birth order in the classroom; and flexibility with promotion issues. Each of these will be briefly discussed.

Interaction, Role Theory, and Modeling

In a multiage classroom, the interaction among students is especially valuable for a number of reasons. First of all, role theory posits that when someone is placed in a role (such as teacher or tutor), the role is highly influential in shaping his or her behavior. Individuals have the tendency to live up to the expectations that others have of them. Second, theorists such as Vygotsky talk about the benefit of spurring learning and development as a result of problem-solving opportunities that occur between learners of different abilities (the zone of proximal development). Learners benefit from each other through interactions in ways that cannot be accomplished alone (Vygotsky, 1978). Others have added to this idea by emphasizing the value of multiple perspectives and models in learning, even when the models aren't necessarily all good ones. The mere presence of perspectives caused by interaction is a powerful learning catalyst (Bornstein & Bruner, 1989; DiLorenzo & Salter, 1965; Piaget 1928, 1977; Trudge & Rogoff, 1989; Webb, 1977; Wood, 1988). This type of learning is an inherent feature of multiage classrooms....

Cross-Aged Tutoring

While role theory suggests that people live up to the expectations others have of them, cross-aged tutoring puts some of this into practice. When students of differing ages and abilities help each other in either incidental or systematic ways, the tutor benefits from the self-esteem and confidence that the new role engenders. There are other equally important advantages. The act of teaching is the most powerful learning tool known. Most teachers have learned this feature of their job, as they discover their own new competence in areas they are required to teach. The same holds true for students of all ages. The act of teaching not only requires synthesis but also prompts one to express these new understandings. The act of translating one's understanding into language is intellectually demanding. One must understand the concept, break it down into parts, describe it with words, and gauge the reaction of the recipient. The sum total of all this is deeper, unforgettable understanding (Drake, 1993; Hedin, 1987; Juel, 1991; Leland & Fitzpatrick, 1994; Lougee, Grueneich, & Hartup, 1977; Teale & Labbo, 1990; Valletutti & Dummett, 1992).

In multiage classrooms, cross-aged tutoring happens both incidentally and explicitly. Sometimes it may be contrived when the teacher assigns an experienced student to help a less experienced one, but more typically these interactions are spontaneous and unplanned, and they last only a few minutes. Parents will worry that their children who are more advanced learners will be used or exploited as teachers in a multiage setting. These concepts need to be discussed with parents to alleviate their concerns and help them understand that the act of teaching is a wonderful and powerful gift. Older students or more advanced ones are not "used" or "exploited" in multiage settings. The milieu becomes one where helping others is simply the normal way of operating among all the students....

Decrease in Aggressive and Competitive Behaviors

One more surprising aspect of the multiage or mixed-aged setting is that individuals in these environments have been observed exhibiting fewer aggressive and competitive behaviors; instead, individuals in these mixed-aged settings show more caring, nurturing, and altruistic behaviors. I consider this a serious effect of a multiage environment because it's one that cannot be duplicated in settings where children are segregated by age. This difference may explain why some principals have observed a decrease in discipline referrals from their multiage classes in comparison with their traditionally grouped ones.

Pratt (1986) discusses the historical perspective of human societies (and other primate societies as well) that socialize their young in mixed-aged groups, generally spanning clusters of about three years. In fact, he contends that all hunting and gathering societies that have survived until the twentieth century have socialized their children in this manner. Outside of school, most of society today clusters youth in similar ways. Camps, sports, recreational programs, scouting, dance, martial arts, and many more activities tend to group children in clusters (or if they do not, it is due to a recent change that has attempted to match school structures). Organizing children in clusters of ages is natural as well as being effective and is the most common human grouping plan, except in schools. The benefits have been noted by others as well (Goldman, 1981; Wolfson, 1967). Some teachers have simply stated that they believe children in multiage classes are just kinder to each other.

Social Development and Self-Esteem

This feature of multiage classrooms may result in part from the characteristics discussed above, including the decrease in competitive behaviors, the use of role theory, and modeling. However, even in comparative studies where academic benefits may or may not have shown up, there have been effects in increased self-esteem, confidence, and positive attitudes among students in multiage settings. For districts beginning multiage classes, this would be useful data to collect. Many instruments exist that address self-esteem. If local parents feel similarly to those in Goodlad's extensive 1984 study who want school to attend to issues beyond academics, then this feature becomes an important one and would be well worth documenting through assessments (Buffie, 1963; Connell, 1987; Goldman, 1981; Hammack, 1974; Piaget, 1977; Pratt 1986; Schrankler, 1976; Wolfson, 1967).

Birth Order in the Classroom

Has anyone ever met a student who, by luck of the draw, was younger and less mature than age-mates in his or her kindergarten class? This student may have been chronologically and developmentally younger than other students in the class because of his or her birth date, or just because he or she was a late bloomer. In these cases, even particularly bright children continue to be at the young end of the developmental continuum as they proceed through schooling. They remain less advanced, less mature, and less confident in their abilities than others in their group. The important question in this instance is, if this child proceeds through school always in the same relatively low position as compared to classmates, how does this effect an overall sense of self? Aspirations? Self-esteem?

I have met many such children, but one in particular comes to mind. He was added to a multiage classroom as a kindergarten-aged student when his class was a K–2, and he had turned five only three days before school began. In addition, this youngster had not attended any preschool, had illiterate parents, and was generally developmentally young. This little boy lacked the social skills most five-year-olds possess. In fact, he was the most immature student I had ever met in any kindergarten. In such a situation, no matter how much or how little progress this student makes during his first year of school, when the subsequent school year begins, he will be older and more experienced about many things than next year's new students. He will, after one year in school, have a new opportunity which he'd likely never have if he were in a grade-level classroom. He may become a mentor to someone else, and, in doing so, he will see how much progress he has made instead of always being the youngest.

In real life, birth order affects parenting and families more than we'd like to believe (Zajonc & Marcus, 1975). We don't control that. But in school, we can manipulate this effect so that everyone can be the younger, middle, and older child at different times, and there are advantages to each. The advantage to being the younger is the help and nurturing from older members of the group. The middle members have opportunities to teach others and still be helped as needed, and to see themselves along the natural continuum of development. The most mature members, however, have the best advantages. One teacher who himself grew up in a multiage situation enjoyed getting help from the older or more advanced learners when he was the little guy. But his favorite time was when he was one of the "big kids." He says he will never forget the feeling he got when he realized he'd first taught something to someone else. Those opportunities to teach and nurture, he believes, helped shape him as a human being and as a future teacher. I have heard stories similar to this from graduates of one-room schoolhouses. Without a doubt, being the eldest is the most prestigious and coveted place to be. Everyone looks forward to getting their turn to be there eventually. In a multiage setting, we can give each learner opportunities to experience the varied benefits of being in different relative positions in classroom birth order. This way, not only do students benefit from each other, but also they will not be adversely affected by being in *any* single position for their entire school career.

Promotion and Retention

Most educators know the dismal statistics on retaining students in order to re-peat a grade level (Goodlad, 1966; Goodlad & Anderson, 1987). Retention simply does not remedy whatever is wrong in most cases. Repeating the same experi-ences doesn't make anything better; children don't develop in predictable or tidy ways. The combination is nasty when decisions have to be made about placement for a child at the end of only one year. This issue, more than any other, caused educators to take a serious look at multiage structures.

In schools where multiage settings exist, either as one alternative or com-pletely, decisions about the promotion of a student can be flexible. Sometimes students begin a primary unit and the expectation is communicated to parents that students graduate from a primary unit to an intermediate one when they are *developmentally* prepared rather than by calendar attendance. Another alter-native is that students can be moved in the middle of a term. These decisions are never made lightly, of course (as makes sense). Parents, teachers, children, administrators, and other professionals make these decisions jointly after con-ferring about the best educational environment for the individual child.

Summary

I believe that the evidence which suggests that a multiage environment can be superior to one of age-segregated settings is overwhelmingly positive. However, several cautions need to be noted. First of all, the structure alone does not make for a better environment. Considerations of curriculum, teacher quality, sense of community, and compatibility between teacher and student all need to be carefully weighed. . . .

Second, the multiage model should not be forced upon teachers, especially not without adequate resources or staff development. Teachers are professionals. Different teachers have different strengths to offer their students. Multiage teaching is one way to serve students better, but teachers may have particular strengths in curriculum or management that still make them excellent teachers, whether or not they choose to use multiage classrooms.

Third, the change to multiage cannot be made smoothly in any situation without adequate education and communication with parents and the community. Grade leveling, however illogical, is currently a deeply ingrained tradition and cannot be changed easily without systematic reeducation. Most of us can track the years of our childhood or those of others by the grade level membership at the time. Traditions, good or bad, die hard.

The most important consideration then, is, what do we want for our children? What are our goals for K–12 education? In light of these discussions, considerations about implementing multiage classes need to be addressed. The arguments that support multiage education are compelling ones.

DeWayne A. Mason and
Roland W. Doepner III

Principals' Views of Combination Classes

Combination classes are an organizational structure in which teachers instruct students from two or more grades for most or all of the school day. These anomalous structures, embedded within a graded system of schooling, have resulted from imbalanced or inadequate enrollments (Knight, 1938; Miller, 1989) and have recently become a hot topic in elementary education. In California, for example, where year-round schools have been encouraged, and in Kentucky, where nongraded programs have been legislated, combination classes have been an unintended consequence of statewide restructuring, proliferating in many districts (Galluzzo et al., 1990; Guskey & Oldham, 1995; Quinlan, George, & Emmett, 1987). Such increases have often caused stakeholders to question the efficacy of this method of grouping students; those concerns have led to debates over whether the classes lead to innovative curriculum and instruction or, conversely, to educational environments that are extremely challenging for teachers and detrimental to students. Unfortunately, in-depth, comprehensive research on combination classes is nearly nonexistent.

In the present study, we explored principals' views about combination classes. Principals, who have typically taught or supervised combinations, are likely to hold insights about this structure. Although those insights may be idiosyncratic and occasionally erroneous, Leinhardt (1988, 1990) explained that such *craft knowledge* can play an important role in understanding the complexities of schooling, the effects of organizational constraints on teaching and learning, and the manner in which practitioners make decisions—knowledge that would enable researchers to identify key issues and valid research designs. Thus, we randomly selected 36 principals and interviewed them about what they think of combination classes, how they assign students and teachers to them, and what curriculum strategies they believe are important for making this format work. We sought this knowledge to guide future research to inform principals and teachers and to enlighten policymakers charged with establishing combination classes.

Background

During the 20th century, combination classes have been a significant feature of schooling, especially in rural areas and other countries (Miller, 1989; Muse,

From DeWayne A. Mason and Roland W. Doepner III, "Principals' Views of Combination Classes," *The Journal of Educational Research*, vol. 91, no. 3 (January/February 1998). Copyright © 1998 by The Helen Dwight Reid Educational Foundation. Reprinted by permission of Heldref Publications, 1319 Eighteenth St., NW, Washington, DC 20036-1802. References omitted.

Smith, & Barker, 1987; Veenman, 1995). For example, in their survey of 12 states, Mason and Stimson (1996) found that 5% of the elementary school classes were combinations. Laükkanen (1978) found 29% of Finland's K–3 students similarly placed, a percentage that parallels reports from England (Her Majesty's Inspectors of Schools [HMI], 1978) and British Columbia (Craig & McLellan, 1987). According to a report from the Netherlands (Commissie Evaluatie Basisonderwijs, 1994), 53% of the elementary school classes there are combinations; Pratt and Treacy (1986) found that 85% of the schools in Western Australia used some type of combination class. Veenman (1995) reported that the incidence of combination classes was "quite significant" and likely to grow in Asian and Pacific countries as equal educational opportunity policies are implemented.

Despite their history and prevalence in many areas, research on combination classes has been limited in scope, superficially analyzed, and lacking in research design. The results from some inquiries on educators' views suggest that combination classes increase social growth, peer tutoring, independent learning skills, and individualized instruction (e.g., Chace, 1961; Hoen, 1972). In contrast, several researchers have reported (a) that teachers and principals prefer single grades because combination classes create extra planning and difficulties with classroom management and curriculum coverage (Brown & Martin, 1989; Galluzzo et al., 1990; Pratt & Treacy, 1986) and (b) that educators attempt to mediate these problems by placing better students and teachers in combination classes (Appalachia Educational Laboratory and Virginia Education Association, 1990; Bennett, O'Hare, & Lee, 1983; Galluzzo et al., 1990; Pratt & Treacy, 1986).

Observational research on combination classes has also been limited. Only one observational study has been conducted in the United States (Foshay, 1948), and most inquiries (including Foshay) have been narrowly conceived with scant evidence presented. Nevertheless, these studies suggest (a) that combination-class teachers generally teach two grade-level groups, especially for reading and mathematics, delivering separate curricula and lessons, in turn, to the two groups, and (b) that this division of the teachers' time between grade-level groups leads to less direct instruction, less curriculum adaptation, more independent work, and more waiting for teachers (e.g., Galton, Simon, & Croll, 1980; HMI, 1978, Pratt & Treacy, 1986; Veenman, Voeten, & Lem, 1987).

Reviewers of the comparative research have offered different conclusions about the effects of combination classes. Veenman (1995), for example, reviewed 45 combination-class outcome studies, computing effects sizes for 34 achievement and 13 affective comparisons. Finding no achievement differences (median effects size of .00) and small affective effects favoring combination classes (median effects size of +.10), Veenman concluded that combination classes "are simply no worse, and simply no better, than single-grade . . . classes" (p. 367). In contrast, Mason and Burns's (1994) review of the literature led them to conclude that outcome studies are generally flawed by the assignment of better students and teachers to combination classes and that because those selection biases have not led to positive effects for these classes, combination classes appear to have a slightly negative effect.

Purpose and Questions of the Study

The present study was part of a comprehensive investigation of combination classes initiated by practitioners from the California Educational Research Cooperative—a consortium of 20 school districts, two county offices of education, and the School of Education at the University of California, Riverside. We sought to explore principals' feelings about combination classes as well as the manner in which this organizational structure is formed and managed by teachers. Such knowledge might guide practitioners and policymakers in the enactment, organization, and teaching of combination classes. This knowledge might also assist researchers in developing theories of school and classroom organization (e.g., see Bidwell & Kasarda, 1980; Slavin, 1989a). Prominent scholars have called for inquiry on alternative school and classroom structures (e.g., Bidwell & Dreeben, 1992; Good, Mulryan, & McCaslin, 1992; Slavin, 1989c). Although Bidwell and Kasarda argued that school organization generally has little effect on classroom processes and student outcomes, Slavin (1989a) explained that organizational structures vary in the instructional tradeoffs they create (e.g., time, appropriate curriculum, quality of instruction) and that "understanding the terms of these tradeoffs is critical for an understanding of how to build effective models of classroom organization" (p. 6)....

In sum, no U.S. or international study has focused primarily on how principals view combination classes. Several of the extant studies are dated, and most inquiries are narrow in scope and quite nonrepresentative. Moreover, recent research and advocacy supporting multiage and nongraded programs may have altered principals' views about combination classes. Therefore, in the present study we sought an updated, more representative, and in-depth picture of combination classes from the principal's perspective. To this end, we explored three sets of related questions:

1. What are principals' views of combination classes? (For example, how do they feel about combinations? Do they prefer to teach them? What do they see as the advantages and disadvantages of these classes? Is their use of combination classes linked to an interest in adopting practices found in multiage or nongraded classes?)
2. How do principals form combination classes? (That is, how do they assign students to combination classes? How are teachers assigned to this structure?)
3. How are combination classes generally taught? (For example, how do combination teachers organize students for instruction? What strategies are effective for delivering curricula in these classes?)

Our reading of the limited literature and preliminary discussions with practitioners led to two major predictions. First, given concerns in the literature about combination classes (e.g., teachers' negative views, divided instructional time, and diminished planning and curriculum coverage), we predicted that a large number of principals would express a preference against and general negative feelings about these classes. However, anecdotal evidence gleaned from local administrators led to a competing prediction that a sizable number of principals would prefer these classes, viewing them as a catalyst for making the transition to more developmental, progressive approaches to curriculum and instruction. Second, the first author's experience in an observational study of mathematics teaching—an inquiry that involved several combination classes (Good, Grouws, Mason, Slavings, & Cramer, 1990)—led to a prediction that combination teachers would predominantly use two grade-level groups for instruction.

Method

Sample

The participants were drawn in a three-stage process: First, we randomly selected 200 of the 768 elementary schools from the 54 districts in the two largest counties in California.... Second, we sorted the 120 elementary school principals who responded to the survey by crossing their experience (novice—less than 5 years as an administrator—or experienced) with type of school (traditional or year-round). Third, we randomly selected 9 principals from each group and used letters and phone calls to solicit their participation.... The 36 principals (16 males, 20 females) represented 36 schools, 14 districts, and a range of small rural to large urban schools. They varied in experience from 0–22 years as a teacher, 0–10 years as a combination teacher, and 8 months to 42 years as a principal.

Instrument and Procedure

We developed the 32-item interview schedule during a series of meetings with 12 educators (6 teachers, 3 principals, 3 assistant superintendents) from three districts. The questions were focused on issues that emerged from a review of the literature and on issues important to practitioners. In addition to background data on the principal, the instrument addressed three major areas: (a) affect, (b) class formation, and (c) the teaching of combination classes (e.g., classroom organization, curriculum)....

Results

Reflecting the three sets of study questions, the results of this investigation are presented in three sections: (a) affect, (b) class formation, and (c) teaching combination classes. We integrated calendar and experience findings into these sections as appropriate.

Affect

Preferences and feelings. Two primary questions were asked to assess the principals' preferences and feelings about combination classes: "Would you prefer to teach combination classes?" and "What is your general feeling about combination classes?" Of the 36 principals, 21 (58%) responded to the preference question by reporting that they preferred not to teach combination classes, 10 principals (28%) expressed no preference or mixed feelings, and 5 principals (14%) preferred these structures. In response to the feelings question, 16 principals (44%) provided remarks that were negative, 7 principals (19%) responded with mixed feelings, and 13 (36%) commented in a generally positive manner.

The comments of those principals who preferred single grades and those who held negative feelings about combination classes focused most frequently on curriculum-coverage problems and teacher and parent concerns. The following comments are representative of this sentiment:

> It is stressful . . . , they [the teachers] have a lot to address from two different curricula and grade levels.

> A lot of parents object to it, and I have a tough time convincing them.

> They [combinations] are fraught with peril because teachers are resistant.

Also mentioned frequently—as illustrated by the following comment—were difficulties with classroom management and divided instructional time:

> I don't like them . . . it's very hard, the time—managing it—trying to do your lesson plans . . . the situation of just trying to make sure that both grades are functioning. And the teacher can't be with both of those grades at all times. And one [group] feels left out, and one doesn't really get a concept, and you don't have time to explain it. You can't do it. A master teacher could not.

The principals with mixed feelings about combination classes typically qualified those same concerns with an explanation of how purposeful student assignment can make this format manageable or even appealing. One principal, asserting that combination classes require the best students, remarked that his preference "depends on the classroom composition"; another stated that she preferred combination classes only if she could assign "appropriate" students to them. Still others, however, reported that they would accept combination classes if teachers had the time and flexibility to develop one in-depth curriculum rather than covering curricula from two grades. Finally, a few principals who expressed mixed feelings commented that combination classes were "a fact of life" and really not that much different from single-grade classes.

The principals who were more positive about combination classes provided fewer comments supporting their views. Several simply commented that combinations are (or can be) good learning environments, but a few principals saw these classes as "an opportunity" to develop innovative teaching, to meet students' social needs, or to provide administrative flexibility to form classes:

> I think they can generate more creative instruction . . . , it can involve students' needs much more in the learning process. It can lead the teacher to be more creative in choosing instructional approaches.

> We hope to keep students with the same teacher for two or three years—students need a sense of belonging.

> As a teacher, I thought it [a combination class] was wonderful.
> As an administrator, a necessity to balance numbers.... I don't
> see it as an advantage, but as an opportunity.

The comments of the 5 principals reporting a preference for teaching combination classes were quite brief and lacking in themes or rationales. Each of these principals had fewer than 4 years of experience as a principal, and only 2 had taught a combination class for more than 1 year. We found no other calendar or experience differences....

Class Formation

Assigning students to combination classes.   The principals were asked, "School-wide, what strategies do you use to organize combination classes? That is, how do you generally assign students? And, how do you determine who goes into combination classes?" ... Twenty-four principals reported collaborating with teachers to form combination classes:

> The teachers get together, and they know which classes are likely to be com-
> binations next year, and they work together to make class lists of students
> that they feel are a mixed group.

In contrast, 17 principals (12 from year-round schools) reported that purposeful class formations were constrained by (a) last-minute enrollments ("We find out we're growing, and we have to form combination classes"), (b) the limited number of students in small schools ("There's only one K–1 teacher"), or (c) track placements in year-round schools ("I have very little control.... It's based strictly on parental choice of track").

In addition to this lack of flexibility and the use of collaborative processes to assign students strategically to combination classes, the principals reported using numerous criteria to form these classes. Cited most frequently were homogeneous ability (22 responses) and independence (21 responses):

> We try to identify students who are independent workers, those who can
> work while others are instructed.... We also look for those who are not
> significantly below grade level.

Also mentioned frequently were good behavior (9 responses) and heterogeneous ability (8 responses).

Assigning teachers to combination classes.   The principals characterized assigning teachers to combination classes by administrative policy (51 responses) and by teacher characteristics (49 responses). In the teacher-characteristic category, experience was most frequently mentioned (18 principals), but 16 principals reported assigning their "best, most able" teachers:

> I look at experience.... It takes a lot of planning, and you have
> to have curriculum [experience] to address for both grade levels.

> They would be my better teachers, more flexible, more able to
> cope with different personalities and different kinds of group-
> ings.

Although these comments usually implied the exclusion of novice teachers, 12 principals stated explicitly that they avoid new teachers:

> A brand new teacher would not be placed in a combination class.... Sometimes, you have to do that, but I would avoid it as much as possible, because I don't think they could handle it.

In the administrative-policy category, 19 principals reported rotating teachers, whereas 16 principals remarked that they usually solicit volunteers.

> Whether or not she had a combination the last year. I try to rotate it.

> Usually I ask who would consider teaching them. I have volunteers, pretty much have them throughout.

Ten principals (8 from year-round schools) noted that teacher assignments were often dictated by whoever was teaching a particular grade or track when imbalanced or inadequate enrollments occurred (as in small schools or year-round schools with parental choice of tracks):

> [It's] pretty much how things fall.... If a teacher is on the green track, and we end up having a [Grade] 5–6 class, that's where they're going to teach.

Finally, as a result of their multiple tracks and teachers' preferences for certain tracks, year-round principals reported inflexible teacher assignment four times more frequently than their traditional school counterparts did.

Teaching Combination Classes

Grouping approach. The principals' responses to questions about grouping, curriculum, and organizing for combination classes suggested that teachers consider grade level, subject area, teacher preference, individual student needs, and class heterogeneity as important factors. For example, several principals noted that ability grouping was used more frequently in mathematics (where skills are emphasized), at the intermediate grades (where student abilities are more varied), and after or along with whole-class presentations (for remediation or enrichment)....

Curriculum strategies. Asked the question, "What specific curriculum strategies do you generally feel are effective in teaching combination classes?" the principals identified four predominant strategies: (a) integrated curriculum, (b) thematic curriculum, (c) cooperative learning, and (d) small-group methods. Nineteen principals reported integration as an effective curriculum strategy; and 15 principals identified thematic approaches:

> I think they should try, with the exception of mathematics, to integrate as much as they can.... I can't believe that a [combination] teacher can present every lesson in the fourth and fifth grade... they can't really cover it all. So they try and combine as much as possible.

> Well, I think the thematic approach is really effective because you can pull in the language arts, even if it's not the same book at both grade levels, if it addresses that theme.

In addition to, and occasionally in contrast to, integrated and thematic curriculum design strategies that would apparently increase the time spent in a whole-class format, 26 principals, reported cooperative learning or small-group strategies as effective for delivering curriculum in combination classes. Fourteen principals identified cooperative learning; of those who identified cooperative learning, 9 mentioned this strategy as effective with thematic or integrated approaches:

> I think cooperative learning is a valuable one [strategy].... The younger ones learn from older ones, and the older ones develop self-esteem by working with the younger ones.... Cross-age collaboration really develops good student habits for both groups.

Twelve principals cited small groups as effective for combinations, although the purposes they expressed for using these groups varied. Some focused on ability grouping across grades: "instruct at ability level rather than grade level." Others focused on ad hoc ability grouping for remediation or enrichment: "Teachers need to pull kids off to the side and give them skill-specific things that are important to those kids.... You may be working with only five or six kids." Still others focused on grouping students by grade after thematic whole-class lessons or for addressing different grade-level curricula.

Discussion

In the present study, we examined principals' views about combination classes. Thirty-six principals from California's two largest counties were randomly selected and interviewed about (a) how they feel about combination classes, (b) how they form combination classes, and (c) how teachers organize and teach combination classes. Four major findings emerged. First, a majority of the principals expressed negative feelings about combination classes. Second, the principals assigned better students and teachers to combination classes. Third, the principals reported that combination-class teachers use a mixed approach to grouping (i.e., whole-class organization for some subject and two grade-level groups, two curriculums, and two instructional presentations for other subjects). Finally, the principals perceived thematic and integrated curriculum and the use of cooperative learning and small-group instruction as effective approaches for teaching combination classes. We discuss these four findings in light of research and theory on teaching and school and classroom organization (Bidwell & Kasarda, 1980; Slavin; 1987, 1989a, 1989b, 1989c; Veenman, 1995; Westbury, 1973).

Principals' Feelings

Collectively, the comments of the principals suggest that combination classes create a complex and challenging learning environment that (a) diminishes curriculums, instruction, and attention to individual students (e.g., monitoring and feedback), (b) requires extensive teacher effort in developing curriculum and in coping with the management demands of students from two grades (or groups); and (c) precipitates the expression of concerns from teachers and parents. Clearly, the principals responded to our questions about the advantages of combination classes with a number of positive beliefs (e.g., "exposes lower grade students to the more appropriate curriculum of the upper grade," "develops social skills," "increases peer tutoring"). A large number of the advantage comments, however, noted that combinations allowed administrators to save money and teachers to have better classes, with higher ability, more independent students. Thus, the principals' disadvantage comments were not only more frequent but their major concerns (e.g., about instruction and classroom management, curriculum coverage, or "opportunity to learn") were arguably more substantive.

That principals were more negative than positive about combination classes confirms U.S. and international research involving more narrow surveys, interviews of teachers, principals, or both (Bennett et al., 1983; Brown & Martin, 1989; Chace, 1961; Knight, 1938; Mason & Burns, 1995; Pratt & Treacy, 1986). Moreover, the diminishment of curriculum and instruction has been reported in observational research exploring combination class processes (e.g., Galton et al., 1980; HMI, 1978; Mason & Good, 1996; Veenman et al., 1987)—and these variables (direct instruction and curriculum coverage or opportunity to learn) have been linked consistently to student achievement (e.g., Brophy & Good, 1986; Cooley & Leinhardt, 1980; Slaving, 1989a, 1989c). However, because combination classes are often mandated by budget constraints or district policies and administrators are generally compelled to publicly support these classes, the principals' actual views about this structure were likely more negative than those expressed.

It is surprising that the rationale that the principals used to support their views about combination classes did not refer directly to research or theory. Indeed, in arguing for or against combination classes, not a single principal expressed awareness of research reviews on the effects of combination classes (Ansah, 1989; Ford, 1977; Miller, 1989, 1990, 1991; Pratt, 1986). Further, no principal mentioned research on related forms of school and classroom organization such as within-class ability grouping, regrouping, or various types of nongraded programs (e.g., Gutiérrez & Slavin, 1992; Slavin, 1987). Similarly, in their identification of instructional tradeoffs that would likely occur with a combination class, no principal referred to common models of teaching or learning (e.g., Carroll, 1963; Good, Grouws, & Ebmeier, 1983; Hunter, 1976; Joyce & Weil, 1992; Slaving, 1989a)....

Teaching Combination Classes

... [T]he principals reported that combination-class teachers most frequently used both two-group and whole-class approaches depending on subject matter, grade level, teacher preference, and the like. Their comments suggested that most teachers used two groups for mathematics; for other subjects, about half used two groups and half used a whole-class approach. For two-group subjects, principals indicated that teachers generally rotated recitation and seatwork between two groups that were nearly always grouped by grade level. That is, while one group was involved in teacher presentation, the other was working independently on a seatwork assignment. This *mixed-approach* finding is consistent with that of a recent investigation on teachers' views of combination classes (Mason & Burns, 1995) as well as that of observational research in other countries (Galton et al., 1980; Veenman et al., 1987)....

Finally, the principals noted that an integrated and thematic curriculum and cooperative learning and small-group instruction are effective strategies for teaching combination classes. However—perhaps reflecting the complexity of the combination classroom or the variety of approaches that teachers use in this structure—the principals provided few specifics about how these strategies should be used. Additional questions may have captured more detailed information about instruction, but we suspect that this lack of specificity reflects the principals' understanding that such answers depend on the goals and context of instruction or, perhaps, a belief that even after specifying particular goals and context, such technologies do not yet exist.

Although the principals did not specify the type of integrated or thematic curriculum that teachers should use, their comments suggest that they prefer a well-developed curriculum that carefully combines, but does not omit, key concepts from each grade level. Again, however, developing this type of integrated curriculum would likely entail careful if not extensive efforts on the part of teachers (Brophy & Alleman, 1991). Still, such efforts may be important to satisfactory student achievement in combination classes, especially if one links reports of combination-class teaching in science and social studies (whole-class teaching) with results of achievement comparisons in these subjects in single-grade and combination classes. Though limited, this research generally indicates that combination-class teachers use whole-class approaches for science and social studies but that combination-class achievement in these subjects tends to be lower than that in single-grade classes (Veenman, 1995). Of the nine studies (five science and four social studies) that Veenman reported, five favored single-grade classes (three significantly so) and four favored combination classes (zero significantly so); the median effects size was $-.16$, favoring single-grade classes.

Conclusion

In this exploratory study, we showed that elementary school principals generally viewed combination classes as complex and challenging assignments for their teachers, as an anomalous, expediently formed structure that exists within a graded system of schooling, and not as a structure that necessarily leads to progressive curriculum and instruction practices associated with nongraded programming. Furthermore, most principals viewed combination classes as creating important curriculum, teacher motivation, and instruction and classroom management tradeoffs. It appears that combination classes are an exception to Bidwell and Kasarda's (1980) general model that school organizational structures have little influence on the allocation of resources to or within classes or on the outcomes of schooling. Indeed, the principals, in an apparent attempt to mediate the constraints that a combination class might otherwise impose on classroom processes and student outcomes, reported differential allocations of resources (students, teachers) to those classes.

Given their widespread and apparently difficult nature, combination classes represent a significant school and classroom structure that deserves in-depth, comprehensive research. Future researchers might further examine principals' tacit or conscious theories of teaching and school and class-room organization. Studies on how students view combination classes and observational research that describes present practice would contribute to the literature. Methodologically sound comparisons of student outcomes in single-grade and combination classes would be especially instructive, as would comparisons of different approaches to teaching combination classes (e.g., two-group, integrated, and mixed approaches). Indeed, understanding how combination-class teachers effectively manage two curriculums while instructing a diverse range of students may provide insights into how single-grade teachers can better address perhaps their greatest challenge—meeting the increasingly wide array of individual needs that they face in their classes.

POSTSCRIPT

Are Multi-Age Programs Best for Young Children?

What qualities make for successful multi-age teaching? Are certain teachers more suited to having successful experiences in multi-age classrooms? Are certain students better equipped to function smoothly in a multi-age class? Can a principal assign teachers and students to multi-age classes that would result in fair and equitable arrangement for all involved? If so, how? These issues surround any discussion on multi-age classrooms in elementary schools and deserve input from all involved—teachers, parents, and administrators.

Critics of multi-age programs argue that there is no specific methodology, standardization, special curriculum, or monitoring to assist teachers in this type of classroom. Teachers may feel overwhelmed when forced to teach more than one grade level simultaneously and teachers who may already feel that they have too many responsibilities are challenged to meet the needs of all the children at their different levels. It can be argued that principals often place the most advanced and independent students with the most skilled teachers when establishing a multi-age classroom. These arrangements may lead to a strain in relationships with colleagues who may have been passed over for a multi-age class or who have a high proportion of students who require a great deal of assistance and attention throughout the day. The following disadvantages to multi-age programs were reported: teachers having to prepare two or more sets of curricula, the lack of time for instruction, problems with class management and organization, and parental concerns over the placement of their child with older or younger children. Should parents be concerned about multi-age programs? Would a multi-age classroom be better for some students than a conventional classroom? Should parents be offered a choice as to what type of classroom their children are enrolled in?

Suggested Readings

Byrnes, D. A., Shuster, T., and Jones, M., "Parent and Student Views of Multi-age Classrooms," *Journal of Research in Childhood Education* (vol. 9, no. 1, 1994).

Kolstad, R. K. and McFadden, A., "Multiage Classrooms: An Age-old Educational Strategy Revisited," *Journal of Instructional Psychology* (vol. 25, 1998).

Stegelin, D. A., "Outcomes of Mixed-age Groupings: Research Highlights," *Dimensions of Early Childhood* (vol. 25, no. 2, 1997).

ISSUE 15

Is the Whole-Language Approach the Best Way to Teach Reading?

YES: Steve Zemelman, Harvey Daniels, and Marilyn Bizar, from "Sixty Years of Reading Research—But Who's Listening?" *Phi Delta Kappan* (March 1999)

NO: National Reading Panel, from "Teaching Children to Read: An Evidence-Based Assessment of the Scientific Research Literature on Reading and Its Implications for Reading Instruction," A Report of the National Reading Panel, http://www.nichd.nih.gov/publications/nrp/smallbook.htm (April 12, 2000)

ISSUE SUMMARY

YES: Steve Zemelman, Harvey Daniels, and Marilyn Bizar, all faculty at the Center for City Schools, National-Louis University, assert that a whole-language approach to reading is supported by 60 years of research that confirms its positive results.

NO: Members of the National Reading Panel conclude that students need a strong foundation in systematic phonics instruction in kindergarten through sixth grade in order to be successful readers.

Learning to read has been the cornerstone of education for hundreds of years. One of the most hotly contested debates in public schools today centers around the best way to teach children how to read. It is clear to see why the battle rages. Reading is a measurable item that can be assessed easily and is often used to determine the success of a school system. Unlike math, which is more difficult to assess, many legislators and administrators can assert that in their school system children will leave third grade knowing how to read.

Does the "best" way to teach students how to read mean the fastest, most long lasting, easiest, or least expensive way? Whatever it is, the battle concerning what is best shows no sign of easing. There are basically two camps in what has been called by many "the reading wars." First, there is the side that supports the *phonetic approach*. Phonics focuses on the way letters and sounds correspond to each other. Phonics helps beginning readers learn how the 26 letters of the

English alphabet are linked to sounds, also called *phonemes*. Phonemes are the smallest units that make up a spoken language and are combined to form recognizable words. The philosophy behind the phonics approach to teaching reading is that when children learn to use the letters in words to blend or segment the sounds, they can learn to read words, any words. For over one hundred years children have been taught to read using the phonetic approach. When teachers follow this approach, they systematically instruct students in a sequential set of phonics elements. Students are exposed to more complex sounds and words as they learn phonetic skills.

The other method discussed in the reading war debate is known as the *whole-language approach*. When children learn to read in a classroom using the whole-language approach, they are read to a great deal. As they hear the same books many times and as they learn letter sounds, they also learn to distinguish words in context to make sense of the story. They use clues from the pictures and print to comprehend the story. Phonics in a classroom using the whole-language approach are presented in what is known as *incidental phonics instruction*. The teacher uses the teachable moment to bring to the students' attention certain components of phonics as they appear in material being read at the time. Proponents of the whole-language approach contend that if children are exposed to good literature, are interested in what they are reading, and have knowledgeable teachers, they will master the technique of reading. In the past 25 years, excellent children's books have been published that make the presentation of high-quality, appropriate literature easier than it was a generation ago. But still, the debate continues. Approximately 100,000 research studies on reading have been published since 1966, with more than 15,000 completed prior to that date.

To examine the issue more closely, two selections have been chosen that represent each side of this debate. In the first, Steve Zemelman, Harvey Daniels, and Marilyn Bizar report that the whole-language approach works, and that there is over 60 years of research to back this assertion up. They conclude that the supporting research is being ignored by those who favor the standard phonetic approach. Zemelman, Daniels, and Bizar are concerned that the results of these research studies have not been disseminated more effectively. They maintain that in general there is a negative attitude toward more progressive methods of teaching.

In the second selection, the National Reading Panel presents findings on the five key areas examined in their report and concludes that systematic, explicit phonics should be taught to all elementary students. Children who are taught phonics beginning in kindergarten will read more proficiently later. Coupled with phonics instruction, the teacher should help students improve fluency and comprehension skills so that they can become successful readers. Due to the length of the panel's report, only the portion that addresses alphabetics, including phonics, is presented in this selection.

Steve Zemelman, Harvey Daniels, and Marilyn Bizar

Sixty Years of Reading Research— But Who's Listening?

Areporter calls to get some background for an article about staff development in language arts. Staff development? We are astonished and delighted that any media outlet—even this modest local magazine—actually wants to cover our neglected field. Since our work involves inservice workshops, classroom consulting, and whole-school renewal projects, we're thrilled to talk. We offer quotes, sources, and anecdotes about teacher development efforts around Chicago—our own and others', modest and ambitious, successes and failures. Then, somewhere in the conversation, the term "whole language" comes up.

"Oh," says the young reporter, as if someone has made a rude noise. "That doesn't work." Her tone is flat and certain.

"What do you mean?" we ask.

"You know," she replies impatiently. "There are no scientific studies that show whole language works."

There's a brief pause while we silently bid farewell to cordiality. "Well, actually, there are lots of scientific studies supporting whole language. As a matter of fact, there are a bunch of them sitting right here on the bookshelf."

"But there *aren't* any studies. It's just opinions. There's no research to back it up."

Through gritted teeth: "Are you saying that these shelves are actually empty? That these studies weren't published? We'd be glad to start faxing you some summaries."

"No, no, no." Now she's annoyed. "That can't be real research. People have done scientific research and proved that phonics works, not whole language."

Within moments our conversation has foundered on the rocks of educational research. Both parties hang up, peeved and polarized.

If research could actually settle the "great debate" over teaching reading —and over the broader character of education in America—the shouting would have died down long ago. In spite of what our reporter friend thinks, the research overwhelmingly favors holistic, literature-centered approaches to reading. Indeed, the proof is massive and overwhelming.

From Steve Zemelman, Harvey Daniels, and Marilyn Bizar, "Sixty Years of Reading Research— But Who's Listening?" *Phi Delta Kappan*, vol. 80, no. 7 (March 1999). Copyright © 1999 by Phi Delta Kappa International. Reprinted by permission of *Phi Delta Kappan* and Harvey Daniels. Notes omitted.

For six decades, leading researchers and writers have steadily produced summaries and meta-analyses that reiterate the key findings of mainstream, long-term research. For example, Constance Weaver has published research summaries on many aspects of progressive, whole-language teaching, in both book and electronic forms. Margaret Moustafa has pulled together the findings about the role of phonics in teaching reading. For more than 20 years, David Johnson, Roger Johnson, and Edythe Holubec have reviewed the hundreds of studies on the collaborative aspects of the progressive classroom. Michael Tunnell and James Jacobs surveyed the studies on literature-based reading instruction from 1968 to 1988. George Hillocks focused his massive meta-analysis on studies of the teaching of writing. And Richard Thompson looked at 40 studies dating back to 1937.

The most recent volumes of the *Annual Summary of Investigations Related to Reading* include several studies showing statistically significant test score gains in whole-language classrooms and 15 additional studies validating particular strategies within whole language. In our own work, we have tried to connect the research base with the emerging national curriculum standards, as detailed in *Best Practice: New Standards for Teaching and Learning in America's Schools; Methods That Matter: Six Structures for Best Practice Classrooms;* and articles such as "Whole Language Works: Sixty Years of Research." Just [recently], Jeff McQuillan's book *The Literacy Crisis: False Claims, Real Solutions* has offered yet another powerful review of the research on reading instruction, debunking faddish phonics claims and pointing to the strong evidence favoring holistic approaches.

Of course, we need to learn still more about the detailed mechanics of reading and other thinking processes. We can argue over the degree to which competent readers use letter/sound relationships as they read, as opposed to sampling larger chunks of information and fitting it into a context. No thoughtful progressive teacher would say that readers don't need phonics knowledge. And no thoughtful student of phonics can deny that a reader must consult the wider context of a passage to make meaning. But the large and clear outlines are there: whole language works.

Yet 60 years of research and thousands of studies that resoundingly validate progressive approaches to literacy learning still haven't produced the strong consensus we might expect. In fact, many schoolpeople—even progressive teachers themselves—act as though this information didn't exist at all or were somehow unreliable, inconclusive, or tainted. We witness this phenomenon every time the promoters of the latest "breakthrough study" seek to overturn decades of solid, workmanlike research with a faddish, mechanistic gimmick such as "decodable text." Curiously cowed by such dubious "evidence," many educators stand mute even as the preponderance of scientific proof shouts just the contrary. So what's up? Clearly, if a shortage of convincing research is not the main reason that progressive methods have failed to be widely acknowledged or supported, then some large and troubling questions are before us:

- Why haven't whole-language teachers and leaders shared their research base more effectively?
- Why does it often seem that back-to-basics proponents have cornered the market on "scientific proof"?
- How is it that one brand-new study can sometimes overturn our confidence in decades of research?
- Why is there so much antagonism toward whole language and other progressive teaching methods these days—especially when they have been so strongly endorsed by the many national standards projects released in recent years?

There are many ways in which research that confirms good practice comes to be misunderstood, ignored, or subverted. Let's start with some of the factors nearest the surface and work toward the deeper ones. First, there's the fact that the teachers who use these practices haven't spoken up very strongly about the research supporting them. One simple reason for this is that many educators simply don't know their own research heritage. When confronted by the authoritative-sounding claims of citation-spewing opponents, they lack ready access to the huge body of knowledge that supports their own practice. In fact, most teachers, whatever their philosophies, select their actions toward children based not on research but on what they see each day in the classroom and on the beliefs they've acquired through their own culture and education.

This is really no different from parents (no doubt including those who challenge the research on whole language), who don't usually make parenting decisions about bedtime or curfews by consulting academic research. Good teachers chose to teach because of their interest in children, not because they encountered some statistically significant experimental finding. The research is valuable in that it may confirm particular practices or call them into question, but culturally, research is a relative newcomer to the calculus of human decision making.

Further, many teachers, both progressive and traditional, look on social science research with broad and well-merited skepticism. They've seen claims and absolute "proofs" come and go over the years. They're wise to the often tortuous attempts of educational, psychological, and cognitive researchers to cloak themselves in the sometimes ill-fitting garb of "science." They worry that, if researchers don't understand the realities of the classroom, their experiments will not reflect those realities. And they know that, even in the best experimental studies, it's impossible to control all the variables associated with dozens or hundreds of human beings in multiple locations over any appreciable span of time. Instead, many thoughtful teachers have learned to pay more attention to qualitative studies that provide a "thicker," more detailed picture of the classroom. They recognize that there are multiple ways of measuring and evaluating a teaching strategy besides conducting statistical studies with large numbers of children that provide only a very sketchy picture of what any given child actually experienced.

With regard to teachers' lack of outspokenness, whether for good or ill teachers are not usually very political creatures. They focus on the intense and immediate needs of the students in their classrooms and on the concerns of the parents, and they have little time or energy left over to mount campaigns to inform a broader public. Attacks on progressive education, on the other hand, tend to come from policy gurus like William Bennett, Diane Ravitch, and E. D. Hirsch, Jr., whose time is fully devoted to the public forum.

Some of these pundits work directly to discredit educational research, and "cultural literacy" guru Hirsch is perhaps the leading debunker. In his latest book, *The Schools We Need and Why We Don't Have Them*, Hirsch introduces himself as a middle-of-the-roader, a peacemaker, an old lion sadly creaking toward retirement in an era of regrettable polarization. He inveighs against the "selective use of research," decrying the "deplorable development" that "research is being cited as a rhetorical weapon to sustain a sectarian position." Then he goes on to describe progressive education as a cancer that has "metastasized" throughout the schools, a vast "conspiracy" to keep American children stupid and to spawn "chaos." Virtually all American educators, he explains, live in an evil "thoughtworld," where phony research undermines knowledge, repels facts, "quashes" debate, and prevents children from becoming literate. Hirsch repudiates the hundreds of studies cited in the reviews we listed earlier, including all the current national standards projects that were, of course, based on that research. He concludes: "No studies of children's learning in mainstream science support these generalizations.... The consensus in research is that [these] recommendations are worst practice, not 'best practice.'"

Hirsch is not the dispassionate, grandfatherly observer of education that he claims, but an aggressive vendor, who sells millions of dollars' worth of books (*A Dictionary of Cultural Literacy, What Every First-Grader Should Know, What Every Second-Grader Should Know*, and so on) to the schools he vilifies and to the parents whom he encourages to distrust their children's teachers.

The news media are no help, either. Hand-wringing stories about falling test scores provide good headlines. So do politicians' and administrators' declarations that they're going to get tough, crack knuckles, and raise standards. A detailed story about the 20 ways a good teacher makes learning happen in a progressive classroom and how those methods have been statistically validated just might make the feature page—but only if it includes a sensational twist, like the principal spending the day on the roof if all the kids get 100% on their spelling tests. David Berliner and Gerald Bracey have made a helpful if quixotic hobby out of identifying misinformation in news reports and then campaigning (with little success) to get errors corrected and to see more balanced reporting in the first place. When test scores go up, there's a mild ripple, a squib on page 12 with a tone of "Well, maybe, but there are still plenty of problems." When they go down, it's a front-page story.

Whatever the difficulty with delivery of the news, however, we must also reflect on why so many people are indisposed to hear anything positive about schools, and particularly about progressive classrooms. Again, let's start with the simplest cause. Progressive innovations usually change the classroom into something considerably different from what parents remember from their own school days. They worry: Is my child getting what she needs from this stuff? Will I be able to help with the homework? They think: I wasn't taught this way, and I turned out okay! It's not news that people resist change.

Of course, the issues go deeper. Recently, a *New York Times* editorial writer argued that education has become an ideological battleground because we've lost the comfortable old arena of communism versus capitalism. People looking for something wrong need somewhere to duke it out. When politicians seek a "hot" issue, public education usually fits the bill. With education's implications for our children and our property values, most Americans can quickly go round the bend about the quality, or lack of it, of our schools.

Actually, the opposition between conservative and progressive views of education has existed for a long time. Conservatives see children as primarily in need of discipline, while progressives see them as creatures seeking opportunities for expression and initiative. Conservatives look to education mainly to supply basic skills for a competent labor force—skills taught one at a time and tested by standardized, impersonal instruments—while progressives want school mainly to nurture active citizens and creative individuals. Conservatives think of education as socializing students to the status quo, while progressives view it as an opportunity to teach students to critique and question the world they've inherited. Many conservatives doubt that public education is even an appropriate domain for government, while progressives see it as the seedbed of democracy.

While it's obvious which side we are on in this debate, we will not try to plumb all the depths or lay out our most cherished arguments here. Rather, we just want to remind people that, when research is touted or when one study is suddenly elevated over decades of previous inquiry, this old, ongoing debate is probably the subtext, and research is not really going to settle it. If people are talking about differing purposes—and thus differing characteristics—of education, then each side will find the other's research irrelevant....

Perhaps there's an even deeper reason that people don't want to hear good news about progressive classrooms. The late education writer James Moffett theorized that some parents are unconsciously terrified of their children's dawning independence, as symbolized by their learning to read and write. A strong phonics program appeals to these parents because it is the only approach to reading that takes meaning out of the bargain. As long as a child spends most of her time enunciating t's and d's and decoding only synthetic, denatured texts, she will never encounter troubling or dangerous ideas, or begin to think and read for herself. This parallels some parents' preference for grammar drills over writing workshops. If children only do exercises and never write original texts, then they can never utter dangerous ideas on paper. Though Moffett would never have said it so inelegantly, people who want to replace whole, balanced reading programs with phonics-only curricula may unconsciously be holding children back, stunting their growth, and keeping them ignorant.

Looked at through Moffett's lens, the "great debate" isn't a clash over phonics or educational research at all, but rather a symbolic skirmish in the broader culture wars between two opposing camps on matters of teaching and learning, of child development, and of human nature. In a sense, research studies and journal articles are beside the point; this is a religious controversy. After all, if you believe that children are intrinsically flawed beings who need to be tightly controlled and amply punished, you will design a very different kind of classroom from the one you would design for people who were seen as basically good, worthy of love and respect, and capable of self-actualization. If you believe that books—especially religious scriptures—have only one correct meaning that is inherent in the text, you are not going to be very friendly to schools that teach children to explore a wide range of books and ideas, to write and discuss their own responses, to make critical evaluations of what they read, and to develop strong and independent voices as authors.

People may say that this is an oversimplified picture, that each side in the debate actually values some of what the other side advocates, and that good teachers choose approaches to create a balance that works for them. All of this is true, of course. We acknowledge that most good teachers take a "balanced" approach, combining activities that give students voice and choice—individually and in small and large groups—with more information and direct instruction on valuable skills and strategies. In fact, many of the studies cited in the research reviews involved classrooms in which the teachers used progressive student-centered strategies along with more traditional teacher-centered instruction.

One of the most frustrating aspects of the debate is that whole language is mischaracterized as merely turning children loose to do their own thing, with no support or guidance from the teacher. In the good whole-language classrooms we've observed, nothing could be further from the truth. Whole language is, in fact, a balanced and mainstream approach to teaching and learning.

Good teachers who "balance" instruction know that one of the most important aspects of teaching is to be a good "kid watcher." Whether in an affluent suburb, a rural community, or the heart of the inner city, good teachers focus on the learner and what she brings to school. Sweeping statements about "the right way" to teach all beginning readers just don't make good sense. If children already have the ability to segment phonemes, why teach it? If, on the other hand, children are unable to hear sounds in words, it is urgent that we help them acquire this necessary skill. If we concentrated on learning, rather than just on teaching, and designed instruction to meet students' needs, we wouldn't be in the predicament that one downstate Illinois teacher reported to us. Her district has mandated direct instruction in "intensive phonics" in all primary grades. This third-grade teacher, under extreme duress, is forced to teach one full hour of phonics a day to children who already can and do read.

We also see some powerful and disturbing crosscurrents as we move away from the simplified picture. Some educators working in troubled urban schools advocate a highly restrictive skill-and-drill approach because they believe that this is the only thing that will work for minority children or in a school culture that has been extremely resistant to change. Yet whole-language advocates observe again and again in strong and well-run whole-language classrooms that these approaches work wonderfully with inner-city students. These students, the whole-language teachers say, need more of what works in privileged, high-achieving schools, not less. Both groups say they want more of the population to enter the mainstream of American social and economic life, and yet they profoundly disagree about how to achieve this goal. It's a challenge to acknowledge cultural differences in social and learning styles and yet not pigeonhole or restrict children as we take account of those differences when we teach.

In spite of these complexities, however, there are clear distinctions between conservative and progressive approaches to education. A classroom in which children are working in small groups on various projects they've chosen looks and feels far different from one in which students are sitting in rows listening to a lecture or filling in worksheets. We've watched children from all backgrounds excel when given lots of opportunities to choose their own reading, writing, and inquiry topics and when classrooms are structured so that the teacher can provide lots of individual attention that's well-tuned to students' personal needs. Students at the Best Practice High School, a small Chicago public high school we helped found in 1996, prove to us every day that progressive ideas can be brought to life in the inner city. And on the other side of the equation, we've observed the failure of punitive approaches, of approaches that assume that young people bring to school no relevant knowledge or abilities of their own, and of lockstep scripts that prevent teachers from using their own judgment to provide what students need at a given moment.

In the latest chapter of the "great debate," the National Research Council brought together a panel of reading experts that included some of the most outspoken researchers and educators on both sides, plus some who occupy the middle ground. In their report, this diverse group not only appealed for an end to the squabbling but endorsed the value of teaching both letter/sound relationships and a range of whole-language strategies, including the extensive use of good literature, a focus on comprehension, and the use of developmental spelling for beginning writers. The real challenge, the panel asserts, is to provide much more training to increase prekindergarten and elementary teachers' knowledge of reading research and effective teaching strategies.

Nevertheless, as many of us try once again to get people to pay attention to and be guided by the research on progressive literacy education, let's remember that the debate is not likely to resolve itself anytime soon. Many of the differences do represent real disagreements about the nature of childhood, the human psyche, government, and society. And parents' anxieties about their children will find expression and, like air squeezed from one side of a balloon, will simply well up somewhere else nearby. Meanwhile, schools and teachers, always lacking the resources to push far enough in any direction, will continue to struggle, sometimes to react politically, and most often to do the best they can with the funds and the knowledge that they have.

Teaching Children to Read

Introduction

Congressional Charge

In 1997, Congress asked the "Director of the National Institute of Child Health and Human Development (NICHD), in consultation with the Secretary of Education, to convene a national panel to assess the status of research-based knowledge, including the effectiveness of various approaches to teaching children to read." This panel was charged with providing a report that "should present the panel's conclusions, an indication of the readiness for application in the classroom of the results of this research, and, if appropriate, a strategy for rapidly disseminating this information to facilitate effective reading instruction in the schools. If found warranted, the panel should also recommend a plan for additional research regarding early reading development and instruction."

Establishment of the National Reading Panel

In response to this Congressional request, the Director of NICHD, in consultation with the Secretary of Education, constituted and charged a National Reading Panel (the NRP or the Panel). The NRP comprised 14 individuals, including (as specified by Congress) "leading scientists in reading research, representatives of colleges of education, reading teachers, educational administrators, and parents." . . .

NRP Approach to Achieving the Objectives of Its Charge and Initial Topic Selection

The charge to the NRP took into account the foundational work of the National Research Council (NRC) Committee on *Preventing Reading Difficulties in Young Children* (Snow, Burns, & Griffin, 1998). The NRC report is a consensus document based on the best judgments of a diverse group of experts in reading research and reading instruction. The NRC Committee identified and summarized research literature relevant to the critical skills, environments, and early developmental interactions that are instrumental in the acquisition

From National Reading Panel, "Teaching Children to Read: An Evidence-Based Assessment of the Scientific Research Literature on Reading and Its Implications for Reading Instruction," A Report of the National Reading Panel, http://www.nichd.nih.gov/publications/nrp/smallbook.htm (April 12, 2000). National Institute of Child Health and Human Development (NIH Publication No. 00-4769). Washington, DC: U.S. Government Printing Office, 2000. References omitted.

of beginning reading skills. The NRC Committee did not specifically address "how" critical reading skills are most effectively taught and what instructional methods, materials, and approaches are most beneficial for students of varying abilities.

In order to build upon and expand the work of the NRC Committee, the NRP first developed an objective research review methodology. The Panel then applied this methodology to undertake comprehensive, formal, evidence-based analyses of the experimental and quasi-experimental research literature relevant to a set of selected topics judged to be of central importance in teaching children to read. An examination of a variety of public databases by Panel staff revealed that approximately 100,000 research studies on reading have been published since 1966, with perhaps another 15,000 appearing before that time. Obviously, it was not possible for a panel of volunteers to examine critically this entire body of research literature. Selection of prioritized topics was necessitated by the large amount of published reading research literature relevant to the Panel's charge to determine the effectiveness of reading instructional methods and approaches. A screening process was therefore essential.

The Panel's initial screening task involved selection of the set of topics to be addressed. Recognizing that this selection would require the use of informed judgment, the Panel chose to begin its work by broadening its understanding of reading issues through a thorough analysis of the findings of the NRC report, *Preventing Reading Difficulties in Young Children* (Snow, Burns, & Griffin, 1998). Early in its deliberations the Panel made a tentative decision to establish subgroups of its members and to assign to each of them one of the major topic areas designated by the NRC Committee as central to learning to read—Alphabetics, Fluency, and Comprehension.

Regional Public Hearings

... The Panel believed that it would not have been possible to accomplish the mandate of Congress without first hearing directly from consumers of this information—teachers, parents, students, and policymakers—about their needs and their understanding of the research. Although the regional hearings were not intended as a substitute for scientific research, the hearings gave the Panel an opportunity to listen to the voices of those who will need to consider implementation of the Panel's findings and determinations. The regional hearings gave members a clearer understanding of the issues important to the public....

Adoption of Topics to Be Studied

Following the regional hearings, the Panel considered, discussed, and debated several dozen possible topic areas and then settled on the following topics for intensive study:

- Alphabetics

  - Phonemic Awareness Instruction
  - Phonics Instruction

- Fluency
- Comprehension

    - Vocabulary Instruction
    - Text Comprehension Instruction
    - Teacher Preparation and Comprehension Strategies Instruction

- Teacher Education and Reading Instruction
- Computer Technology and Reading Instruction.

In addition, because of the concern voiced by the public at the regional hearings that the highest standards of scientific evidence be applied in the research review process, the methodology subgroup was tasked to develop a research review process including specific review criteria.

Each topic and subtopic became the subject of the work of a subgroup composed of one or more Panel members. Some Panel members served on more than one subgroup. The subgroups formulated seven broad questions to guide their efforts in meeting the Congressional charge of identifying effective instructional reading approaches and determining their readiness for application in the classroom:

1. Does instruction in phonemic awareness improve reading? If so, how is this instruction best provided?
2. Does phonics instruction improve reading achievement? If so, how is this instruction best provided?
3. Does guided oral reading instruction improve fluency and reading comprehension? If so, how is this instruction best provided?
4. Does vocabulary instruction improve reading achievement? If so, how is this instruction best provided?
5. Does comprehension strategy instruction improve reading? If so, how is this instruction best provided?
6. Do programs that increase the amount of children's independent reading improve reading achievement and motivation? If so, how is this instruction best provided?
7. Does teacher education influence how effective teachers are at teaching children to read? If so, how is this instruction best provided? . . .

Methodological Overview

In what may be its most important action, the Panel then developed and adopted a set of rigorous research methodological standards. . . . These standards guided the screening of the research literature relevant to each topic area addressed by the Panel. This screening process identified a final set of experimental or quasi-experimental research studies that were then subjected to detailed analysis. . . .

It is the view of the Panel that the efficacy of materials and methodologies used in the teaching of reading and in the prevention or treatment of reading disabilities should be tested.... rigorously. However, such standards have not been universally accepted or used in reading education research. Unfortunately, only a small fraction of the total reading research literature met the Panel's standards for use in the topic analyses....

Findings and Determinations of the National Reading Panel by Topic Areas

Alphabetics

Phonemic Awareness Instruction

Phonemes are the smallest units composing spoken language. For example, the words "go" and "she" each consist of two sounds or phonemes. Phonemes are different from letters that represent phonemes in the spellings of words. Instruction in phonemic awareness (PA) involves teaching children to focus on and manipulate phonemes in spoken syllables and words. PA instruction is frequently confused with phonics instruction, which entails teaching students how to use letter-sound relations to read or spell words. PA instruction qualifies as phonics instruction when it involves teaching children to blend or segment the sounds in words using letters. However, children may be taught to manipulate sounds in speech without any letters as well; this does not qualify as phonics instruction. PA is also frequently confused with auditory discrimination, which refers to the ability to recognize whether two spoken words are the same or different....

Findings and determinations The results of the meta-analysis were impressive. Overall, the findings showed that teaching children to manipulate phonemes in words was highly effective under a variety of teaching conditions with a variety of learners across a range of grade and age levels and that teaching phonemic awareness to children significantly improves their reading more than instruction that lacks any attention to PA.

Specifically, the results of the experimental studies led the Panel to conclude that PA training was the cause of improvement in students' phonemic awareness, reading, and spelling following training. The findings were replicated repeatedly across multiple experiments and thus provide converging evidence for causal claims. While PA training exerted strong and significant effects on reading and spelling development, it did not have an impact on children's performance on math tests. This indicates that halo/Hawthorne (novelty) effects did not explain the findings and that indeed the training effects were directly connected with and limited to the targeted domain under study. Importantly, the effects of PA instruction on reading lasted well beyond the end of training. Children of varying abilities improved their PA and their reading skills as a function of PA training.

PA instruction also helped normally achieving children learn to spell, and the effects lasted well beyond the end of training. However, the instruction was not effective for improving spelling in disabled readers. This is consistent with other research showing that disabled readers have difficulty learning how to spell.

Programs in all of the studies provided explicit instruction in phonemic awareness. Specifically, the characteristics of PA training found to be most effective in enhancing PA, reading, and spelling skills included explicitly and systematically teaching children to manipulate phonemes with letters, focusing the instruction on one or two types of phoneme manipulations rather than multiple types, and teaching children in small groups. . . .

Phonics Instruction

Phonics instruction is a way of teaching reading that stresses the acquisition of letter-sound correspondences and their use in reading and spelling. The primary focus of phonics instruction is to help beginning readers understand how letters are linked to sounds (phonemes) to form letter-sound correspondences and spelling patterns and to help them learn how to apply this knowledge in their reading. Phonics instruction may be provided systematically or incidentally. The hallmark of a systematic phonics approach or program is that a sequential set of phonics elements is delineated and these elements are taught along a dimension of explicitness depending on the type of phonics method employed. Conversely, with incidental phonics instruction, the teacher does not follow a planned sequence of phonics elements to guide instruction but highlights particular elements opportunistically when they appear in text. . . .

Questions guiding the NRP analysis of phonics instruction   The NRP examined the research literature concerning phonics instruction to answer the following questions: Does phonics instruction enhance children's success in learning to read? Is phonics instruction more effective at some grade levels than others? Is it beneficial for children who are having difficulties learning to read? Does phonics instruction improve all aspects of reading or just decoding and word-level reading skills? Are some types of phonics instruction more effective than others and for which children? Does phonics instruction have an impact on children's spelling?

To address these questions the NRP performed a literature search to identify studies published since 1970 that compared phonics instruction to other forms of instruction for their impact on reading ability. The initial electronic and manual searches identified 1,373 studies that appeared relevant to phonics instruction. Evaluation of these studies to determine adherence to the general and specific NRP research methodology criteria identified 38 studies from which 66 treatment-control group comparisons were derived. Data from these studies were used in a meta-analysis, including the calculation of effect sizes.

The meta-analysis indicated that systematic phonics instruction enhances children's success in learning to read and that systematic phonics instruction is significantly more effective than instruction that teaches little or no phonics.

Findings and determinations   The meta-analysis revealed that systematic phonics instruction produces significant benefits for students in kindergarten through 6th grade and for children having difficulty learning to read. The ability to read and spell words was enhanced in kindergartners who received systematic beginning phonics instruction. First graders who were taught phonics systematically were better able to decode and spell, and they showed significant improvement in their ability to comprehend text. Older children receiving phonics instruction were better able to decode and spell words and to read text orally, but their comprehension of text was not significantly improved.

POSTSCRIPT

Is the Whole-Language Approach the Best Way to Teach Reading?

What is the best way to teach young children how to read? Should it be the same way they learn to walk and talk—through trial-and-error practicing, making mistakes, practicing some more, and then finally succeeding? Or should it be by direct instruction where the proper method of decoding words is taught specifically in a very structured way?

With so much money being spent on early literacy materials, children's literature, formal reading materials, and supplemental texts and instructional materials, this issue is garnering a great deal of interest. Colleges and university faculty who prepare future teachers want to make sure that the most appropriate methods are being taught. School administrators are concerned that their limited funds are spent wisely on programs that will actually yield proven results. Much more research needs to be conducted, both quantitative and qualitative.

Suggested Readings

Butler, J., Liss, C., and Sterner, P., "Starting on the Write Foot: Helping Parents Understand How Children Learn to Read and Write," *Texas Child Care* (Winter 1999).

Lemann, N., "The Readings Wars," *The Atlantic Monthly* (November 1997).

Manzo, K. K., "Whole Language Lives," *Teacher Magazine* (vol. 10, 1999).

Palmaffy, T., "See Dick Flunk," *Policy Review* (vol. 86, 1997).

Tunnell, M. O. and Jacobs, J. S., "Using 'Real' Books: Research Findings on Literature-based Reading Instruction," *The Reading Teacher* (vol. 42, 1989).

ISSUE 16

Is Class Size Reduction the Most Effective Way to Improve Educational Performance?

YES: John A. Zahorik, from "Reducing Class Size Leads to Individualized Instruction," *Educational Leadership* (September 1999)

NO: Eric A. Hanushek, from "Class Size Reduction: Good Politics, Bad Education Policy," *The High School Magazine* (January/February 1999)

ISSUE SUMMARY

YES: John A. Zahorik, a professor emeritus at the University of Wisconsin–Milwaukee, asserts that the research on class size reduction indicates that smaller class size translates into higher academic achievement in the primary grades.

NO: Eric A. Hanushek, the Paul and Jean Hanna Senior Fellow at the Hoover Institution of Stamford University, states that the small academic gains, found mainly among poor kindergarten children, do not warrant the cost of nationwide class size reduction programs.

There never was a magical number devised for the perfect-sized classroom in elementary schools. Guidelines for class size ratios for the number of teachers to children in preschools vary from state to state. North Dakota and New York have the lowest adult-to-child ratio with one adult required for every seven preschoolers. Texas has the highest ratio with one adult required for every seventeen preschoolers. The other 47 states and the District of Columbia fall in between with the average being one adult required for every ten preschoolers. That changes when children attend kindergarten. Public and private schools typically do not have to follow specific licensing standards for class size. Some teachers' contracts may specify a specific class size and if that class size is exceeded, the teacher may get a classroom aide or additional pay.

Historically, when a town built a one-room school, all the children in that town would attend. When too many families moved into that town for all of the children to be accommodated in one classroom, a second school may have been built. In other cases, children shared benches and books and the teacher managed to squeeze more children in as they moved into town. When larger schools started to be built, a uniform class size was used to assign children to a room. Over 100 years ago class size averages were in the 30s. They have steadily decreased over the years. Today, many parents and teachers strongly believe that the smaller the class the more the students will learn. Is that true? Does smaller class size indeed translate into higher student achievement?

John A. Zahorik presents data from some of the more well known class size studies, including one by the Student Achievement Guarantee in Education (SAGE) program in Wisconsin and one entitled the *Student/Teacher Achievement Ratio (STAR)*, conducted in Tennessee. When class size in these two states dropped significantly, below 17 students per teacher, children benefited, particularly urban and rural children from poor families who were in kindergarten through third grade. Zahorik advocates for smaller class sizes, asserting that teachers will be able to get to know their students better and therefore will provide opportunities for individualization.

Eric A. Hanushek found that even though class size has been shrinking over the past 25 years in general, there has not been a marked improvement in academic achievement. Student/teacher ratios have fallen 35 percent nationally from 1950–1995, but scores on national assessment tests have not increased. Hanushek reports data that does support smaller class size for kindergarten classes, but states that there is little that would support continuing smaller class size *after* kindergarten.

All across the nation school board members are discussing class size issues. California legislators passed a law which calls for a 20:1 class size. What are the ramifications of legislation such as this? Are there enough certified teachers to cover all of the additional classes that will be needed? With overcrowding already an issue in many schools, are the funds available to support building and equipping additional classrooms for the new, smaller-sized classes? Does the research support these added costs?

Teachers working in schools with a large number of challenging children find that smaller classes give them the opportunity to give the extra help needed. Years ago, when parents provided stricter discipline and supported the educational process, teachers could rely on them to follow through with teaching their children after they returned home. Today this is often not the case. Many teachers express concern over having to be both a teacher and a parent to needy children and contend that with fewer students in the class, they would be able to offer more assistance.

In the following selections, Zahorik maintains that many more opportunities for individualization occur when children are enrolled in classrooms with fewer children. Hanushek asserts that he would like to see money spent on teacher effectiveness rather than on policies designed to lower class size. He states that real changes in learning will occur when all children have access to high quality teaching.

John A. Zahorik

Reducing Class Size Leads to Individualized Instruction

In California, Texas, Wisconsin, and other states, reducing class size is being used as a way to increase student achievement in the primary grades. The approach makes sense intuitively, and research supports it. Although Slavin (1989), Hanushek (1996), and others claim that any benefits of reduced class size are minimal and that other ways to increase achievement may be more effective and less costly, the Student/Teacher Achievement Ratio (STAR) project in Tennessee in the 1980s offered convincing evidence of the positive effects of reduced class size (Word et al., 1994).

Class size, of course, cannot influence academic achievement directly. It must first influence what teachers and students do in the classroom before it can possibly affect student learning. A reasonable expectation of teaching in a small-size class is that students receive more individual attention, and this is one of the main findings from research by Cahen, Filby, McCutchen, and Kyle (1983), Robinson and Wittebols (1986), and Johnston and Davis (1989). How individualization comes about in small-size classes and the type of individualization that is used are topics being investigated in the Student Achievement Guarantee in Education (SAGE) program (Maier, Molnar, Smith, & Zahorik, 1997; Molnar, Smith, & Zahorik, 1998).

SAGE

SAGE is a five-year program featuring class-size reduction that is being implemented in 80 Wisconsin schools. The program, initiated in 1996 by the Wisconsin Department of Public Instruction, provides resources for schools that enroll children from poor families to reduce class size to a 15:1 student-teacher classroom ratio in kindergarten through 3rd grade.

Because of individual school requirements, the 15:1 student-teacher ratio occurs in four formats: 15:1 Regular (one teacher and 15 students); 15:1 Shared Space (one teacher and 15 students sharing a room with another teacher and 15 students); 30:2 Team Taught (two teachers team teaching 30 students); and 30:2 Floating Teacher (one teacher and 30 students except during reading, language arts, and mathematics, when another teacher joins the class to reduce the ratio to 15:1).

We are conducting a longitudinal study of the effects of reduced class size on achievement and classroom events in 30 SAGE schools. Achievement results, based on pre- and post-tests using the Comprehensive Testing Basic Skills, Terra Nova, Complete Battery, show that SAGE students in grades 1 and 2 consistently outperform students in 14 comparison schools, but we have found no differences among the types of SAGE classrooms.

To determine the effects of reduced class size on classroom events, our research team collected data through teacher logs, teacher questionnaires, teacher interviews, and classroom observations for the past three years. These data have resulted in a model of teaching in small classes that illustrates the importance of individualization.

The Emergence of Individualization in Small-Size Classes

Small class size has three main effects that lead to increased individualization: fewer discipline problems and more instruction, more knowledge of students, and more teacher enthusiasm for teaching. In small-size classes, there is less misbehavior. When misbehavior does occur, it is more noticeable, and teachers can treat it immediately before it becomes a major problem. This reduced, if not totally eliminated, time spent on discipline leads to more time available for instruction.

More knowledge of individual students is an important result of smaller class size. Teachers come to know students personally, and they have a much greater understanding of each student's place in the learning cycle. A caring, family-like atmosphere develops in the classroom.

When classes are small, teachers experience less stress from disciplining, correcting papers, and not having time to do what needs to be done. As stress is reduced, enthusiasm and satisfaction increase, and educators begin to implement teaching procedures that they know will benefit students.

The main result of more instructional time, knowledge of students, and teacher enthusiasm is individualization. Often the individualization is one-to-one tutoring, but it also occurs in other ways. Teachers individualize when they form and instruct small groups on the basis of perceived need. And teachers individualize during whole-class instruction when they provide numerous opportunities for each student to express his or her understanding.

The product of this emphasis on individualization is greater coverage of content and, to some extent, greater in-depth treatment of content. Many teachers completed the grade-level curriculum well before the end of the year. The outcome of this broader, and possibly deeper, content coverage is greater student achievement.

Although individualization is the main product of teaching in small-size classes, some increase in the use of hands-on activities, such as manipulative activities, interest centers, and cooperative groups, occurs because of less student misbehavior and greater teacher enthusiasm. These activities, then, also contribute to increased student achievement.

The Nature of Individualization in Small-Size Classes

The individualization that occurs in small-size classes is more procedural than substantive. Teachers generally do not alter the curriculum for individual students; they expect each student to acquire the same content. Even when students complete the grade-level content before the end of the year, as is the case in many small-size classrooms, the additional content that teachers provide is the established content for the next grade. It is not enrichment content tailored to students' interests.

What teachers do alter for individual students is instruction. Teachers identify the learning problems of individual students; they provide help to individual students that includes explanations, analogies, examples, demonstrations, and tasks; and they constantly check on the progress of individual students. As one teacher said,

> If a child is having problems, you can see it right away. You can take care of it then. You don't have to wait until they turn in their papers.... You can get around to each child.... I can take care of it [a problem] right then before they practice it wrong. It works a lot better for the children.

With the exception of the slight increase in the use of hands-on activities found in small-size classes, the dominant mode of teaching remains direct instruction. Teachers continue to structure, manage, and pace all activities. The teacher gives information, asks questions, praises correct responses, and controls interactions with students in other ways. The students are largely passive in that their role is to listen and to follow the teacher's directions. It usually is not to engage in problem solving, creating, and decision making.

In summary, small-size classes are clearly moving toward more individualization of instruction. The individualization that occurs, however, involves methods that the teachers have always used. They simply repackage methods for use with individual students.

As teachers change from teaching normal-size classes to teaching small-size classes, what happens may not be too different from what happens to chefs as they change from cooking in a restaurant to cooking for their families. In the restaurant, the chef prepares many menu meals. Each meal generally does not differ in elements, portions, or presentation. One plate of chicken and pasta, for example, is identical to every other, and the chef serves it night after night. At home, the chef can pay more attention to the needs of family members. Although the chef does not prepare a different meal for each family member, he or she varies the menu by not putting broccoli on Alice's plate, reducing the amount of salt for Grandma, and giving Joe two pieces of fish. The actual food preparation in the two settings is probably very similar, however. Like teachers shifting from large to small class sizes, the chef alters his or her behavior as he or she moves from the restaurant to the home. But planning for chefs—and for teachers—does not alter significantly.

Continuing Research on Individualization

The present understanding of individualization in small-size classes will undoubtedly be clarified as the SAGE project evaluation continues. One focus of future research is differences in the four types of SAGE classrooms. Our research has revealed few differences to date. If differences are not found in the future, results would suggest that obtaining additional classrooms for districts embarking on small-class-size programs may not be an issue, because sharing classrooms does not harm achievement.

Another focus is the question of when teachers begin to individualize. At present, they appear to individualize as soon as the school year begins. If individualization starts instantly—if small class size permits teachers to do what they have always wanted to do and know how to do—staff development may not be needed in small-class-size programs.

Still another focus is who receives the individualization in classes. Do all students receive equal attention from the teacher? Our tentative findings indicate that both able students and problem learners receive comparable amounts of individual attention, as do typical students. If all students receive individualization, the need for future remedial and gifted programs may be reduced because of small-size classes.

As an answer to the problem of poor achievement, small class size has much promise. Understanding its process and outcomes can provide guidance to states and districts as they consider whether to reduce class size in their schools.

Eric A. Hanushek

 **NO**

Class Size Reduction: Good Politics, Bad Education Policy

Since California Governor Pete Wilson demonstrated the political popularity of reducing class sizes governors and politicians at all levels in both political parties across the nation have been tripping over themselves in a rush to mandate and to fund smaller classes. It is masterful politics, combining concern for education with the righteous support of parents and school personnel. Unfortunately, it is bad education policy. It is minimally an expensive policy with little hope of improving overall student performance. It is arguably an expensive policy that does actual damage.

The arguments for reduced class size seem unassailable. Smaller classes permit more individual attention by teachers and may reduce teachers' burden of managing large numbers of students and their work. Unfortunately, the evidence does not suggest any changes typically occurring (as opposed to potentially occurring) that add up to significant improvements in student performance.

No aspect of education has been studied as thoroughly as the effect of class size on student performance, and a wide range of information points to no effect. First, class sizes have been falling nationally for at least the last quarter century, but average student performance is essentially unchanged. Allowing for changes in student backgrounds does not help to explain these results. Second, international comparisons of math and science performance are unrelated to differences in intensity of teacher hiring. Third, some 300 high quality statistical studies show some positive effects of class size but an almost equal number of negative effects, suggesting nothing consistent or systematic. Finally, Project STAR in Tennessee indicates that large reductions in class size at kindergarten will perhaps improve student performance. But there is no indication that class size reductions after kindergarten have any consistent impact. Moreover, STAR is silent about more modest reductions (i.e., less than the movements to class sizes of 14–16 students), although prior analyses suggest little to no effect of class size reductions not going down to class sizes of 15 or fewer students.

All this evidence concerns a simple question: Is there reason to believe there are ANY gains in student achievement to be expected from class size reductions? My conclusion at this point is that there is no reason to expect improvements, although by selecting specific evidence (e.g., the kindergarten evidence from Project STAR) and ignoring other pieces one might conclude there is reason to expect some positive results. But educational policy decisions require answering a tougher question: Are the gains in student performance that one might expect worth the costs? Here the answer is unambiguous: NO. Reducing class size is very expensive, and it could only make sense if there were no other uses for the money.

My candidate for alternative uses of funds centers on the quality of teaching. While the research evidence on the effects of class size suggests no real effects, the research does show dramatic differences in the performance of teachers. The research confirms some teachers are much better than others and differences in teacher effectiveness completely dwarf any possible differences due to class size variations. Given this, it seems much more productive to channel money toward attracting and retaining particularly effective teachers than toward continuing to pursue a failed policy.

With that background, several oft-mentioned things should be addressed. First, it is almost certainly true that smaller classes yield significant performance gains for particular students, for particular teachers, and for particular subject matters. Nothing in current proposals, however, focuses resources on the areas where they would be most beneficial—implying that general policies mix effective and ineffective circumstances. Second, modest changes in class size, ones that have the most manageable fiscal implications, also lead to modest changes in teacher behavior—and a lack of results should not be a surprise. Third, nothing in the current proposals ensures that new teachers hired to reduce class sizes are better (or as good as) current teachers. If worse, the class size policy could easily harm students. Indeed, as the California policy was implemented, it appears that suburban districts raided urban districts for experienced and qualified teachers—probably leading to a worsening of schools for disadvantaged students.

Improving our schools should be a national priority. But not every policy that directs resources toward schools is the same. Overall class size policies of the type currently being debated simply do not appear to be effective even though they are very expensive.

POSTSCRIPT

Is Class Size Reduction the Most Effective Way to Improve Educational Performance?

When looking for solutions to educational problems, all possibilities must be thoroughly researched. Hanushek is concerned that in the rush to lower class size, inferior or large numbers of new teachers will be hired. He states that lower class size policies could actually harm children. If a large number of wealthy suburban districts lower class size and suddenly need to hire many more teachers to work in their modern, well-equipped schools, would children who attend less financially secure schools lose their teachers to suburban schools? Would the problems of poor academic performance, especially among urban, poor children, be exacerbated with the mass exodus of quality teachers to new classrooms? Deans at some of the largest teacher preparation institutions in the United States question if they can prepare enough teachers to meet the demand of lower class sizes. There are growing teacher shortages in areas all across the country, with large cities being the hardest hit. Are there enough people wanting to pursue a career in education to meet the demand? Without compromising quality, can the need be met? The large numbers of new hires that would need to be made would mean that some schools would have a large percentage of first- and second-year teachers on their staff.

Do smaller class sizes mean that better quality teaching will occur? If so, will this lead to improved academic performance? Zahorik contends that more individualization will be evident because three factors are present in smaller size classes. They are: fewer discipline problems, a better understanding by the teacher of the needs of each student, and more enthusiasm from the teacher for his or her job. Teachers who feel better about being in the classroom and who are not overburdened will teach better.

Lower class size has put a great strain on the public school system in many areas. School districts without enough classrooms to accommodate the new classes may have to move to a year-round program where, for example, four classes of one grade would share three classrooms. With a schedule of nine weeks in school, and three weeks off, one class would always be off and not need a classroom. One teacher and his or her class would be designated as the roving group and move into an empty classroom every three weeks. This may not be an ideal teaching or learning situation, but it is one solution to the overcrowding issue.

There are some who assert that teachers and their union leaders support class size reduction not because it improves students' academic performance, but because it allows for more teachers to be hired, therefore increasing the number of teachers who could join a union. When teachers are asked, many overwhelmingly support lowering class size. Administrators and school board members, however, want empirical evidence that a change in practice would improve the performance level of the students.

Hanushek asks us to carefully decide if lowering class size is the best use of limited education dollars. He worries about the children in the urban schools in California who lost their teachers to more affluent districts in the suburbs when California moved to a 20:1 ratio policy. He argues that sometimes the most expensive option is not the best buy. He supports programs that assist teachers in becoming skilled at their craft. There is great variance in the methods used by teachers and excellent teaching should be the hallmark of any program to improve academic performance.

Suggested Readings

Gursky, D., "Class Size Does Matter," *Education Digest* (vol. 64, no. 2, 1998).

Korostoff, M., "Observing From the Inside: Teaching and Learning in California's 20:1 Reduced-Size Classrooms," *Teacher Education Quarterly* (vol. 26, no. 1, Winter 1999).

Murray, G. J., "Class Size: Major Implications for School Leaders," *NASSP Bulletin* (vol. 84, 2000).

Ross, R., "How Class Size Reduction Harms Kids in Poor Neighborhoods," *Education Week* (May 26, 1999).

Turley, S. and Nakai, K., "Coping With Class-Size Reduction in California," *Educational Leadership* (vol. 55, 1998).

ISSUE 17

Is Grade Retention a Sound Educational Practice?

YES: Joellen Perry, from "What, Ms. Crabapple Again?" *U.S. News & World Report* (May 24, 1999)

NO: William A. Owings and Susan Magliaro, from "Grade Retention: A History of Failure," *Educational Leadership* (September 1998)

ISSUE SUMMARY

YES: Joellen Perry, a writer for *U.S. News & World Report,* states that for many families, grade retention is successful. She asserts that to many parents and children, the only solution for getting back on the right track in school is to start again. For these children, repeating a grade offers them a chance at having a positive learning experience.

NO: William A. Owings, superintendent of Accomack County Public Schools in Virginia, and Susan Magliaro, an associate professor at Virginia Tech, maintain that grade retention is not a positive experience for children when it happens or later in their school careers. Grade retention does more harm than good in the long run and other options should be considered before retaining a child.

Retention is often called a gift of time. It allows a child who is having difficulty keeping up academically with his or her peers the time to catch up and feel comfortable in a school setting. Although it is not currently used as often as it was in the past, retention still receives a great deal of attention from presidents, researchers, and school administrators. Is retention the answer for children who are not able to keep up with their peers? Would another year in the same grade yield more success the second time around? Could retention harm a child socially? Would it be better to promote a student, in what many call a *social promotion,* just so the student could remain in class with those who are his or her same age?

Teachers are often told in October to begin to keep a list of those children that they think they might recommend for retention at the end of the school year. Grade retention is not always readily accepted by parents, but is offered as a solution for the constant academic struggle their child may be undergoing. Children themselves have the summer to accept the idea and by September many begin to embrace being in the same grade again. Many gain new respect from classmates because they are chronologically older and more experienced than the rest of the class.

What is the criteria that teachers use to determine if a student is a candidate to be retained? The list varies among teachers and school districts, but some of the most frequently occurring criteria used by early childhood educators include: chronological age younger than peers, small size for age, poor self-concept or lack of social skills, poor academic performance—especially in reading, and, if in kindergarten, lack of previous school experience. One factor that is not related to the student at all has to do with the academic requirements of the next grade level. James L. Hymes, Jr., one of the most influential early childhood educators of the twentieth century, called it the "dribble down disease," but it is often called the "push down curriculum." What used to be taught in second grade is now part of the curriculum for first grade. What was once part of the first grade experience is now expected to be mastered in kindergarten. With rigorous academic requirements in place throughout the country young children who may developing normally are having an increasingly difficult time keeping up with the expectations of the next grade level. Early childhood educators may have colleagues in the grade above them demanding that the students who enter their class be well prepared in certain academic skills. As a result, teachers may be torn when they have colleagues who put unrealistic demands on pupils. Some teachers view retention as a gift to the child to better prepare her or him to deal with the academic pressure she or he will face in September. But many ask, is this the best way to handle academic expectations?

Just as children walk and talk at different ages, they acquire academic skills at different rates. Accommodating for varying abilities is the mark of a good early childhood teacher. When children are not progressing as rapidly as their peers, support services need to be in place to assist that child in acquiring the necessary skills. Instead of making a retention decision in April, would a gift of time over the summer be a better option? The student may be able to receive help that could assist him or her in being successful in the next grade. Some of that help may include summer school, small group tutoring efforts, after-school help, and information and assistance for the families to help the child at home.

In the following selections, Joellen Perry asserts that many parents view retention as an ideal solution for combating educational difficulties and are pleased that they decided to retain their child. Perry maintains that for certain children and families, retention can be a successful experience and should be presented as a viable option for school success. William A. Owings and Susan Magliaro present a history of the practice of retention and strongly urge educators to abandon this practice. They argue that it may seem like a good short-term solution to a problem, but when looking long-range at the total educational experience, grade retention does not help a child to be more successful and can, in fact, cause more harm than good.

What, Ms. Crabapple Again?

To kids, the only thing worse than repeating a grade is the thought of losing a parent or going blind. That's the finding of a classic 1980 study on childhood stress. Academics tend to agree, and not only because of the stigma. Research shows that repeaters rarely catch up with classmates and are more likely to drop out of school.

Tell that to the Yee family in Kailua, Hawaii. Last year, Luana Yee's daughter Keolamau struggled as the youngest, smallest first grader at Punahou School. Academically, the 6-year-old held her own, but older classmates drowned her out of discussions and teased her. Keolamau's self-confidence crumbled; she began squinting excessively and urinating nearly 15 times a day. When academic and medical testing ruled out a mental or physical disability, Keolamau's parents requested that she repeat first grade. Keolamau accepted the decision reluctantly—at first. But as she finishes her second year of first grade, her physical symptoms have disappeared and she is a well-liked class leader.

Like the Yees, a significant number of parents are using voluntary retention as a way to aid a failing or flailing child. The trend has not been quantified, but based on anecdotal evidence, repeating a grade is clearly becoming part of a parent's arsenal of school-management tools.

What about studies showing that retention doesn't work? Educators argue that retention is not a solution for academic failure. Neither, according to research, is "social promotion"—pushing kids through school to buoy their self-esteem. But the cautionary studies don't distinguish between students forced to repeat a failed grade and those who voluntarily stay back for developmental reasons, and children who voluntarily repeat a year. The latter group is but a tiny minority among the nearly 20 percent of students held back each year. In addition, classrooms can have a wide age spread to the clear disadvantage of the young and the immature. Nearly 1 in 10 children enters kindergarten a year late, redshirted by parents hoping to hone an academic or athletic edge. As a result, a child with a birth date right before the cutoff for entering kindergarten may be a year or more younger than at least a few classmates.

There is no sure-fire way for parents to know if a child will benefit from being retained, but certain signs may help identify a potential candidate. Children who feel developmentally out of sync with classmates might form close bonds with youngsters in the grade below. Second or third graders with late-blooming fine motor skills, lacking the hand-eye coordination to deftly maneuver a pencil, can struggle with writing. Other students may find the school day physically exhausting. Kindergarten wiped out Christine Morris by midweek. "By Wednesday," recalls her mother, Valerie, "she just didn't want to go." Christine attended a yearlong transitional program before first grade; today she is in the top 5 percent of her junior class at a metropolitan Atlanta high school.

Gift of time   Preparing children to repeat a year is perhaps the most dreaded hurdle of the retention process. Presenting the second year as a "gift of extra time" helps kids view repeating as an issue of development, rather than personal failure, educators say. "Reassure children that some people just need more time than others," counsels Lilian Katz, professor of education at the University of Illinois. Parents of children born prematurely, and of those who are chronologically young for their grade, or physically small for their age, have tangible reference points for why children might need more time. Luana Yee recalls that her daughter Keolamau, born three months prematurely and two months before her school's entrance cutoff date, accepted the logic that her brain and body simply needed time to catch up to those of her older classmates.

Some parents do a public-to-private switch that eliminates the debate over retention. While public schools often have a fall birth date as a cutoff for entering a grade, private schools frequently use a spring date. If the retention is engineered within the confines of the public school system, parents might consider switching teachers, or even schools, to lessen the stigma or allay fears that the coming school year will be a boring rehash of the past year.

If a child remains "unalterably opposed" to repeating, though, counsels Garry Walz, professor emeritus of education at the University of Michigan, a second year in the same grade could be disastrous. Parents should consider promotion coupled with intensive tutoring or counseling to give the child both self-confidence and strategies for succeeding in school.

Other difficulties   The results of retention should be clear after just a few months, says James Uphoff, professor emeritus of education at Wright State University in Dayton, Ohio. A child whose academic or social struggles intensify or plateau in the repeated year likely has issues that run deeper than developmental immaturity. Perhaps the problem is an undiagnosed learning disability or a chemical imbalance triggering, for instance, depression or an attention disorder. But a midyear switch up a grade is not recommended, says Uphoff, as the child will have missed months of crucial material. He suggests that students remain in the repeated grade while parents and school staff continue to seek the true source of the difficulties.

But when a child simply needs extra time, retention can work wonders. In 1993, third grade overwhelmed Sterling Collins-Hill of Oakland, Maine. Tough math problems could reduce him to tears. Even sloppily tied shoelaces might upset him. "He was hanging on by his fingernails," says his father, Steven Collins. Sterling recalls feeling "pretty alone" returning to third grade while his friends went ahead, but the feeling faded fast. Now 15 and a freshman on the honor roll and lacrosse team at Messalonskee High School, he says, "When I look back, I see it turned out for the best."

The Risks of Retention

Academics point out that there are many reasons not to retain, starting with the stigma. Slow learners or students with attention disorders will encounter the same difficulties the second time around, while enduring the shame of repeating a grade. Educators also warn of a lingering, powerful "should be" syndrome. Years later, many retained children believe their rightful place is in the grade above.

For these reasons, most experts advise parents to consider retention as a last resort. They recommend testing first to rule out learning disabilities, then exploring other interventions—tutoring, therapy, or medication, for example— suggested by teachers, administrators, school counselors, and doctors.

NO

**William A. Owings
and Susan Magliaro**

Grade Retention: A History of Failure

For almost 50 years, research has shown that grade-level retention provides no academic advantages to students. Yet, the practice is gaining increasing attention as schools face political pressure to demonstrate accountability for student achievement. Publications including *USA Today* (Ritter, 1997) and *Education Week* (Reynolds, Temple, & McCoy, 1997) have addressed the topic, and President Clinton in his 1997 and 1998 State of the Union Addresses called for increased retention of students with low scores on standardized tests, stating that a child should not move from grade to grade "until he or she is ready." Research suggests that retention is on the rise. According to one study (Roderick, 1995), from 1980 to 1992 the national percentage of retained students increased from approximately 20 percent to nearly 32 percent.

The overly simplistic view of retention as a panacea for education woes ignores its negative impact on children. A walk through history reminds us of what we have learned about retention.

History of Grade Retention

It was not until about 1860 that it became common in U.S. elementary schools to group children in grade levels, with promotion dependent on mastery of a quota of content. The New York City school system was reporting the results of promotion and retention as early as the turn of the century. Maxwell's (1904) age-grade progress study became the standard vehicle for school system reports on retention, promotion, and dropouts. Within the next two decades, researchers started to examine the efficacy of retention in terms of student achievement.

The goal of grade retention was to improve school performance by allowing more time for students to develop adequate academic skills (Reynolds, 1992). By the 1930s, researchers were reporting the negative effects of retention on achievement (Ayer, 1933; Kline, 1933). Goodlad (1954) summarized the research between 1924 and 1948 related to grade retention. This synthesis showed that retention did not decrease the variation in student achievement levels and had no positive effect on educational gain. Otto (1951) suggested that retention had no special educational value for children and that the academic

From William A. Owings and Susan Magliaro, "Grade Retention: A History of Failure," *Educational Leadership*, vol. 56, no. 1 (September 1998). Copyright © 1998 by The Association for Supervision and Curriculum Development. Reprinted by permission of ASCD; permission conveyed through Copyright Clearance Center, Inc. References omitted.

gain of nonpromoted students was smaller than the gain of their promoted counterparts.

In the mid-20th century, researchers began to investigate the relationship between retention and dropouts. One study (Berlman, 1949) indicated that students who were retained might be more likely to drop out of school than those who were not retained. This article appeared at a time when the literature was emphasizing the need to keep students in school (Anderson, 1950; Holbeck, 1950; Moffit, 1945; Nancarrow, 1951; Sandin, 1944).

In the 1960s and the 1970s, the pendulum moved toward the social promotion of students. After the publication of *A Nation at Risk* (National Commission on Excellence in Education, 1983), a time of reduced public confidence in schools, many school systems instituted more stringent promotion and retention policies—in spite of the lack of supportive research evidence (Roderick, 1994). For the public at large, it was counterintuitive to think that retention was not useful in helping students to reach basic skill levels (Natale, 1991).

Current Practice and Research

No precise national data record the exact numbers of retained students. However, a number of studies suggest that retention has persisted and possibly has increased. The Center for Policy Research in Education (1990) reported that by the 9th grade, approximately 50 percent of all U.S. school students have been retained. Roderick (1995) reported that the proportion of overage students entering high school has risen almost 40 percent since 1975. One synthesis of research indicated that the current level of retention matches that of the early 20th century (Shepard & Smith, 1990).

Of 66 articles on retention written from 1990 to 1997, only 1 supported retention (Lenarduzzi, 1990). These articles and Holmes's (1984) and Holmes and Matthews's (1989) meta-analyses document the effects of retention.

Many studies show the association between retention and dropping out of school (Cairns, Cairns, & Neckerman, 1989; Dawson, 1991). These studies control for the effects of other influencing factors. Grissom and Shepard (1989) determined that retention significantly increases the probability of dropping out, controlling for prior achievement, sex, and race.

Demographic data show that retained students tend to come from lower socioeconomic (SES) backgrounds than nonretained students (Thomas et al., 1992). Meisels (1993) found that approximately 40 percent of repeaters come from the lowest SES quartile, whereas approximately 8.5 percent come from the highest SES quartile. Meisels (1993) also determined that more than two-thirds of all retentions take place between kindergarten and 3rd grade. Other studies have shown that retained students tend to be male and African American, with parents who are less educated than the parents of nonretained students (Byrd & Weitzman, 1994; Dauber, 1993; Foster, 1993; Meisels, 1993). In California, George (1993) found that retention rates for African Americans and Hispanics are twice the rate for whites. Byrd and Weitzman (1994) examined social and health factors associated with retention. Poverty, gender, mother's education level, hearing and speech impairments, low birth weight, enuresis, and exposure to household smoking are significant predictive factors. Learning disabled students may also be retained more frequently than the general population (McLeskey, Lancaster, & Grizzle, 1995).

The long-held belief that early retention is best for students continues to be refuted in the literature (Johnson, 1990; Mantizicopoulos & Morrison, 1992; Thomas et al., 1992). Studies of retention in kindergarten indicate that retained students have significantly lower scores on standardized achievement tests than do nonretained students (Dennebaum & Kulberg, 1994). Another study shows no differences in achievement for retained kindergarten students and the matched control group (Shepard & Smith, 1987). Some research indicates that early retention may produce a short-lived increase in achievement; however, this gain vanishes in two or three years (Butler, 1990; Karweit & Wasik, 1992; Snyder, 1992).

Research indicates that retention produces negative social implications. Kindergarten students who were retained indicated a slightly more negative attitude toward school than did a matched control group (Shepard & Smith, 1987). Retained students may have more behavioral problems than those who are not retained (Meisels, 1993). Rumberger (1987) suggests that retention contributes to a permanent disengagement from school.

Research also shows that retention may have negative effects on long-term student achievement. Holmes's (1989) meta-analysis reviewed 63 controlled studies that compared the progress of retained students with that of lower-achieving promoted students; 54 studies showed negative achievement results for the retained students. Holmes then reviewed only those studies with the greatest statistical control. The negative achievement effects were again demonstrated. These findings were substantively identical to those of Goodlad's analysis in 1954. Subsequent studies have provided little new evidence to contradict Holmes's synthesis of research.

Other studies indicate an increased, cumulative negative effect of retention on achievement for at-risk students (Reynolds, 1992). Retained children may continue to decline in reading achievement over time compared with nonretained students. Whether this cumulative decline occurs in mathematics achievement is uncertain.

Retention Harms Learners

Historically, educators have viewed retention as a means of reducing skill variance in the classroom in an attempt to better meet student needs. Clearly, this practice has not achieved its goal. In the process we have harmed our clients. Physicians take an oath that guides their professional practice—first, do no harm. Educators would do well to take a similar oath. Retention harms an at-risk population cognitively and affectively. Alternatives to consider include requiring summer school, offering intensive remediation before and after school, changing teacher and administrative perceptions, and increasing teacher expectations.

One indicator of a profession is that a body of research guides its practice (Darling-Hammond & Goodwin, 1993). A body of research exists on the subject of retention, and it should guide our practice. If we are to treat our "patients" professionally, we need to stop punishing nonlearners and instead provide opportunities for success.

POSTSCRIPT

Is Grade Retention a Sound Educational Practice?

Finances play a role in many decisions made in public schools and many wonder if that is often the case when it comes to grade retention. Is it financially advantageous for a school district to retain students? When a district can receive 14 years of funding from the state for educating a student in what could have been only 13 years, are administrators more inclined to recommend retention? What incentives are in place for a school district to provide additional support to students that it retains or to students that it contemplated retaining, but did not? Should students who are retained be treated like all of the other students in a grade level? What services would ensure their success?

Retention decisions require careful consideration from a committee of educators and from the family of a child who may be retained. However, of greater concern are the students who are recommended to be retained again after having already been retained. What responsibility does the school district have to that student and his or her family?

When students are retained in kindergarten, what are the ramifications in high school? When freshmen are old enough to drive, are other problems present that educators and parents may not have thought of when the child was 5 years old? Do students who are 19 and still in high school pose additional concern for educators? Retention decisions are not to be made lightly and require careful consideration from all involved. Deciding what is best for each student is no easy task.

Suggested Readings

Bergin, D. A., Osburn, V. L., Cryan, J. R., "Influence of Child Independence, Gender, and Birthdate on Kindergarten Teachers' Recommendations for Retention," *Journal of Research in Childhood Education* (vol. 10, 1996).

Grant, J. and Johnson, B., "Preventing Retention in an Era of High Standards," *Principal* (vol. 76, 1997).

Mantizcopoulos, P. Y., "Do Certain Groups of Children Profit From Early Retention? A Follow-up Study of Kindergartners With Attention Problems," *Psychology in the Schools* (vol. 34, no. 2, 1997).

Mohr, K., "Seth's Story: The Tale of a Self-Determined Retention," *Childhood Education* (vol. 74, no. 1, 1997).

ISSUE 18

Do Multi-Year Assignments With the Same Teacher Improve Primary Students' Learning?

YES: Karen Rasmussen, from "Looping—Discovering the Benefits of Multiyear Teaching," *Education Update* (March 1998)

NO: Allan S. Vann, from "Looping: Looking Beyond the Hype," *Principal* (May 1997)

ISSUE SUMMARY

YES: Karen Rasmussen, associate editor for *Educational Leadership,* states that classroom teachers spend a great deal of time at the beginning of the school year developing positive working relationships with students and their families. Multi-year assignments allow these relationships to flourish over a minimum of a two-year period of time, making possible more learning progression in the second year.

NO: Allan S. Vann, principal at the James H. Boyd Intermediate School, counters that there may be significant disadvantages in having a child stay with the same teacher and peers for more than one school year. The disadvantages often outweigh the potential benefits of multi-year assignments.

We all remember teachers in whose class we would want to spend another year. They were caring, passionate teachers who made learning meaningful. However, we also remember teachers we were not sad to say goodbye to at the end of the school year. How long should each teacher have to influence young children? If one year is too short, are two or more years too long? Multi-year assignments, also called looping, have been gaining in popularity in recent years. Despite the lack of research conducted on the subject, multi-year assignments are being embraced by school districts all over the United States.

Staying with the same teacher for more than one year is not uncommon, particularly in early childhood settings. Preschool children are often enrolled in multi-age classrooms and have the same teacher throughout their preschool years.

Traditionally, when children enter kindergarten, the time limit with the teacher has been one academic year. However, some teachers have been challenging that tradition by requesting that they be allowed to move up to teach the first grade and to keep their class intact for the following year. This may occur when enrollments increase and a teacher needs to be added to the next grade level. Multi-year assignments are sometimes also prompted by a teacher who has had an extremely successful year with a group of students and who wants to continue the progress into the next year. Teachers who believe that they have received support from the families of the students in their class are also most likely to explore the option of multi-year assignments.

When a school district allows multi-year assignments as an option, are these teachers who are most often classified as the "good" teachers placed into multi-year assignments, leaving the teachers with less favorable ratings for those students in single-year assignments? Teachers who feel confident in their abilities and who want to be challenged as professionals are those who most often volunteer for multi-year assignments. Taking on new responsibilities and work is usually a trait found in high-performance teachers.

There are students who do not care which teacher they are assigned; they are more concerned with not being in the same classroom as a certain student. When children are in a multi-year assignment, they may have to deal with the negative consequences of having the same child or children bully them for two years as opposed to one year.

In general, multi-year assignments have not been found to be significantly advantageous to academic performance, but they have not been found to be harmful, either. The question then becomes, Should we endorse educational practices that have not been found to significantly improve performance? Are we just throwing more twists and turns into the academic setting without any concrete improvement?

In the following selections, Karen Rasmussen maintains that there are benefits to multi-year assignments, even though they may not be evident in current studies. Rasmussen asserts that teachers and students in a multi-year assignment can progress at a faster rate, especially in the beginning of the second year. Allan S. Vann counters that there are disadvantages to multi-year assignments, including students being exposed to a teacher's weaknesses for two consecutive years and the ridicule that some students may face from the same peers for two years.

Karen Rasmussen  **YES**

Looping—Discovering the Benefits of Multiyear Teaching

On the first day of school, the 2nd graders in Stephanie Jones's class run eagerly into the room to greet their teacher and one another. They quickly put away their lunches, jackets, and school supplies. As the bell rings, Jones invites the students to sit in a circle. They compare what they have written in their journals over the summer and then get started right away on a new writing assignment.

Students in Jones's class are able to start learning on the first day of school because they were all 1st graders in Jones's class the previous year. "Last year on the first day of school, the kids were crying and wouldn't let go of Mom and Dad," she relates. "I spent the morning learning the students' names and teaching them how to introduce themselves to one another. The second half of the day we spent going over bus schedules and procedures."

Buying Time

Jones is one of four teachers at Maple Dale Elementary School (Cincinnati, Ohio) who are involved in looping. Looping—which is sometimes called multiyear teaching or multiyear placement—occurs when a teacher is promoted with her students to the next grade level and stays with the same group of children for two or three years.

"After a year with my students, I felt like I was just beginning to know them," Jones explains. She first learned about looping three years ago from an article in *Education Update*. "It seemed that there was no down time in looping, so I would have more time for teaching."

"September 1 of the second year of looping is the 181st day of school for those in the class," says Jim Grant, who directs the Society for Developmental Education and codirects the National Alliance of Multiage Educators. Teachers who loop have fewer transitions to make at the beginning of the school year and can introduce curriculum topics right away at the start of the second year, he explains.

"Looking places kids in a developmental continuum," says Carol Cummings, staff development coordinator for the Raising Healthy Children Project at the University of Washington (Edmonds, Wash.). "It can take from three to six weeks at the beginning of the school year to establish classroom routines and expectations." By allowing students and teachers to remain together, says Grant, "looping literally buys time."

A Richer Curriculum

More time for teaching translates into a richer curriculum, say teachers. Since she began looping, Jones says, the most significant way her curriculum has changed is the addition of more social learning at the beginning of the 1st grade. Because she knows she'll have extra time in the second year, Jones spends the first several weeks building a sense of community. Once students have the skills to cooperate and communicate, she says, "you reap the benefits in the second year."

With their extra time in the second year, Jones and her students pursued topics they were interested in. During a heritage unit, the class studied quilts. Their fascination with tessellation led them to an in-depth study of math, science, and the work of Dutch artist M. C. Escher. Using a computer, students created their own designs and made quilts out of paper.

Sara Oldham, a 1st and 2nd grade teacher at Shelton Elementary School in Golden, Colo., appreciates that looping, in addition to giving her more teaching time, permits her to address topics when children show they are ready for them.

Oldham discovered looping when she and two other teachers at her school decided to investigate multiage configurations for their school. "The more I learned, I found I liked some aspects of multiage," she says. "But I didn't want such an age span in my class. In a single grade I think you have enough of a developmental span in the class."

Oldham views the 2nd grade curriculum as an extension of what happens in 1st grade. "Students read and write in 1st grade every day, and they do in 2nd, too, only it's more sophisticated."

Although Oldham is responsible for covering 1st and 2nd grade curriculums, she can address topics when she thinks students are ready for them. For example, math standards for place value and money are in the 1st grade curriculum, says Oldham. But "I've taught 1st grade long enough to know that money is a hard concept for 1st graders to understand."

At the end of 1st grade, Oldham introduces money to her students and then asks parents and children to practice using money over the summer. She resumes studying it in the 2nd grade, by which time most of the students have practiced exchanging money and getting change.

Because looping allows teachers to decide when to introduce curriculum topics, Oldham suggests that teachers who loop keep records of what they have taught during the first year so they don't repeat themselves. "Sometimes I'll pull out a book and a child will say, 'We read that last year.'"

Meeting the Needs of Each Student

Another benefit of looping cited by teachers is the opportunity to get to know students over two years. After a year, Oldham says, she has learned a lot about each student's skills and strengths. During the summer, "I think about certain children who are having behavior or academic problems and ask myself, 'What can I do to help this child?'" With looping, "you don't have to start from scratch with each child."

Grant believes that building a bond between teachers and students is at the heart of looping: "Teachers have tried everything and now they are getting back to the basics, which is that strong student, parent, and teacher relationships are important."

These strong relationships help all students, but are especially important to students with special needs, say experts. In her class, Oldham has a child who is paraplegic, three ESL [English as a Second Language] students, and two hearing-impaired students. The parents of the wheelchair-bound and hearing-impaired students chose the looping program because they believed the teacher should know a lot about their children's needs, says Oldham.

"This helps both the students and the teacher because the teacher can get used to having the child's aide in the room and students get used to seeing their friend in a wheelchair or brace." By being together for two years, the students feel more comfortable with their peers and will take risks, she explains.

Postponing High-Stakes Decisions

At the same time that looping helps teachers meet special needs of students, it also allows them time to consider the best interests of the children. "Looping allows teachers to postpone high-stakes decisions," says Grant. "If a teacher thinks a child may need a special education referral or an ADD [attention-deficit disorder] diagnosis—decisions that could dramatically affect the life of the child—they can put it off for a year until they can better observe the child."

Jones remembers a child in her 1st grade class who was having social and academic problems and was physically small for his age. Although she thought repeating 1st grade might give him a chance to mature, she worried that he would feel punished. "On the first day of 2nd grade, I started with him where he'd left off the previous year. That year he took off." He passed all proficiency tests and began to interact more comfortably with his peers, she says. "He skyrocketed and was at grade level by the end of 2nd grade."

Young children are not the only students who benefit from the strong teacher-student relationships and individual attention provided by looping, say experts. Patricia Crosby, a 7th and 8th grade language arts and social studies teacher at Robert J. Coelho Middle School in Attleboro, Mass., cites many of the same benefits of looping as her colleagues in elementary schools. In addition to those benefits, Crosby states that the trust a student has in a teacher can become even more important as children become adolescents. "They ask you questions they don't always think they can ask their parents," she says. "And because you know them so well you can observe any changes in behavior that might indicate problems, such as drug or alcohol abuse."

"Looping is a K–8 thing right now," says Grant, "but it could work at the high school level. Think how great it would be. Adolescence is a tough time. Many young people's lives have been saved because they found a mentor in high school and were able to form a bond with a teacher through having him or her as a teacher for more than one class."

Helping At-Risk Students Succeed

Jan Jubert, a 1st and 2nd grade teacher at Lac du Flambeau Public School in Lac du Flambeau, Wisc., agrees with Grant that looping provides opportunities for students who might otherwise fall through the cracks of the education system. Of her 15 students, most come from low socioeconomic backgrounds and have been identified as at-risk. Additionally, one child in Jubert's class is deaf and requires an interpreter, and the students' ability levels range from learning disabled to gifted and talented. Jubert believes that equal opportunity, which requires equal education, will enable the children to set and reach their life goals.

"Children today join gangs because they want to feel they are a part of a group and feel accepted," says Jubert. "Looping makes children feel secure. At-risk kids are starving for this." Because many parents work two jobs or are single parents, she explains, students need to feel a bond with one another and with adults. "It takes the entire first year to build a level of trust," she says.

By staying with a teacher who really knows them and whom they trust, students are given time and high-quality instruction to succeed, says Jubert. Because she has more time to teach and to consider the needs of each child, Jubert says, she covers more material, offers more hands-on activities to her students, and designs activities using multiple intelligences theories that will help children learn the way they learn best.

Jubert believes that looping has helped her reach her goal to make a difference for her students. She cites high attendance, increased test scores, improved self-esteem, and a love of learning as the results. "The children love to be at school. They come in at 6 a.m. and stay as long as they can or until the bus leaves."

Parent Involvement

Not only do students who loop enjoy school more, but teachers say that parents of those students feel more comfortable talking to teachers. "Increased parent involvement is a nice by-product of looping," says Grant.

Because families get to know teachers, parents relax in the second year, Oldham says. Some parents feel uncomfortable in schools or may not have had a positive education experience themselves, explains Oldham. "For those parents who tend to be a little more reserved, looping helps them because they know the teacher and communication can take place on a deeper level.

Especially if a child is struggling, the teacher and parents can work closely together."

"Knowing that parents and I will be in a partnership for two years changes our ideas about what our relationship will be," says Jones. To lay a foundation for parent-teacher communication, Jones routinely invites parents to visit the class and calls parents with positive remarks and reports about their child during the first year of the loop. By the second year, "the parents know your expectations for their child," she says. "Sometimes, the parents have different expectations than you, and the parents speak more frankly in the second year."

Fostering a good relationship between parents and the teacher benefits the child in the end, says Jones. "Because parents are comfortable with the teacher, the teacher learns how to help parents and parents learn how to help the teacher."

Making Smooth Transitions

For students, leaving a looping class can be scary, says Oldham. To help prepare them, students in grades 1–3 work on projects together throughout the year so the children can meet other students and teachers. In December, for example, they decorated cookies and took them to local nursing homes.

As the end of the school year approached last year, Jones knew that the children in her class would be divided into six 3rd grade classes. With another 2nd grade teacher she held writing workshops during the last month of school so the students could get to know one another. Still, this wasn't enough, she says, because she would see her former students clinging together on the playground during recess this year. In response, she and her colleagues have instituted "Fabulous 1st Graders" assemblies once a month so students can interact.

Despite its benefits for students, teachers, and parents, Grant concedes that looping isn't for everyone. "The entire school shouldn't adopt looping. One teaching model won't work for everyone."

He warns that looping by itself will not cause student achievement scores to skyrocket. Jubert agrees, saying, "Looping is not a cure-all and it may not be for everyone. It is a means rather than an end."

Nevertheless, Jubert calls looping "the most rewarding opportunity to help children I've ever engaged in." For her, looping has allowed her to "see the children be the best they can be—to see them read, cooperate and work together, and to see joy in them as they learn."

NO

Allan S. Vann

Looping: Looking Beyond the Hype

Looping," the practice of having teachers stay with the same class for two consecutive grade levels, has been getting a lot of favorable attention lately in professional publications and at educators' conferences. What looping advocates often don't mention, however, is that this grouping strategy has been around since the one-room schoolhouse, and that while looping has been successfully implemented in many schools, there is no body of research supporting greater cognitive or affective growth in children who have experienced it. . . .

Advantages of Looping

If I were to advocate looping, I would probably cite three reasons for implementing such a practice:

1. If teachers move up with their classes, the first weeks of the second year will probably be more productive because the teachers will not need the days or weeks usually taken to become familiar with each child's learning style, strengths, weaknesses, interests, or home situation.
2. For the many children coming to school from fragile homes, looping teachers provide familiar and welcome "significant others" in their lives, giving them a greater sense of security.
3. If teachers believe that looping is beneficial, the "Hawthorne effect" may prevail—i.e., when people feel strongly about a concept and are willing to work hard to make it succeed, it probably will.

Disadvantages of Looping

Looping is not for everyone, however, and certainly should not be mandated or forced on an unwilling staff. Even with enthusiastic participation, there may be disadvantages in having a child remain with the same peers and teacher for a second year, such as:

1. Time may be lost at the beginning and throughout the school year as the looping teacher strives to master the new curriculum. The higher the grade level, the more curriculum content there is to be mastered.
2. Despite the best efforts to match teaching styles with children's learning styles, there will always be mismatches. Continuing those mismatches for a second year is unfair to both teacher and child.
3. Every teacher has strengths and weaknesses. As children move from grade to grade in the traditional system, they may go from a teacher who is gifted at teaching one subject to a teacher who is strong in a different subject. But looping relegates children to two consecutive years with an instructor who may not teach an important curriculum area as well as other grade-level teachers, or who may not be able to bring out the best in a particular child's area of special interest.
4. Each year, there are some children who are ridiculed or even ostracized by peers who perceive them as too smart, too dumb, too tall, too short, too fat, too thin, or too this or that. Looping extends the negative consequences for both those children and their classmates. Also, remaining with the same class for a second year limits a child's opportunities to make new friends in the classroom setting. . . .

Two Pitfalls to Avoid

Some advocates argue that looping teachers should view their curriculum as a two-year course of instruction. Such an approach, however, can have negative outcomes for children who opt out, and for new children placed in the class the second year. The scope and sequence of their instruction will have serious gaps if the looping teacher omits certain topics from the customary grade-level curriculum the first year in the expectation of teaching them the second year. It may be prudent for the teacher to cover the graded curriculum one year at a time.

Some looping proponents also feel that teachers must implement nontraditional teaching strategies to ensure success. However, looping is essentially a grouping strategy and its success or failure has not been shown to be dependent on its environment, be it structured or unstructured, teacher-centered or child-centered. Attempts to wed looping to a particular learning environment should be discouraged, as this may limit the number of available teachers, as well as the ability of principals to match student learning styles with teaching styles. It may also create unfair expectations in the minds of parents.

I see no outstanding advantages for looping, nor do I see any insurmountable disadvantages.

POSTSCRIPT

Do Multi-Year Assignments With the Same Teacher Improve Primary Students' Learning?

Are we asking too much to have teachers teach a different curriculum every year? If, as Vann suggests, multi-year assignments are a completely voluntary experience, will the most committed teachers volunteer to take on these assignments, leaving those teachers not willing to undertake new learning opportunities to teach the rest of the students for single years? If school administrators who are committed to providing alternatives for the parents divert some resources to those teachers most willing to undertake new innovations they may leave the other teachers with limited resources. With no proof that multi-year assignments improve academic performance or social and emotional development, should they be offered as an alternative at all? How will students and teachers be selected for participation? Should there be any systematic evaluation of the program? If so, how can the evaluation be carried out?

If a student moves to a school and is assigned to a classroom in its second year of a multi-year assignment, will that student feel more out-of-place than if he or she was placed in a single-year class? Many in the media have raised the issue of school bullying due to the rash of school shootings that have taken place in recent times. Could multi-year assignments exacerbate this problem?

What should administrators do when faced with the dilemma of a teacher requesting to have a multi-year assignment with his or her class for a third year? Should that be allowed? Are there greater advantages or disadvantages for being with the same teacher and peers for three years?

Suggested Readings

Bellis, M., "Look Before You Loop," *Young Children* (vol. 54, no. 3, 1999).

Chapman, J., "A Looping Journey," *Young Children* (vol. 54, no. 3, 1999).

Forsten, C., Grant, J. and Richardson, I., "Multiage and Looping: Borrowing From the Past," *Principal* (vol. 78, no. 4, 1999).

Hanson, B. J., "Getting to Know You: Multi-year Teaching," *Educational Leadership* (vol. 53, no. 3, 1995).

Nichols, G. W. and Nichols, J. D., "Looping: The Impact on Parental Attitudes in the Educational Environment," *International Journal of Educational Reform* (vol. 8, no. 3, 1999).

Contributors to This Volume

EDITOR

KAREN MENKE PACIOREK is a professor of early childhood education at Eastern Michigan University in Ypsilanti, Michigan. She edits, with Joyce Huth Munro, *Annual Editions: Early Childhood Education* and *Sources: Notable Selections in Early Childhood Education,* also published by McGraw-Hill/Dushkin. Paciorek has served as president of the Michigan Association for the Education of Young Children and chair of the Michigan Early Childhood Education Consortium. In addition, she serves on many committees addressing the needs of young children in her community and state. She earned a B.S. from the University of Pittsburgh, an M.A. from George Washington University, and a Ph.D. from Peabody College of Vanderbilt University, all in early childhood education. She presents at local, state, and national conferences on curriculum planning, guiding behavior, preparing the learning environment, and working with families.

STAFF

Theodore Knight   List Manager
David Brackley   Senior Developmental Editor
Juliana Gribbins   Developmental Editor
Rose Gleich   Administrative Assistant
Brenda S. Filley   Director of Production/Design
Juliana Arbo   Typesetting Supervisor
Diane Barker   Proofreader
Richard Tietjen   Publishing Systems Manager
Larry Killian   Copier Coordinator

AUTHORS

KELLY KING ALEXANDER is a contributing editor for *Parents* magazine and writes on a variety of issues that affect children and their families. She writes for numerous other national magazines, as well. She lives with her husband and three children in Prairieville, Louisiana, where there is still plenty of playtime.

SHARON BEGLEY is senior editor for *Newsweek* and writes extensively on scientific theories and issues. Begley earned a B.A. from Yale University and has received numerous awards for her work.

MARILYN BIZAR teaches at the Center for City Schools of National-Louis University in Chicago, Illinois. She is the author, with Harvey Daniels and Steven Zemelman, of *Rethinking High School: Best Practice in Teaching, Learning, and Leadership* (Heinemann, 2001) and, with Harvey Daniels, of *Methods That Matter: Six Structures for Best Practice Classrooms* (Stenhouse Publishers, 1998).

DAVID F. BJORKLUND is a professor in the department of psychology at Florida Atlantic University in Boca Raton, Florida. He is the author of *Children's Thinking: Developmental Function and Individual Differences,* 3rd ed. (Wadsworth, 2000). Bjorklund received his B.A. from the University of Massachussets–Amhurst, his M.A. from the University of Dayton, and his Ph.D. from the University of North Carolina–Chapel Hill.

NADINE BLOCK is director of the Center for Effective Discipline. The center is headquarters for and coordinates the NCACPS (National Coalition to Abolish Corporal Punishment in Schools) and EPOCH-USA (End Physical Punishment of Children) programs.

BRENDA J. BOYD is an assistant professor in the department of human development at Washington State University in Pullman, Washington. She teaches in the areas of child development, early education, and parent-child relationships. Her research interests include the play of young children and the professional development of child-care providers.

JOHN T. BRUER is president of the J. S. McDonnell Foundation in St. Louis, Missouri. He established the McDonnell-Pew Program in Cognitive Neuroscience, a new mind-brain science that links systems neuroscience and psychology in the study of human cognition. He is the author of *The Myth of the First Three Years: A New Understanding of Early Brain Development and Lifelong Learning* (The Free Press, 1999). Bruer received his B.A. from the University of Wisconsin and his Ph.D. from Rockefeller University.

PATRICIA CLARK is an assistant professor of elementary education at Ball State University in Muncie, Indiana.

MARK J. COOPER is an assistant professor in the college of education at the University of Central Arkansas in Conway, Arkansas.

HARVEY DANIELS teaches at the Center for City Schools, National-Louis University in Chicago, Illinois. He is the author of *Literature Circles: Voice and Choice in Book Clubs and Reading Groups,* 2d ed. (Stenhouse Publishers,

2001) and, with Steven Zemelman and Arthur A. Hyde, *Best Practice: New Standards for Teaching and Learning in America's Schools*, 2d ed. (Heinemann, 1998).

ROLAND W. DOEPNER III was a graduate student at the University of North Carolina–Chapel Hill at the time of the writing of his selection.

SIEGFRIED ENGELMANN is director of the National Institute for Direct Instruction in Eugene, Oregon, and was presented with the Fred Keller Award of Excellence in 1994 by the American Psychological Association. He is the author of *War Against the Schools' Academic Child Abuse* (Halcyon House, 1992) and, with Douglas Carnine, *Theory of Instruction: Principles and Applications* (ADI Press, 1991).

JONATHAN L. FREEDMAN is a professor of psychology at the University of Toronto in Ontario, Canada.

MARJORIE HAMPTON is the director of First Presbyterian Preschool in Arlington, Texas. The program serves more than 200 children. In addition, she is an individual and family therapist.

ERIC A. HANUSHEK is the Paul and Jean Hanna Senior Fellow at the Hoover Institution of Stanford University, as well as a research associate at the National Bureau of Economic Research. He specializes in the economics and finance of schools. Hanushek is the editor, with Dale Jorgenson, of *Improving America's Schools: The Role of Incentives* (National Academy Press, 1996). He has published numerous articles in professional journals.

ELIZABETH HARVEY was a professor in the department of psychology at the University of Connecticut at the time of the writing of her selection. She is currently at the University of Massachusetts–Amherst. Harvey is the author of "Parental Employment and Conduct Problems Among Children With Attention-Deficit/Hyperactivity Disorder: An Examination of Child Care Workload and Parenting Well-Being as Mediating Variables," *Journal of Social and Clinical Psychology* (vol. 17, 1998). Her research interests include the early development of attention-deficit/hyperactivity disorder (ADHD) and oppositional defiant disorder (ODD) as well as parents' beliefs about father involvement among dual-earner families with elementary school-aged children.

SUSAN W. HAUGLAND is currently a professor at the Metropolitan State College of Denver and professor emeritus in child development at Southeast Missouri State University in Cape Girardeau, Missouri. She is also the president of K.I.D.S. & Computers, Inc., which provides training for teachers, consulting, and evaluations of the developmental appropriateness of children's software and Web sites.

CAROL HUNTSINGER is a professor of education and psychology at the College of Lake County in Grayslake, Illinois. Her research interests include the study habits of young children.

WENDY C. KASTEN is an associate professor of curriculum and instruction at Kent State University in Kent, Ohio. She is 1996–2002 president of C.E.L.T. (Center for the Expansion of Language and Thinking). She is the author, with Elizabeth M. Lolli, of *Implementing Multiage Education: A Practical Guide* (Christopher-Gordon Publishers, 1998). Kasten earned her B.S. degree from Rowan University in New Jersey, her M.Ed from the University of Maine, and her Ph.D. from the University of Arizona. Her research interests include whole-language learning, action research, literature-based reading instruction, literature circles, multi-age education, struggling readers, the writing process, reading assessment, teacher reflection, and children as informants in research.

NANCIE L. KATZ is a freelance writer for the *Christian Science Monitor*.

KATHLEEN KELLEY-LAINE is project officer at the Organization for Economic Cooperation and Development in Paris, France. She is the author, with Caroline St. John-Brooks and John Townshend, of *Parents as Partners in Schooling* (Organization for Economic Cooperation and Development, 1997).

ELIZABETH KIRK is an assistant professor of teacher education at Miami University in Middletown, Ohio.

LAWRENCE KUTNER is a clinical psychologist and professor at Harvard University Medical School, where he is codirector of the Harvard Center for Mental Health and Media. He is a contributing editor of *Parenting, Family Life,* and *BabyTalk*. Kutner is the author of *Your School-age Child* (Morrow/Avon, 1997) and *Toddlers and Preschoolers* (Morrow/Avon, 1995).

SUSAN MAGLIARO is an associate professor of educational psychology/educational technology at Virginia Tech in Blacksburg, Virginia. She is the author, with R. Neal Shambaugh, of *Mastering the Possibilities: A Process Approach to Instructional Design* (Allyn & Bacon, 1997). Magliaro received her B.S. from East Stroudsburg University, her M.S. from Iowa State University, and her Ph.D. from Virginia Tech.

DeWAYNE A. MASON is currently an adjunct professor at the University of Southern California.

SAMUEL J. MEISELS is a professor of early childhood education and associate dean for research in the school of education at the University of Michigan in Ann Arbor, Michigan. He is the author, with Helen L. Harrington, of *Thinking Like a Teacher: Using Observational Assessment to Improve Teaching and Learning* (Allyn & Bacon, 2001). His research interests include long-term consequences of high-risk birth, early intervention policy, developmental screening of young children, and performance assessment for children from preschool through the elementary years.

MARY H. MOSLEY is an associate professor in the College of Education at the University of Central Arkansas in Conway, Arkansas.

DEBORAH OLSEN was a post-doctoral fellow at Yale University at the time of the writing of her selection.

WILLIAM A. OWINGS is superintendent of Accomack County Public Schools in Virginia and past president of Virginia's Association for Staff and Curriculum Development.

ANTHONY D. PELLEGRINI is a professor in the College of Education and Human Development at the University of Minnesota and was a visiting professor at the University of Cardiff in Wales at the time his selection was written. He is the author of *Observing Children in Their Natural Worlds: A Methodological Primer* (Lawrence Erlbaum Associates, 1996). Pellegrini's research interests include observational research methods, children's peer relations, and social contextual influences on classroom achievement.

JOELLEN PERRY is a writer for *U.S. News & World Report*.

KAREN RASMUSSEN is a staff writer and editor for the Association for Supervision and Curriculum Development's Newsletters and Special Publications Unit and an associate editor of *Educational Leadership*.

ROMESH RATNESAR is a staff writer at *Time* and writes about a variety of issues affecting education. Prior to writing for *Time*, Ratnesar worked as a reporter-researcher at *The New Republic* where he wrote about business, politics, society, and entertainment.

LYNN ROSELLINI is a writer for *U.S. News & World Report*.

MARY ELLIS SCHREIBER had been a teacher of young children for sixteen years before becoming a consultant for the Early Childhood Conflict Resolution Program. She is also an adjunct faculty member at New York University in New York City.

LAWRENCE J. SCHWEINHART is chair of the Research Division at the High/Scope Educational Research Foundation in Ypsilanti, Michigan. He is the author, with David P. Weikart, of *Lasting Differences: The High Scope Preschool Curriculum Comparison Study Through Age 23* (High/Scope Press, 1997) and, with Ann S. Epstein and L. McAdoo, of *Models of Early Childhood Education* (High/Scope Press, 1996).

BETTY JO SIMMONS is a professor of education in the Department of Education, Special Education, and Social Work at Longwood College in Farmville, Virginia. She is the author of numerous articles on early childhood education. Simmons received both a B.A. and an M.S. from Longwood College and received an Ed.D. from The College of William and Mary.

KELLY STALSWORTH is a professor of education at Longwood College in Farmville, Virginia.

ANDREW PEYTON THOMAS is an attorney in Phoenix, Arizona, and the author of *Crime and the Sacking of America: The Roots of Chaos* (Brassey's, 1994). He has written for the *Wall Street Journal, Weekly Standard, National Review,* and other publications.

ALLAN S. VANN is principal of James H. Boyd Intermediate School in Huntington, New York.

DAVID P. WEIKART is founder and former president of the High/Scope Educational Research Foundation in Ypsilanti, Michigan. Weikart remains an active member of the High/Scope Board of Directors.

HEATHER WENTZEL is a professor of education at Longwood College in Farmville, Virginia.

JOHN A. ZAHORIK is a Professor Emeritus in the School of Education at the University of Wisconsin–Milwaukee. He earned an M.S. from the University of Wisconsin–Milwaukee and a Ph.D. from the University of Wisconsin–Madison. Zahorik is currently an investigator of the Student Achievement Guarantee in Education Program (SAGE), focusing on the reduced class size effects on teacher classroom behavior.

STEVE ZEMELMAN is a faculty member at the Center for City Schools, National-Louis University in Chicago, Illinois, and a director of the Illinois Writing Project. He is the author, with Harvey Daniels and Arthur A. Hyde, of *Best Practice: New Standards for Teaching and Learning in America's Schools*, 2d ed. (Heinemann, 1998).

EDWARD ZIGLER is the Sterling Professor of Psychology and director of the Bush Center in Child Development and Social Policy at Yale University. He has played a key role in major policies affecting children and families since the early 1960s. He received the National Head Start Founder's Award in 1995.

Index